CULTURE JIHAD

HOW TO STOP THE LEFT FROM KILLING A NATION

TODD STARNES

Post Hill
PRESS

A POST HILL PRESS BOOK

ISBN: 978-1-64293-166-2

ISBN (eBook): 978-1-64293-167-9

Culture Jihad:

How to Stop the Left from Killing a Nation

© 2019 by Todd Starnes

All Rights Reserved

Cover art by Cody Corcoran

Post Hill Press

New York • Nashville

posthillpress.com

Published in the United States of America

This book is dedicated to the freedom-loving, flag-waving patriots of Starnes Country.

Proclaim liberty throughout the land unto all the inhabitants thereof.
- Leviticus 25:10[1]

---

1   Leviticus 25:10 (English Standard Version), https://biblehub.com/leviticus/25-10.htm.

TABLE OF CONTENTS

CHAPTER 1

THE CULTURE JIHADISTS LIVE AMONG US

VICE PRESIDENT MIKE PENCE delivered a terse warning to Christians: be prepared to be discriminated against because of your religious beliefs.

"The truth is, we live in a time when the freedom of religion is under assault," the vice president said during the 2019 commencement address at Liberty University.

"We live in a time when it's become acceptable and even fashionable to ridicule and even discriminate against people of faith," Pence told the Class of 2019.

"Throughout most of American history, it's been pretty easy to call yourself Christian," Pence said. "It didn't even occur to people that you might be shunned or ridiculed for defending the teachings of the Bible."

The vice president was widely ridiculed for his stark assessment of the state of Christianity in American. But the truth is in recent years Christians have faced unrelenting attacks in the public marketplace from secularists and a small, but vocal, mob of LGBT activists.

"Some of the loudest voices for tolerance today have little tolerance for traditional Christian beliefs," the vice president said.

He told the assembled crowd they must be prepared when the day comes when they "will be asked to bow down to the idols of popular culture."

"You're going to be asked not just to tolerate things that violate your faith; you're going to be asked to endorse them," he said.

The fact is that in some states Christians are being treated as second-class citizens—forced by the government to renounce the religious beliefs for the sake of political correctness.

Just a few weeks later House Democrats passed the so-called Equality Act, a piece of legislation that would expand the 1964 Civil Rights Act to include sexual orientation and gender identity.

The law would completely obliterate the 1003 Religious Freedom Restoration Act, a law that stops the government from encroaching on a person's religious liberty. In other words, the Equality Act effectively puts a bull's-eye on every person of faith in the nation.

The Christian Broadcasting Network warned that "Christians will be forced to violate their beliefs." Tony Perkins, the president of the Family Research Council called the legislation "Orweillian" and predicted a "catastrophic loss of religious freedom in America."

Representative Jody Hice, a Republican lawmaker from Georgia, told me the bill would flat-out erode the First Amendment.

"This is an attempt to silence the Christian voice," he said.

Christian churches would be forced to host events that are contrary to the Bible's teachings on marriage and sexuality. Christian schools would be required to accommodate the preferences of transgender students and many Christian-owned businesses would be forced to violate their deeply held religious beliefs.

The vice president's dire warning turned out to be a modern-day prophecy.

I wrote this book because I love America and I love freedom. I love the freedom to practice my religion in the public marketplace. I love the freedom to read *To Kill A Mockingbird* on a warm summer day in Bryant Park. I love to watch parents doting over their newborn child. But our freedoms are in danger, grave danger.

In the pages of this book, you will read about a Catholic farmer banned from selling blueberries because of his religious beliefs. You will read stories about modern-day book bans. You will even read about attempts to slander our Founding Fathers as racist bigots.

The truth is, our nation is under attack and the enemy lives among us. They have already overrun our public school system and judicial system and now they are infiltrating our church houses.

They want to destroy life, liberty, and the pursuit of happiness. They want to open our borders and cede our national sovereignty to an invading horde of illegal aliens. Quite literally, they want to silence our voices and bully us into submission. Opinions contrary to the those of leftists are now designated as hate speech.

Many years ago, I wrote in *God Less America* that our values have been turned upside down. Wrong is right, right is wrong. Truth is no longer absolute. And neither is gender. Cherished traditions like marriage are scorned. Patriotism is no longer a virtue. It truly is a bloodless jihad, a cultural jihad.

President Trump has been fighting for the American people and our way of life, but Congress has been fighting him every step of the way—even members of his own political party.

Charlie Daniels, the country music singer, once told me it's time for the politicians to knock off the backstabbing and bickering and get to work for the American people.

"All you guys in the Senate and all you guys in Congress stop and listen—we're not getting (anything) done—nothing," he said. "You're sitting over there—Chuck Schumer on that side—and you're sitting over there—Mitch McConnell on that side and you guys act like you're dealing with a devil."

"Get your act together and sit down and do something," he said. "You're not hurting the party, you're killing America. Do you want to be known for killing America? You want to be the S.O.B.'s that took America down the drain?"

Could you imagine Charlie giving Republicans and Democrats the "what for"? What a day in American history that would be. Then again, it's unlikely to happen because lawmakers can't handle the unvarnished truth.

"They'd throw me in jail for contempt of Congress," Charlie said.

There's no greater patriot I know than Charlie Daniels. This guy loves God, he loves America, and he loves our troops. He understands the heartbeat of "We the People" and he understands that we've taken a wrong turn.

"I think we have forgotten to count our blessings," he said. "I think a lot of people have forgotten what America is. America is the greatest country the world has ever known. Nobody can hold a candle to the United States of America."

Charlie believes the only way to restore traditional American values is to engage the political process—to take a stand.

"Why do people from every corner of the Earth do everything in their power to come to this country and be a citizen," he said. "It's because this is the best place on Earth. We can't let that slip away from our national conscience."

I thought about Charlie's words in early 2019 when I was invited to be a guest of Georgia Congressman Jody Hice at the State of the Union Address.

It was one of those uniquely American moments, where strangers sat together, many of opposing political views, united in the belief that we are a free people, one nation under God.

My seatmate was a Democrat from Illinois. She runs a non-profit food pantry in Aurora. We found common ground by talking about food—the belief that no American should ever have to go to bed hungry.

Also in my section was an investment guy from Silicon Valley, a Packers fan from Wisconsin, and a decorated Army Ranger from Texas. He was gracious as all of us shook his hand and thanked him for his service.

There were also some illegal aliens in the crowd and one was seated in my section of the gallery. She was a guest of Congressman

Mike Levin, a Democrat from California. The illegal alien had been an intern on his campaign in 2018. The congressman could have selected a law-abiding, American taxpayer to watch the State of the Union, but instead, he chose someone who does not even legally belong in the country. *What makes that person so special?* I wondered.

As near as I could tell, there were not too many fans of President Trump sitting in my section of the gallery. More than once, I was the only person giving the president a standing ovation. And I might have triggered a few microaggressions when I hollered, "Amen!" when the president delivered a passionate defense of the unborn and newborn.

He used graphic language to call out New York lawmakers who passed a law allowing mothers to abort their babies in the birth canal.

"Lawmakers in New York cheered with delight upon the passage of legislation that would allow a baby to be ripped from the mother's womb moments before birth," the president said. "These are living, feeling, beautiful babies who will never get the chance to share their love and dreams with the world."

Trump went on to publicly shame Virginia Democratic Gov. Ralph Northam for affirming "that he would execute a baby after birth."

Trump continued, "To defend the dignity of every person, I am asking the Congress to pass legislation to prohibit the late-term abortion of children who can feel pain in the mother's womb. Let us work together to build a culture that cherishes innocent life. And let us reaffirm a fundamental truth—all children—born and unborn—are made in the holy image of God."

The Republicans rose with a mighty force and roared their affirmation of the president's remarks. It was, in my estimation, the most passionate and emotional moment of the evening.

But the reaction from Democrats was stunning, albeit predictable. They refused to stand in agreement that newborn children deserve the right to live. There they sat for the nation to see, many dressed in white, as they sat stone-faced in their seats.

A few days later, I caused a bit of an uproar when I said on *Fox News @ Night* that there was an evil in the Democratic Party. After what I saw in the House chamber, I absolutely stand by those words. There is something demonic happening within the ranks of the Democrats. There is something demonic happening within the ranks of Leftists. And maybe they should consider swapping their white dresses and cloaks for sackcloth and ashes.

David Horowitz, the conservative writer and founder of the David Horowitz Freedom Center, was a guest on my Fox Nation show in spring 2019. He offered a rather unique perspective of the crisis facing the nation as a self-described agnostic Jew.

"We are a Christian country," he said. "Every value and every principle we hold dear—the basis of our freedom—equality, inclusion, tolerance, pluralism, individual accountability and individual freedom—these are all Christian ideas."

Horowitz went on to tell me that 98 percent of the people who originally settled America were Protestant Christians.

"America could only be created and our freedoms only created by Protestant Christians. It could not be done by Catholics. It could not be done by atheists and certainly could not be done by Muslims," he said.

Horowitz said it's time for the sleeping Christians of the nation to wake up and face the reality of the situation—the leftist assault on Christianity is an assault on America itself.

"This is an existential battle for the life of this country," he said. "This is a very serious moment in our country. Christians stand in the way of the Left—which wants to destroy this country."

His two-word call to arms for people of faith: get active.

The other day I thought about a well-worn quote attributed to the great Irish statesman Edmund Burke, "The only thing necessary for the triumph of evil is for good men to do nothing."

Recently, Barna Research released a study showing that half of American pastors worry they will offend someone if they preach a message about a controversial issue. In other words, good men have done nothing and evil has triumphed.

Back home in the Deep South, the revival preacher would always deliver a hellfire-and-brimstone message. He'd have just about everybody in the church squirming in the pews. And before the church organist could belt out the first line of "Just As I Am," there would be a stampede to the altar.

In a way, this book is a hellfire-and-brimstone message to America. We've gone astray and it's time to return to our heritage, our roots. There may be a few chapters that make you uncomfortable and there may be a few that make you downright angry. But there are also chapters that will give you cause to smile and laugh and even cheer.

Culture Jihad is not meant to be a book about our nation's demise. It's about hope—hope for a better future. And I still have hope. I have hope in America because my hope is not built on a political party. My hope is not built on celebrities. My hope is built on nothing less than Jesus's blood and righteousness.

So, as you read the following pages, I would urge you to consider a beloved passage of Scripture paraphrased from the Holy Bible: Let now your heart be troubled, America.

CHAPTER 2

LET'S GET GOING, WE'VE GOT A COUNTRY TO SAVE

IMAGINE WAKING UP in the year 2030 and seeing this news item appear on your smartphone:

> *Ft. Leavenworth, Kansas (AP) - Rev. Oliver Criswell Hart, the last president of the Southern Baptist Convention, died in a federal prison today. He was ninety-two.*
>
> *Hart, who once headed the nation's largest Protestant denomination, had been imprisoned for felony violations of federal hate crime laws.*
>
> *The Southern Baptist Convention was disbanded by the federal government in the early 21st century after it was declared a domestic hate group by the Department of Homeland Security.*
>
> *Ironically, Hart was a direct descendant of one of the Southern Baptist Convention's most renowned ministers, Revolutionary War hero Rev. Oliver Hart.[2]*
>
> *The elder Hart had been pastor of The First Baptist Church of Charleston, South Carolina just before the outbreak of the*

---

2   Turner, Helen Lee. "Hart, Oliver (1723-1795)." *South Carolina Encyclopedia. University of South Carolina, Institute for Southern Studies, April 15, 2016.* http://www.scencyclopedia.org/sce/entries/hart-oliver/

Revolutionary War. He was heralded for preaching sermons about freedom from the pulpit.

Hart had refused to comply with federal agents, who demanded he stop reading and preaching from the Holy Bible. He was also found guilty on multiple counts of discriminating against Muslims and LGBT-Americans during sermons he delivered from church pulpits.

The original translations of the Bible were banished by special legislation enacted under the 2025 Hate Crimes Act. Most religious books were confiscated by federal authorities and replaced with a government-approved text that removed all verses deemed controversial or hateful by censors.

Democrats reclaimed majorities in both the Senate and the House of Representatives by campaigning on a promise to pass the legislation. The president signed it into law in a ceremony heralded by protected people groups as well as the Muslim Brotherhood.

The Supreme Court rejected an emergency appeal filed by religious liberty advocates. In their landmark 7–2 decision, the Court ruled that gay rights trump religious liberty.

"Discrimination in the name of God is an abomination that must not be tolerated in a free society," the majority wrote in their opinion. "Religion disguised as bigotry and hate has no place in a tolerant and diverse society."

Followers of extremist religions were then expelled from public service and banned from holding public office. At least one hundred Catholic and Evangelical members of Congress, mostly Republicans, were removed from office after they acknowledged they followed the teachings of Christ.

The president offered to pardon Hart provided he make a public renouncement of his faith and his beliefs that homosexuality is a sin and that Islam is an evil religion.

He refused to do so and was immediately taken into federal custody. The Internal Revenue Service shut down the Southern Baptist Convention headquarters in Nashville along with other Baptist organizations in Atlanta and Richmond, Virginia.

Hart's death came just two weeks after the anniversary of the Day of Sorrows, marking the worst terrorist attacks on American soil. Islamic radicals staged suicide raids on more than two dozen Christian mega-churches on Easter Sunday. Nearly 10,000 worshipers were killed in what became the worst terrorist attack on American soil.

A congressional investigation found that many of the attackers were agents of the Islamic State who had immigrated to America posing as refugees.

Two weeks later, the radical Islamists blew up Christian schools in Colorado Springs, Nashville, and Atlanta and attacked a crowded Chick-fil-A restaurant in Dallas. The carnage was horrific. Several hundred people died—mostly children.

The bloody attacks sparked what would become a de facto holy war. An angry president argued that Christians bore some responsibility for the attacks because of their teachings against Islam. He demanded that Christian pastors stand down and stop "the flaming passions of hatred from the pulpit."

"Christians must turn the other cheek," the president declared.

But the Southern Baptist Convention and other major denominations scoffed at those demands and led a coalition of Evangelical Christian denominations who vowed to ignore the pleas from Washington, D.C.

With the Islamic Radicals threatening to launch even more attacks, Congress decided to take action. To appease the radicals, Congress outlawed all public displays of religion that were contrary to Sharia Law.

A bipartisan committee established what would eventually become the United Church of America, a government-approved, state-sponsored religion. Tax-exempt status for every Christian church was immediately revoked and the IRS confiscated all church property.

Church buildings underwent a religious cleansing. Any relics deemed offensive were destroyed—including crosses, hymnals, and Christian flags. Many former sanctuaries were turned into convention halls and community centers.

A national ministerial registry was created. Pastors were required to obtain government credentials authorizing them to preach—but only from government-approved texts.

Hundreds of preachers, mostly Baptists and Pentecostals, defied the law and were subsequently charged and sentenced up to five years in prison.

The Department of Education immediately ceased all funding to Christian colleges and universities. Professors who advocated for Creationism were sent to re-education camps. Many schools were forced to close.

Prayer was formally banned in public schools. The federal government also rescinded legislation making Christmas a federal holiday. Easter, St. Patrick's Day, and Valentine's Day were banned as well.

Education officials soon implemented a mandatory LGBT education curriculum.

The Department of Homeland Security shut down the Fellowship of Christian Athletes, AWANA, and a number of other Christian-themed clubs.

Gideon's International, a ministry that provided Bibles to school children and hotels and hospitals, was designated as a domestic hate group.

The Pentagon court-martialed hundreds of chaplains who refused to stop praying in the name of Jesus. And Christians were eventually banned from serving in the Armed Forces, as well as government sector jobs.

Christian business owners were required to sign a statement declaring they would not discriminate against protected people groups. They were also required to mark their stores and shops with the ithacus fish—the sign of Christianity. Those who refused, were shut down.

"You must leave your religion at home," the president warned Americans.

The Christian cleansing of the nation did not come easily. There were pockets of resistance in areas of what was once known as the Bible Belt.

The Department of Inclusion and Diversity, a cabinet level office created during the second term of the Michelle Obama presidency, launched a massive sweep of the region during the winter of 2027.

Anyone of the Christian faith caught proselytizing faced a mandatory three-year prison sentence. Jails became so over-crowded that the government was forced to shorten prison terms and instead place convicted Christians in a national database.

Hart had warned Christian Americans that such a day was coming during the historic presidential election of 2016. He conducted a nationwide bus tour, urging Evangelical Christians to pray and vote.

"The church needs to vote. The church needs to show up at the polls," Hart told a gathering at the state capitol in New Mexico.

"Secularism has come into Washington, and Washington is taking God out of [it]," he said in Santa Fe. "We as Christians are being pushed further and further to the back, and I say let's take our country back."

And yet Christians did not heed the pastor's warning.

The 2020 presidential election proved pivotal. Just hours after being sworn into office, the new president nominated a liberal justice to the Supreme Court—permanently altering the ideological makeup of the bench.

Two years later, the president replaced two of the remaining three conservative justices with liberals—marking the end of conservative influence in the judiciary.

Historians have concluded that Hart was correct in his 2020 presidential prediction. Had Christians bothered to vote, they could have swayed the outcome of the election.

"I don't care who wins and who's out there, you have to vote," Hart told the Christian Broadcasting Network at the time. "And I'm not going to tell people who to vote for. I'm not going to do that. Let God tell you who to vote for. You may have to hold your nose. You may have to decide which is the least heathen of the two heathen."

Arrangements are being made to transfer Hart's body to the newly formed Republic of Texas, where he will be buried.

There's really no gentle way to break this to you, America. But the "fake news" report published above is a lot closer to reality than you might believe.

The Left is waging a stealth jihad on our faith, our families, and our heritage. There is a clear and present danger to the American way of life. And unless "We the People" rise up and take a stand, I fear the home of the brave will no longer be the land of the free.

And make no mistake, good readers, this militant mob of godless millennials and malcontents is taking the war directly to the Bible Belt and every Bible-believing community in the nation.

This book will expose a dangerous effort being waged in the shadows and back rooms of government to undermine the very foundations of the Republic.

Some of you might be wondering, "Wait a second. President Trump has made America great again. Jobs are booming. We can say 'Merry Christmas' again. I've got a dinner table filled to overflowing with fried chicken and biscuits and butter beans."

Do not be fooled by the great successes of the Trump Administration in protecting religious liberty and the Second Amendment. Do not be lulled into a sense of security by the vast numbers of conservative judges appointed to the federal courts. Storm clouds are gathering, friends.

Socialism is on the rise. Patriotism is frowned upon. American families are under assault. Freedom of speech and association are nearly bygone vestiges. Government-run schools have been turned into indoctrination centers. In Chapter Six, for example, we will explore a national crusade to introduce children to drag queens at public libraries.[3] One of the queens literally said their goal is to groom children for their lifestyle choice. If that doesn't ruffle your feather boa, I'm not quite sure what will.

Beloved institutions like the Boy Scouts have been morally bankrupted and many churches have been neutered by social justice warriors. Polling data suggests that more than half of the nation's Christians don't even bother to vote.[4] And many pastors are fearful of addressing important issues of the day lest they offend parishioners or stir the wrath of militant activists.

Instead of salt and light, the American church has hidden itself under a bushel and subsists on a low-sodium diet. Truth has become

---

3   Prestigiacomo, Amanda. "WATCH: Drag Queen Admits To 'Grooming' Children At Library 'Story Hour' Events." *The Daily Wire.* Last modified November 29, 2018. https://www.dailywire.com/news/38818/watch-drag-queen-admits-grooming-children-library-amanda-prestigiacomo.

4   Overbeck, Joy. "If Christians Don't Vote, More Christians Will Be Persecuted." *Townhall.* https://townhall.com/columnists/joyoverbeck/2014/10/31/if-christians-dont-vote-more-christians-will-be-persecuted-n1911516.

irrelevant. The violent cultural winds of the day have unmoored our nation from its founding documents and, as a result, the rights afforded to us by the Constitution are in mortal danger.

The great Southern Baptist leader Adrian Rogers warned of such times in a booklet titled *Will God Impeach America?*[5]

"There is a virtual tidal wave of filth sweeping across America," he wrote. "That's America - the home of the immorally free and brave."

"Something is happening in America that is very un-American. We have become a nation riddled with every vile form of immorality and corruption. If you want to find out more, all you have to do is consult the front page of any newspaper," he wrote.

Dr. Rogers, the longtime pastor of Bellevue Baptist Church in Memphis, Tennessee, sounded the warning many years ago—that God could very well take down the hedge He built to protect the United States.

If Dr. Roger's prophecy turns out to be true, that could explain our current predicament—where a radical band of culture jihadists have declared a political fatwa on the Red, White, & Blue. And they will not cease until they have turned the Bill of Rights into a heaping pile of rubble.

In 2017 *Rolling Stone* published a disturbing profile of Tim Gill, an openly gay technology giant who weaponized his $500 million fortune and unleashed a horde of anti-Christian jihadists on the Southern states.[6]

Rolling Stone detailed Gill's mission—to stop states from passing legislation that would protect Christian wedding planners and florists and bakers from LGBT activists—under the guise of equal rights.

---

5   Rogers, Adrian. "Will God Impeach America?" *Oneplace.* Accessed May 23, 2019. https://www.oneplace.com/ministries/love-worth-finding/read/articles/will-god-impeach-america---15740.html.

6   Kroll, Andy. "Meet the Megadonor Behind the LGBTQ Rights Movement." *Rolling Stone*, June 23, 2017. https://www.rollingstone.com/politics/politics-features/meet-the-megadonor-behind-the-lgbtq-rights-movement-193996/.

In response to the Supreme Court's decision to redefine what God had already defined, many state lawmakers introduced religious freedom restoration acts. The legislation would provide legal cover for churches and Christian business owners.

Gill and his followers successfully stopped the legislation in the Republican stronghold of Georgia and helped to unseat the Republican governor of North Carolina over the issue of transgender bathrooms. We'll get into that issue a bit later in the book.

And the election of President Trump only emboldened Gill's militancy.

"We're going into the hardest states in the country. We're going to punish the wicked," he told *Rolling Stone*.

And by wicked, he means every Bible-believing Christian in America, from pastors preaching in the pulpit to sweet grandmothers serving fried chicken at the church potluck.

In 2018, Hollywood mega-producer Ryan Murphy, the creator of hit television programs like *Glee* and *American Horror Story*, echoed Gill's declaration of war.

"I want these hateful and wrong politicians to go and to stop polluting our moral and ethical ether," he told a gathering of sycophants at a pro-LGBT gala in Los Angeles, California. "I think it's now possible to create a movement to protect and nourish our own."[7]

And by "our own" he was referring to the LGBT community. Murphy announced the creation of a multimillion-dollar organization that will target anyone running for office that they consider to be anti-gay.

---

7   Gonzalez, Sandra. "Ryan Murphy funds aims to get 'anti-LBGTQ' candidates out of office in 2020." CNN. Last modified December 3, 2018. https://www.cnn.com/2018/12/03/entertainment/ryan-murphy-2020-politics/index.html?utm_medium=social&utm_content=2018-12-04T00%3A01%3A56&utm_source=fbCNN&utm_term=link&fbclid=IwAR18ho10L1JzeflTZA1OEh3OfcvruRrb_WpuU_ADY7x_NVIFgUIwFbTKkVQ.

"Why don't we consider ever targeting the people that are causing the problem here - the homophobes, the trans-naysayers and the small, restricted and dangerous minds who are causing so many young people to needlessly hate themselves and doubt themselves in our country, when what they should be receiving from us is love and support and understanding."

And just in case all of you folks who live in Mayberry and Hazzard County haven't quite figured out Murphy's nefarious scheme, he spelled it out for you.

"We are going to send a message which says you cannot make discrimination against us a political virtue anymore. You cannot keep killing our vulnerable young people by promoting and nationalizing your rural, close-minded, anti-constitutional viewpoints," he declared.

President Obama used similar language when he was running for the presidency in 2007. He said the folks who lived in the Rust Belt were clinging to their guns and their religion. He called them bitter.[8]

Hillary Clinton took the slur a step further when she said half of President Trump's supporters were a bunch of homophobic, xenophobic, Islamophobic bigots. A basket of deplorables, she surmised. Irredeemable.[9]

In 2018, at a dinner for the radical Human Rights Campaign, former Vice President Joe Biden took direct aim at social conservatives and he was loaded for bear.

"These forces of intolerance remain determined to undermine and roll back the progress you all have made," the vice president snarled. "This time they - not you - have an ally in the White House. This time they have an ally."

---

8   Pilkington, Ed. "Obama angers midwest voters with guns and religion remark." *The Guardian* (London), April 14, 2008. https://www. theguardian.com/world/2008/apr/14/barackobama.uselections2008.

9   Reilly, Katie. "Read Hillary Clinton's 'Basket of Deplorables' Remarks About Donald Trump Supporters." *TIME*, September 10, 2016. http:// time.com/4486502/hillary-clinton-basket-of-deplorables-transcript/.

He went on to call the "Make America Great Again" crowd "virulent people - some of them the dregs of society."

The applause was thunderous from the LGBT activists and their supporters. How ironic that an organization that supposedly opposes bullying and intolerance cheered for a man who was advocating bullying and intolerance.[10]

So when Tim Gill called us "wicked" and Ryan Murphy called us "rural," they were talking in code.

They were referring to all of us gun-toting, Bible-clinging, flag-waving patriots who live in the Heartland. You see, people like Murphy and Gill and Obama and Clinton and Biden seem to believe that we are wicked people who must be silenced—and then punished.

I was talking to a caller from Alabama on my nationally syndicated radio program a while back and the dear lady was frustrated over the Left's hatred of President Trump. But I explained to her that as much as they hate the president, they hate his followers even more.

People like Gill and Murphy despise traditional American values, our way of life. They hate concepts like God and Country. They loathe church and Sunday school.

That's why former President Obama promised to fundamentally transform America. That's why his administration never truly embraced the idea that we are an exceptional nation. That's why he spent a good many days apologizing for our values while standing on foreign soil.

But let's step back for a moment and examine exactly why the Left used such loaded language to attack those of us who love America. They called us irredeemable, bitter, dregs of society, wicked.

It's not that much of a stretch to imagine that the Leftists were giving their followers a wink, wink, nod, nod to engage in political

---

10   Chasmar, Jessica. "Joe Biden: 'Dregs of society' support Donald Trump." *The Washington Times* (Washington, D.C.). September 17, 2018. https://www.washingtontimes.com/news/2018/sep/17/joe-biden-dregs-society-have-ally-donald-trump/.

warfare against Conservatives. After all, if someone is irredeemable, they must be beyond redemption. Right? In other words, those kinds of people get what's coming to them.

That's why so many of President Trump's supporters were left bloodied and beaten in the streets. That's why pro-Trump teenagers have been attacked in restaurants and classrooms for wearing "Make America Great Again" hats.[11]

That's why so many stars of stage and screen have used their bully pulpits to call for the assassination of the president. That's why Representative Maxine Waters summoned an angry mob to "absolutely harass" members of the Trump administration.[12]

So, I'm not at all surprised that a low-class, foul-mouthed political hack like Joe Biden called all of us flag-waving patriots a bunch of virulent dregs of society. And to be perfectly honest, I'd rather be a gun-toting, Bible-clinging, dreg of society than an unemployed, pajama boy leftist living in his mother's basement.

In my "fake news" report, I also posited the theory that it might one day be against the law for Christians to hold public office. As it turns out, the notion that the religious beliefs held by Catholics and Evangelicals might disqualify them from political and judicial life is not far-fetched; it's a modern-day reality.

In 2017, Dr. Mark Green was forced to withdraw his nomination as Secretary of the Army because of his Christian beliefs.[13]

---

11   Phillips, Kristine. "Man accused of taking teen's 'Make American Great Again' hat and throwing soda in his face faces theft charges." *The Chicago Tribune* (Chicago), July 6, 2018. https://www.chicagotribune.com/news/nationworld/ct-trump-hat-stolen-20180706-story.html.

12   Killer, Megan. "Maxine Waters mocks: I threaten Trump supporters 'all the time.'" *The Hill* (Washington, D.C.), September 10, 2018. https://thehill.com/homenews/house/405877-maxine-waters-i-threaten-trump-supporters-all-the-time.

13   Kaczynski, Andrew, Ryan Browne, and Dan Merica. "Mark Green withdraws his nomination for Army secretary." CNN. Last modified May 5, 2017. https://www.cnn.com/2017/05/05/politics/mark-green-army-secretary-withdrawal/index.html.

Dr. Green is a West Point graduate and a decorated Iraq war veteran. At the time of his nomination, he was serving as a Tennessee state senator.

He faced the wrath of a social justice mob because he believes that people should use the bathrooms that correspond with their God-given plumbing. He also believes that marriage is between one man and one woman. And as CNN noted, he is a "self-identified creationist."

Clearly, the Trump White House had no interest in battling the militant LGBT bullies so early in the administration. So, Dr. Green's nomination was sacrificed on the altar of political correctness.

"Tragically, my life of public service and my Christian beliefs have been mischaracterized and attacked by a few on the other side of the aisle for political gain," he continued. "While these false attacks have no bearing on the needs of the Army or my qualifications to serve, I believe it is critical to give the President the ability to move forward with his vision to restore our military to its rightful place in the world."

Dr. Green was just the first of many Trump nominees who were interrogated by Democrats in what became modern-day versions of the Salem Witch Trials.

In 2019, Brian Buescher, President Trump's nominee for the U.S. District Court in Nebraska, was a victim of this blatant form of religious bigotry. Buescher came under attack by Senators Kamala Harris, D-Calif., and Mazie Hirono, D-Hawaii, for his membership in the Knights of Columbus, a revered and highly respected Catholic charitable organization.[14]

Both lawmakers posed a series of written questions demanding to know if he would end his membership in the Knights of Columbus should he be confirmed.

---

14   Richardson, Valerie. "Harris, Hirono accused of anti-Catholic 'bigotry' for targeting Knights of Columbus." *The Washington Times* (Washington, D.C.), December 30, 2018. https://www.washingtontimes.com/news/2018/dec/30/kamala-harris-mazie-hirono-target-brian-buescher-k/.

"The Knights of Columbus has taken a number of extreme positions," Hirono wrote in the questionnaire. "For example, it was reportedly one of the top contributors to California's Proposition 8 campaign to ban same-sex marriage."

Harris referred to the group as an "all-male society" and took issue with their positions on abortion and other culture war issues.

"Were you aware that the Knights of Columbus opposed a woman's right to choose when you joined the organization?" Harris queried.

The condemnation from conservatives was swift.

"This isn't just about the Knights of Columbus or Catholics, this is an ongoing attack from the extremist left of the Democratic Party to silence people of faith and run them out of engaging in public service based on their religious beliefs," Penny Nance, the president of Concerned Women for America, wrote in a statement.

Senator Ben Sasse, the Republican Senator and moonlighting Uber driver from Nebraska, introduced a resolution stipulating that it is unconstitutional to disqualify a nominee from public office based on their membership in the Knights of Columbus.[15]

"There are many people on the left who act like every political fight is going to bring about heaven or hell on earth—and so there are a lot of folks for whom politics is a religion," Sasse told The Daily Caller News Foundation after the resolution was adopted. "I think America at its best has affirmed the dignity of every individual and their right to free speech, free press, and freedom of worship."

Now, in a surprise move, Congresswoman Tulsi Gabbard, a Democrat from Hawaii, issued a blistering rebuke of her colleagues in the Senate. Yes, you read that correctly, Representative Gabbard is a Democrat. She accused members of her own party of "weaponizing religion."

---

15   Daley, Kevin. "Ben Sasse Corners Democrats on Knights of Columbus Dispute in Judicial Nomination." *The Daily Caller*. Last modified January 16, 2019. https://dailycaller.com/2019/01/16/ben-sasse-knights-of-columbus/.

"We must call this out for what it is—religious bigotry," she wrote in a scathing op-ed in *The Hill*. "I stand strongly against those who are fomenting religious bigotry, citing as disqualifiers Buescher's Catholicism and his affiliation with the Knights of Columbus. If Buescher is 'unqualified' because of his Catholicism and affiliation with the Knights of Columbus, then President John F. Kennedy, and the 'liberal lion of the Senate' Ted Kennedy would have been 'unqualified' for the same reasons."[16]

Miracles do happen, right?

I respected Representative Gabbard's bold declaration that "no American should be asked to renounce his or her faith or membership in a faith-based, service organization in order to hold public office." But based on recent history, I'm afraid she may be in the minority within her party.

In 2012, Democrats removed God from their party platform.[17] And in 2016, delegates heckled a preacher attempting to deliver a prayer during the national convention.[18] That could explain why modern-day congressional confirmation hearings now seem to resemble religious inquisitions.

---

16 Condon, Ed. "Congresswoman blasts 'religious bigotry' against Knights of Columbus, Catholic nominees." *Catholic News Agency. Last modified January 9, 2019.* https://www.catholicnewsagency.com/news/congresswoman-blasts-religious-bigotry-against-knights-of-columbus-catholic-nominees-99597.

17 Markoe, Lauren. "Democrats under fire for removing 'God' from party platform. *The Washington Post (Washington, D.C.), September 5, 2012.* https://www.washingtonpost.com/national/on-faith/democrats-under-fire-for-removing-god-from-party-platform/2012/09/05/61b3459a-f79e-11e1-a93b-7185e3f88849_story.html?utm_term=.4eb1a93f5ce9.

18 Gibson, David. "Who boos an opening prayer? The Berniacs of 2016, that's who." *Religion News Service. Last modified July 26, 2016.* https://religionnews.com/2016/07/26/who-boos-an-opening-prayer-the-berniacs-of-2016-thats-who/.

In 2017, Notre Dame law professor and mother of seven Amy Coney Barrett was grilled by Sen. Dianne Feinstein, D-Calif., over her orthodox beliefs.[19]

"When you read your speeches, the conclusion one draws is that the dogma lives loudly within you, and that's of concern when you come to big issues that large numbers of people have fought for, for years in this country," Feinstein declared.

Sen. Dick Durbin (D-IL) interrogated Barrett over her use of the term "orthodox Catholics"—in reference to an article she wrote on capital punishment.

"Do you consider yourself an orthodox Catholic?" Durbin asked.

"If you're asking whether I take my faith seriously and I'm a faithful Catholic, I am," she told the senator. "Although I would stress that my personal church affiliation or my religious belief would not bear on the discharge of my duties as a judge."

During that same year, Sen. Bernie Sanders (I-Vt.) viciously attacked the religious faith of Russell Vought, the president's nominee to be deputy director of the White House Office of Management and Budget.[20]

Sen. Sanders deemed Vought unsuitable for office because the nominee believes that salvation is found alone through Jesus Christ. He said someone with that kind of religious belief system is "really not someone who this country is supposed to be about."

---

19 Blake, Aaron. "Did Dianne Feinstein accuse a judicial nominee of being too Christian?" *The Fix. Last modified September 7, 2017.* https://www.washingtonpost.com/news/the-fix/wp/2017/09/07/did-a-democratic-senator-just-accuse-a-judicial-nominee-of-being-too-christian/?utm_term=.c3817362d57a.

20 Green, Emma. "Bernie Sanders's Religious Test for Christians in Public Office." *The Atlantic, June 8, 2017.* https://www.theatlantic.com/politics/archive/2017/06/bernie-sanders-chris-van-hollen-russell-vought/529614/.

Sen. Sanders: *"'Muslims do not simply have a deficient theology. They do not know God because they have rejected Jesus Christ, His Son, and they stand condemned.' Do you believe that that statement is Islamophobic?"*

Mr. Vought: *"Absolutely not, Senator. I'm a Christian, and I believe in a Christian set of principles based on my faith…"*

Sanders: *"…Forgive me, we just don't have a lot of time. Do you believe people in the Muslim religion stand condemned? Is that your view?"*

Vought: *"Again, Senator, I'm a Christian, and I wrote that piece in accordance with the statement of faith at Wheaton College…"*

Sanders: *"I understand that. I don't know how many Muslims there are in America. Maybe a couple million. Are you suggesting that these people stand condemned? What about Jews? Do they stand condemned too?"*

Vought: *"Senator, I'm a Christian…"*

Sanders *[shouting]: "I understand you are a Christian, but this country [is] made of people who are not just—I understand that Christianity is the majority religion, but there are other people of different religions in this country and around the world. In your judgment, do you think that people who are not Christians are going to be condemned?"*

Vought: *"Thank you for probing on that question. As a Christian, I believe that all individuals are made in the image of God and are worthy of dignity and respect regardless of their religious beliefs. I believe that as a Christian that's how I should treat all individuals…"*

Sanders: *"…Do you think that's respectful of other religions? … I would simply say, Mr. Chairman, that this nominee is really not someone who this country is supposed to be about."*

Salvation through Jesus Christ alone is the core biblical tenet of Christianity. And there was Senator Sanders, on national television, berating an honest man for being a faithful follower of Jesus Christ. The noted socialist administered a religious litmus test on Mr. Vought, a practice that is outlawed by the United States Constitution. He literally told the Wheaton College alumnus that America is not supposed to be about people of the Christian faith. If Senator Sanders had his way, 71 percent of American adults would be disqualified from public service because they follow the teachings of the Holy Bible.

The Democrats may as well have asked, "Are you now or have you ever been a follower of Jesus Christ?"

It's not just religious bigotry, but it comes dangerously close to violating Article 6 of the U.S. Constitution—there "shall be no religious test" for any American seeking to serve in public office. In other words, a religious litmus test for public office is against the law.[21]

Senators Harris and Feinstein and Durbin and Sanders and Hirono are either woefully ignorant of the law or they are, in fact, religious bigots. I contend they are both, making them undeserving of a place in Congress.

Oh, and one more note about Representative Gabbard. Not too long after she called out her colleagues, she was viciously attacked in the mainstream media. Gabbard had declared her intent to run for president. Reporters quickly pounced on reports that she had worked with her parents to defend traditional marriage in Hawaii. Gabbard was seventeen years old at the time. She later apologized, multiple times, for slighting the LGBT community, but it was not enough. Gabbard was officially marked with a scarlet letter.[22]

---

21   "U.S. Constitution—Article 6." *USConstitution.net*. Last modified January 25, 2010. https://www.usconstitution.net/xconst_A6.html.

22   Kaczynski, Andrew. "Tulsi Gabbard once touted working for anti-gay group that backed conversion therapy." CNN. Last modified January 17, 2019. https://www.cnn.com/2019/01/13/politics/kfile-tulsi-gabbard-lgbt/index.html.

So why is it that Democrats and Socialists and Atheists are singling out American Christians and Jews? Dennis Prager, the syndicated radio talk show host, explained why during an interview on *Starnes Country*, my Fox television program.

"The only organized opposition to leftism comes from within Judaism and Christianity," Prager told me. "The orthodox Jew, the faithful Mormon, the traditional Catholic, the Evangelical Protestant, these are the only organized opponents to leftism, and they know it, and they will do anything they can to suppress it."

And so far, the culture jihadists have been successful. They have taken over Hollywood and the Democratic Party. They have conquered public education and many Mainline Protestant denominations. They have even conquered cherished institutions like the Boy Scouts, professional football, and country music.

Now, you might be wondering, "Well, sweet mercy, Todd. If we've already lost the battle, why did I spend my hard-earned money on this book?"

Rest easy, friends. And let not your heart be troubled by this culture jihad. The purpose of this book is not to frighten or to discourage you, but to challenge you and spur you into action. If we want to restore the Judeo-Christian foundation of our country, it's going to take every last one of us.

But the fight cannot just be waged in the halls of Congress or in the hills of Hollywood. First, we must retake our homes and our neighborhoods from the enemy forces. We must establish that our front yard is the forward operating base in this war to reclaim the culture.

In his 1989 farewell address to the nation, President Reagan touched on that theme.

"All great change in America begins at the dinner table. So, tomorrow night in the kitchen I hope the talking begins. And children, if your parents haven't been teaching you what it means to be an American, let 'em know and nail 'em on it. That would be a very American thing to do."[23]

President Reagan understood that waging a fight to restore American values in Washington, D.C. is a losing battle unless the war is fought first on the home front.

To restore America, we must first restore our homes. Parents must take on the mantle of teaching their little ones about the virtues of liberty. They must be the ones to raise up an army to resist the fascists in our midst.

At the close of the Constitutional Convention of 1787 a woman approached Benjamin Franklin and asked, "What have we got - a republic or a monarchy?" Franklin's response has been passed down by generations: "A republic if you can keep it."[24]

My fellow countrymen, I believe we can keep the Republic. I truly do. But we must take the pledge taken so many years ago by our Founding Fathers. I'm reminded of Reagan's beautiful speech delivered in 1964. The speech was titled, "A Time for Choosing."[25]

"Freedom is never more than one generation away from extinction. We didn't pass it to our children in the bloodstream. It must be fought for, protected, and handed on for them to do the same, or one day we will spend our sunset years telling our children and our children's children what it was once like in the United States where men were free," Reagan told the assembled crowd.

23　McLaughlin, Dan. "We Should Have Heeded This Warning From Ronald Reagan." *National Review*, June 20, 2017. https://www.nationalreview.com/corner/ronald-reagan-warned-us-about-we-should-have-listened/

24　Beeman, Richard R., Ph.D. "Perspectives on the Constitution: A Republic, If You Can Keep It." *National Constitution Center*. Accessed May 23, 2019. https://constitutioncenter.org/learn/educational-resources/historical-documents/perspectives-on-the-constitution-a-republic-if-you-can-keep-it.

25　"A Time for Choosing." *Teaching American History*. Accessed May 23, 2019. https://teachingamericanhistory.org/library/document/a-time-for-choosing/.

The Founding Fathers made known the implications of their decision to support the Declaration of Independence. They signed with their John Hancock knowing that Almighty God would be their protector. They pledged their lives, their fortunes, and their sacred honor. And now I believe every generation of Americans must follow suit.

So, as we move forward into the chapters of this book, I challenge you to follow the example set by our Founding Fathers. Let us pledge our lives, our fortunes, and our sacred honor for the sake of Liberty. My fellow countrymen, let's put it all on the line. We've got a country to save.

CHAPTER 3

TRUMP DERANGEMENT SYNDROME

An epidemic of biblical proportions is spreading across the fruited plain at this very hour. The Centers for Disease Control and the American Psychological Association have yet to identify the malady, but it seems to be an isolated outbreak impacting liberals, millennials, fashion designers, Hollywood celebrities, and the entire prime time lineup at CNN.

The affliction is called Trump Derangement Syndrome (TDS). Symptoms include delusional ranting and a feverish flop sweat. Those infected with the disease are especially sensitive to red ball caps.

Representative Maxine Waters, the Democrat from California, showed signs of early onset TDS during a political gathering in her congressional district. She called on her minions to specifically target Trump staffers.

"If you see anybody from that Cabinet in a restaurant, in a department store, at a gasoline station, you get out and you create a crowd and you push back on them, and you tell them they're not welcome anymore, anywhere," she said. "If you think we are rallying now you ain't seen nothing yet."[26]

---

26   Ehrlich, Jamie. "Maxine Waters encourages supports to harass Trump administration officials." CNN. Last modified June 25, 2018. https://www.cnn.com/2018/06/25/politics/maxine-waters-trump-officials/index.html.

Her charge came about the same time as White House Press Secretary Sarah Sanders was told to leave the Red Hen restaurant in Lexington, Virginia because LGBT employees objected to her politics.[27]

"Already you have members of your cabinet that are being booed out of restaurants, who have protesters taking up at their house," Waters said in a message to the president. "No peace, no sleep. No peace, no sleep."[28]

Waters doubled down on her threats during an interview on MSNBC.

"I have no sympathy for these people that are in this administration," she said. "[T]hese members of his cabinet who remain and try to defend him, they won't be able to go to a restaurant, they won't be able to stop at a gas station, they're not going to be able to shop at a department store."[29]

And that's exactly what the leftist mob has been doing—targeting Trump staffers, Republican lawmakers, Trump supporters, and especially teenagers who want to make America great again.

"The people are going to turn on them. They're going to protest. They're absolutely going to harass them until they decide that they're going to tell the president, 'No, I can't hang with you,'" Waters declared on MSNBC.

Trump Derangement Syndrome is a cruel disease that has even impacted the nation's religious community.

27   Eliahou, Maya and Christina Zdanowicz. "Red Hen—the restaurant that asked Sarah Sanders to leave—reopens amid protests." CNN. Last modified July 6, 2018. https://www.cnn.com/2018/07/06/us/red-hen-reopens-trnd/index.html.

28   Fearnow, Benjamin. "Maxine Waters: 'No Peace, No Sleep' For Trump Cabinet Members, Applauds Public Shaming." *Newsweek*, June 24, 2018. https://www.newsweek.com/maxine-waters-trump-harass-kirstjen-nielsen-stephen-miller-sarah-huckabee-993173.

29   Hains, Tim. "Maxine Waters Warns Trump Cabinet: 'The People Are Going To Turn' On You." *RealClear Politics*. June 24, 2018. https://www.realclearpolitics.com/video/2018/06/24/maxine_waters_the_people_are_going_to_turn_on_trump_enablers.html.

In 2017, All Saints Episcopal Church in Pasadena, California decided to refrain from mentioning the president-elect's name during prayers over fears it might trigger micro-aggressions among parishioners.[30]

Reports of some congregants spontaneously combusting upon hearing Trump's name have been proven untrue. There are also unconfirmed reports that San Francisco, Brooklyn, and Los Angeles have been designated as sanctuary cities to house the afflicted.

My sources at the Centers for Disease Control says the illness is incurable. So if you come across an afflicted liberal, please direct them to the nearest safe space or containment zone. In the meantime, check out some of the most egregious episodes of TDS.

CHURCH REFUSES TO PRAY FOR PRESIDENT TRUMP

Parishioners at a California Episcopal church will no longer pray by name for the president of the United States over fears that the name "Donald Trump" might trigger microaggressions among sanctified snowflakes.

Mike Kinman, the rector of All Saints Church in Pasadena, broke the news to the congregation in a blog posting that was filled with all sorts of liturgical lunacy.[31]

"If you come to All Saints this Sunday, you'll notice that we have removed the proper names from our prayers for those in authority. Whereas before we prayed for 'Barack, our president,' we are now

30   ENS Staff. "Episcopalians approach Donald Trump's inauguration with prayer." *Episcopal News Service*. January 19, 2017. https://www.episcopalnewsservice.org/2017/01/19/episcopalians-approach-donald-trumps-inauguration-with-prayer/.

31   "Pasadena Church Won't Pray for President-Elect Donald Trump By Name." *PasadenaNow*. January 12, 2017. http://www.pasadenanow.com/main/pasadena-church-wont-pray-for-president-elect-donald-trump-by-name/.

praying for 'our president, our president-elect, and all others in authority.' This practice will continue for at least the near future," he wrote.

Kinman went on to say the safety of the congregation could be jeopardized by the mere mention of the president-elect's name.

"We are in a unique situation in my lifetime where we have a president elect whose name is literally a trauma trigger to some people—particularly women and people who, because of his words and actions, he represents an active danger to health and safety," he wrote.

Then this pious punk went on to compare Trump to a wife-beater.

"As I have said before, for some it could be as if we demanded a battered woman pray for her abuser by name. It's not that the abuser doesn't need prayer—certainly the opposite—but prayer should never be a trauma-causing act," he wrote.

During Trump's inauguration, the church held a "Weekend of Prayer and Resistance."

"We will stand in resistance to the systemic evils that oppress and marginalize any member of our human family—including but not limited to racism, sexism, nativism, homophobic, anti-Semitism and Islamophobia," reads a description of the event on the church's website.

Sadly, there was no potluck meal provided, so participants had to bring their own halal sandwiches and jugs of herbal tea.

While it seems there has been some debate over the issue, the rector told the congregation his "pastoral" decision will stand.

"There are indeed people in our congregation for whom the anticipation of praying for Donald Trump by name in the worship service is legitimately triggering trauma and compromising the safety of the worship space," the rector wrote. "I am talking about the clinical definition of trauma, not just 'I don't like it' or 'It's really hard for me.'"

It sounds like a good many people parked in the pews at All Saints Church may be slap crazy.

Lord, have mercy.

ELDERLY JEWISH MAN BERATED OVER MAGA HAT

An elderly Jewish man sitting inside a Palo Alto, California Starbucks was viciously berated by a left-wing political thug because he was wearing an iconic Make America Great Again ballcap.

Rebecca Parker Mankey, the co-chair of the Bayshore Progressive Democrats, screamed at the man, calling him a "hater of brown people" and "Nazi scum."

She posted a detailed account of the ugly encounter on her Facebook and Twitter accounts.

"I am going to publicly shame him in town and try to get him fired and kicked out of every club he is in," the crazed woman wrote on Twitter. "I am going to go to his house march up and down carrying a sign that says he hates black people. I am going to organize protests where he works to make him feel safe as unsafe as he made every brown person he met today."[32]

The victim, identified only as Victor, gave a detailed accounting of the attack to the *Palo Alto Daily Post*. The seventy-four-year-old retired technical writer said there is an "atmosphere of fear" around being a Trump supporter in Palo Alto.

"People have always been allowed to wear a political button or shirt," he told the newspaper. "Now to wear a Trump button is considered a provocation."

Victor told the newspaper he thought Mankey was "on drugs or something."

"I'm surprised that the Starbucks manager or someone didn't call the police with this woman raving in the store like that," he said.

He thought it was ironic that she would call a Jewish man a Nazi.

---

32   McDonald, Leah. "Music store employee who abused an elderly man wearing a MAGA hat outside a Palo Alto Starbucks and boasted about it online is fired after her boss finds out." *DailyMail* (London), April 4, 2019. https://www.dailymail.co.uk/news/article-6888165/Elderly-Jewish-man-74-abused-called-Nazi-Starbucks-woman.html.

"I would call that just utterly irrational. Anyone with a high school education should know about the Nazis and the Ku Klux Klan," he said.

Mankey posted on Facebook that she was angered because other customers and Starbucks staffers did not join her political lynch mob.

Instead, conservatives rose up to defend Victor.

Mankey has since been fired from her job and she has resigned her position within the Progressive Democrats.

Clearly, it is unsafe for conservatives to live, shop, or drink coffee in Palo Alto, California. The Make America Great Again crowd would be wise to take their business to a more tolerant part of America. Any red state will do.

STUDENTS BANNED FROM WATCHING TRUMP'S INAUGURATION

Students at Independence High School in Williamson County, Tennessee, were not allowed to watch President-elect Donald Trump's inauguration during class. Senior Olivia Roberts was so surprised by the ban she decided to write a Facebook post.[33]

"To preface this, I am not one to post or debate anything political on Facebook but wanted to hear thoughts on this: I go to public school and we are not allowed to watch the inauguration tomorrow… Teachers were banned (from showing it).

"Teachers are also not allowed to discuss anything about politics or religions which is understandable but this is a nationwide event in history that I think an [sic] a US citizen (whether you are happy

---

33   Sullivan, Maureen. "Should Students Watch Donald Trump's Inauguration As President Or Walk Out Of School?" *Forbes* (New Jersey), January 20, 2017. https://www.forbes.com/sites/maureensullivan/2017/01/20/should-students-watch-donald-trumps-inauguration-as-president-or-walk-out-of-school/#28caa7644684.

about it or not) should be watched to honor and support the president of The United States of America (no matter who it is) And pay respect to the country we are privileged to live in. We watched the last 2 presidential inaugurations in school."

Suzanne Roberts is Olivia's mother. She thought it was really strange that teachers would not be allowed to show such a historic event in the classroom. So she picked up the phone and called the principal.

Instead of getting answers, she said she received a lecture from the principal.

"I asked her if there was a policy regarding inaugurations but instead of answering she asked me, 'Why is it important for you personally that your child see the inauguration live?'"

"I was a little thrown off," she told me.

"[The principal] told me that Independence High School is going to focus on learning and moving forward and staying on curriculum and they would not be stopping class for the inauguration," Mrs. Roberts said. "She told me that news happens every day in this country and they won't be stopping class to watch the news."[34]

Meanwhile, fourth graders at a Michigan grade school were not allowed to watch President Trump's inaugural address because their teacher feared he might use "inflammatory and degrading" language.[35]

Conservative radio host Steve Gruber obtained a letter purportedly written by teacher Brett Meteyer and sent to parents at Explorer Elementary School in the small town of Williamston.

---

34   Starnes, Todd. "Seriously? Schools reportedly to black out Trump's inaugural address." Fox News. January 19, 2017. https://www.foxnews.com/opinion/seriously-schools-reportedly-to-black-out-trumps-inaugural-address.

35   Dulle, Brian. "Michigan elementary school teacher says class won't watch inauguration." *KSNT.com*. Last modified January 19, 2017. https://www.ksnt.com/news/national/michigan-elementary-school-teacher-says-class-wont-watch-inauguration/901298588.

Meteyer said he was concerned about children being exposed to inappropriate language and behavior.

"I am anxious about showing Mr. Trump's inaugural address, given his past inflammatory and degrading comments about minorities, women, and the disabled," he wrote. "I am also uneasy about Mr. Trump's casual use of profanity, so I sought an assurance that as their teacher, I would not be exposing children to language that would not appear in G or PG-rated movies."[36]

Did the teacher really think that the president-elect was going to deliver his inaugural address while dropping f-bombs from sea to shining sea? "Ask not what your country can do for you, ask what you can do for your f*****g country."

I've covered a lot of educators acting moronically over the past few years, but this guy takes the cake.

"I put in a request to the Trump team to preview the speech, but I have not heard back from them," he reportedly wrote to parents.

I'm going to go out on a limb here and suggest that the president-elect's transition team had more pressing matters to attend to than being lectured by a fourth grade school teacher.

The school district sent me a statement acknowledging they were "aware of discourse within the community regarding a teacher parent communication surrounding the Presidential inauguration."

"The district administration expects teachers to present a balanced perspective consistent with the curriculum and demonstrate good judgement in their communications with families," the statement read. "Administrators do not preview nor censor communications sent by teachers."

---

36   "Michigan 4th Grade Teacher Won't Let Students Watch Trump Inauguration Speech." Fox News Insider. January 18, 2017. https://insider.foxnews.com/2017/01/18/michigan-4th-grade-teacher-wont-let-students-watch-donald-trump-inauguration-speech?page=6&nmsrc=email&utm_source=newsletter&utm_campaign=scoop&utm_medium=email.

What a load of pretentious pomposity.

President Trump is going to have a difficult time making America great again with educators like this stinking up our nation's classrooms.

A TEENAGER'S BEEF OVER THE MAGA HAT

A sixteen-year-old Trump supporter wearing a "Make America Great Again" cap was viciously attacked by a left-wing goon inside a San Antonio Whataburger restaurant.[37]

Hunter Richard and his friends were eating burgers when a grown man came over and ripped the iconic red hat off his head. The teen said some of his hair was torn from his scalp.

One of his friends videotaped a portion of the attack when the menacing thug grabbed a beverage and threw it in Hunter's face.[38]

"You ain't supporting s*** n***** little b**** a** mother*****!" the foul-mouthed creep screamed at the boy.

As he stormed off, the attacker continued to hurl obscenities.

"This is going to go great in my f****** fireplace b****," he said.

Hunter told our Fox television affiliate in San Antonio that the attack was unprovoked.

"I support my President and if you don't let's have a conversation about it instead of ripping my hat off. I just think a conversation about politics is more productive for the entire whole rather than taking my hat and yelling subjective words to me," he said.

---

37   Zavala, Elizabeth. "Man accused of grabbing 'MAGA' cap, throwing drink in teen's face indicted." *mySA*. Modified August 31, 2018. https://www.mysanantonio.com/news/local/article/Man-accused-of-grabbing-MAGA-cap-throwing-13193988.php.

38   "Man assaults teen wearing 'MAGA' hat at San Antonio Whataburger restaurant." *YouTube*. Video File. July 5, 2018. https://www.youtube.com/watch?v=AmWUv8aDDgE.

Police are investigating the incident, but the attacker has not been positively identified, television station KABB reports.

The owner of Rumble, a local bar, posted a message on Facebook acknowledging that one of their part-time employees was "captured on cell phone video assaulting another person at a local eatery. The assault took place, presumably, because this employee did not agree with the other individual's political stance."

"We have since terminated this employee, as his actions go against everything that this establishment stands for," the statement read.

"I didn't think it was going to generate the amount like what people are doing, I was looking at the comments by some people and 'they are like this is uncalled for' and other people are like mixed opinions but I didn't think it would blow up to what it is now," Hunter said.

I told you this was going to happen, folks. I told you that conservatives were going to be hunted and attacked by low-life, left-wing predators. I blame the mainstream media and Maxine Waters for this debauchery. Their rhetoric led to a sixteen-year-old boy being brutally attacked. But I doubt that will satisfy their bloodlust.

TEACHER COMPARES PRESIDENT TRUMP TO HITLER

A classroom conversation about President Donald Trump's inauguration took a very ugly turn when a California high school teacher drew a caricature of the president as Adolf Hitler.

It happened when an English teacher at Verdugo Hills High School drew a Hitler mustache on President Trump's face. A student in the classroom reportedly posted a video of the image on Snapchat. A source with ties to the school sent me a series of photos taken from the video.[39]

---

39   Starnes, Todd. "Heil No! Teacher draws Trump as Hitler." Fox News. January 20, 2017. https://www.foxnews.com/opinion/heil-no-teacher-draws-trump-as-hitler.

"The teacher told the students that Trump and Hitler are one in the same," said the person who sent me the photographs.

The Los Angeles Unified School District would not confirm the identity of the teacher, so I will not name the individual. However, the district did say they were aware of the incident.

"While all personnel matters are confidential, the District is aware of this incident and will take appropriate action," a spokesperson told me.

So, what is the appropriate action to take against a school teacher who compares an American president to an evil dictator who was responsible for the slaughter of millions of people?

In-school suspension? Lunch duty?

"The District is committed to providing a civil and respectful learning and working environment," the spokesperson added. "All employees are expected to conduct themselves in a professional manner at all times."

Clearly, this teacher's actions were both uncivil and disrespectful. Do we really want to squander American tax dollars on a public school teacher who seems to genuinely believe that President Trump is Hitler?

TEACHER PRETENDS TO KILL TRUMP IN VIDEO

A Texas high school art teacher was placed on administrative leave after video surfaced showing her "shooting" President Donald Trump inside a classroom while screaming, "Die!"

The teacher, at W. H. Adamson High School in Dallas, posted the video to her Instagram account along with the following message: "Watching the #inauguration in my classroom like…#no #stop #denial #squirtgun #hypocrisy #powerless #saveusall #teachthembetter #atleastitsfriday."[40]

---

40   Smith, Corbett. "Dallas ISD suspends Adamson teacher over faux-assassination of Trump with water gun." *Dallas Morning News* (Dallas), January 2017. https://www.dallasnews.com/news/dallas-isd/2017/01/26/dallas-isd-teacher-hot-water-overfaux-assassination-trump-water-gun.

In the video, voices can be heard in the background—but the school district would not say if students witnessed the teacher's disturbing demonstration.

Video of the inauguration was being broadcast inside the classroom on a whiteboard. The video shows the teacher lunging at President Trump and firing the squirt gun numerous times while shouting, "Die!"

It is disturbing, to say the least. Dallas Independent School District seemed to be taking the matter quite seriously.

"We were made aware of a social media posting being circulated involving a teacher at W. H. Adamson High School," a district spokesperson told me. "The teacher has been placed on administrative leave and the district has opened an investigation. This is a personnel matter and as such we cannot comment."

I wonder which offense the school district found worse: a faux assassination or a teacher using a squirt gun on school property.

Since the 2016 presidential election, liberal educators across the fruited plain have gone slap crazy. I wrote about these phenomena in my book, *The Deplorables' Guide to Making America Great Again.*

Some teachers have even turned their classrooms into breeding grounds for anti-Trump propaganda—going so far as to portray the commander in chief as a modern-day Adolf Hitler.

And I lost count of the number of educators who refused to broadcast the inauguration ceremony over fears that some fragile snowflake might take offense.

But what happened in Dallas is yet another example of how our public schools have been turned into social engineering petri dishes festering with rancorous rhetoric and hate.

What kind of a person would stage a faux assassination attempt in Dallas, of all places? It's simply repulsive.

Let's hope the Dallas Independent School District was able to muster the moral courage to take swift action to rebuke this teacher and send a message that this kind of hate has no place in a public school classroom.

STUDENT ART SHOW INCLUDES
"BURN IN HELL, TRUMP" EXHIBIT

A New York school district has launched an investigation into a student art show that included profane references to President Trump.

The art show at Shen High School featured a dozen drawings of the president's face. Above the drawings was a sign that read, "Draw on Me." On a nearby table was a box filled with markers.

Let's just say, the youngsters did not hold back.

"Burn in Hell, Trump," wrote one person. Another person scrawled the word, "a**wipe."[41]

"I think it's horribly disrespectful," parent Erica McGowan told me.

She said the art display inside a classroom reflected what she called the school district's glaring hypocrisy.

"They preach tolerance and no bullying and safe spaces and all that nonsense - as long as you are not a conservative," she said. "If somebody had put up pictures of Hillary Clinton or Barack Obama - they would mow you down."

Mrs. McGowan told me her son Peter was lectured about wearing an iconic "Make America Great Again" ball cap to school.

"They told him it was hate speech," she said.

Peter told me the art display was "awfully disgusting."

"It's hypocritical for the school to pledge tolerance and then allow photos of a sitting president to burn in hell," he said.

But the Shenendehowa Central School District said the art exhibit has been removed—and it was never meant to include derogatory or profane messages about President Trump.

A spokesperson told me they believe someone vandalized the artwork with graffiti.

---

41   Starnes, Todd. "High School Art Display: 'Burn in Hell, Trump.'"
      Fox News. June 5, 2017. https://www.foxnews.com/opinion/
      high-school-art-display-burn-in-hell-trump.

"Once we noticed this, it was immediately taken down," the spokesperson said.

If that's true, why was there a sign posted above the artwork inviting students to write messages? And why was a box of markers left nearby? I reckon we will just have to wait for the school district to complete its investigation.

The art exhibit has drawn the ire of the New York-based Saratoga Conservative Chicks. Their group called the exhibit "outrageous and unacceptable."

"There are some pretty ugly things on those pictures," Marnie Messitt, a member of Conservative Chicks, told me. "It's all about hate speech and division and indoctrination. There's no place for that in the school."

She said people are getting sick and tired of public schools disparaging the president.

"There is no doubt there is an anti-Trump bias in the public schools," she said. "The teachers are trying to force a liberal agenda on our kids."

If nothing else, the folks at Shen High School have demonstrated that liberal indoctrination is indeed an art form.

GAY PRIDE PARADE BANS PRO-TRUMP GAYS

Those who preach tolerance and equality are normally the least tolerant and least egalitarian of all.

That's why I was not terribly surprised to learn from Fox 46 that organizers of a gay pride parade in Charlotte, North Carolina banned a group of pro-Trump gays.[42]

---

42   Sentendrey, David. "Backlash against Charlotte Pride after gay Trump supporters denied spot in parade." Fox 46. Modified June 8, 2017. http://www.fox46charlotte.com/news/local-news/backlash-against-charlotte-pride-after-gay-trump-supporters-denied-spot-in-parade.

Gays for Trump had submitted an application to display a float during the annual Charlotte Pride parade.

"It was going to support Donald Trump," group spokesman Derek Van Cleve told me. "It was going to be a patriotic float with American flags and a few 'Make America Great Again' flags."

He also said the float would be populated with a number of drag queens dressed as Uncle Sam and the Statue of Liberty.

"We wanted to have a couple of drag queens on the float dancing in 'Make America Great Again' dresses," he said.

"All we wanted to do is let the community know the gay community does not speak for every single gay - just like the mayor of Pittsburgh does not speak for every single person in Pittsburgh," Mr. Van Cleve said.

Nothing controversial, just patriotic.

"Not every single lesbian, gay, bisexual or transgender citizen is anti-Trump," he said. "Some of us love him and some of us support him - including myself."

Mr. Van Cleve told me he was surprised when Charlotte Pride rejected their application. To be clear, the organization did not explain why they rejected the Gays for Trump entry.

However, a spokesperson for Charlotte Pride issued a statement to Fox 46 defending its right to "decline participation at our events to groups or organizations which do not reflect the mission, vision and values of our organization."

"In the past, we have made similar decisions to decline participation from other organizations espousing anti-LGBTQ religious or public policy stances," the statement read.

Charlotte Pride went on to say they envision a world in which "LGBTQ people are affirmed, respected and included in the full social and civic life of their local communities, free from fear of any discrimination, rejection, and prejudice."

It's unfortunate that Charlotte Pride does not practice what it preaches.

"For a group of people to claim to want tolerance, acceptance, and give it to every single person you can imagine to give it to, for them to sit back and judge me for exercising my right as an American to choose my leader without judgment is hypocritical," Gays for Trump organizer Brian Talbert told Fox.[46]

Mr. Van Cleve told me there's not all that much diversity in the local LGBT organization.

"I've been to many pride festivals in the past and it's pretty much a big DNC convention," he said. "It's extremely liberal."

Charlotte Pride has a right to pick and choose who they wish to parade with—that issue is not in dispute. But their decision to ban Gays for Trump smells of narrow-minded political bigotry. Charlotte Pride should be celebrating diversity. Instead, it appears they are shoving gay Republicans back into the closet.

CITY HALL REFUSES TO HONOR TRUMP

The folks who run the Town Hall in Jackson, Wyoming proudly displayed a portrait of President Obama during his terms in office. But they won't be extending the same respect to President Trump.[43]

Mayor Pete Muldoon removed portraits of President Trump and Vice President Pence, replacing them with a portrait of Chief Washakie, a renowned Native American warrior.

The mayor told me in a lengthy email that he stands by his decision—even though he acknowledged that Trump "won the election under the rules we have in place."[44]

---

43   Wootson, Cleve R., Jr. "'Our respect is earned, not demanded': Mayor removes Trump and Pence portraits from town hall." *Washington Post* (Washington, D.C.), June 13, 2017. https://www.washingtonpost.com/news/post-nation/wp/2017/06/13/our-respect-is-earned-not-demanded-mayor-removes-trump-and-pence-portraits-from-town-hall/?utm_term=.f4c2cce58a9d.

44   Starnes, Todd. "Mayor Removes Trump Portrait: 'We Do No Live in a Dictatorship.'" *Todd Starnes* (blog). June 12, 2017. https://www.toddstarnes.com/uncategorized/mayor-removes-trump-portrait-we-do-not-live-in-a-dictatorship/.

"Dictators like Joseph Stalin required their portraits to be displayed everywhere," Mayor Muldoon said. "Luckily, we do not live in a dictatorship."

The mayor said that since the town government is a non-partisan body and they do not work for the federal government, there is no requirement to display a picture of the president.

"The Town of Jackson is not in the president's chain of command," the mayor said. "The idea that we are required to display a portrait of the president at Town Hall is simply not true. There's a tradition of hanging portraits of the president in federal offices within the executive branch—not unlike how grocery stores display pictures of the manager."

He suggested there were only two reasons for displaying the president's portrait: for education purposes or to honor the commander in chief.

"I see no educational value in such a display," the mayor said.

Neither did he find a reason to honor the president.

"Donald Trump is an extremely divisive figure," he said. "Whether you agree with his opinions or not, it's undeniably true that many residents intensely dislike him, and find his political views odious."

He said honoring "such a divisive person" would be seen as the town leaders "taking sides against some of its residents."

"If Barack Obama was still president, I would make the same decision," the mayor responded, presumably with a straight face.

Paul Vogelheim, the chairman of the Teton County Republicans, blasted the mayor's decision.

"I find this totally disrespectful and dishonoring of the position of the president," Vogelheim told *Jackson Hole News*. "Even more so, the concern is that it's bringing ugly national partisan politics into our community."

Mayor Muldoon disputed the notion he was thumbing his nose at President Trump.

"The United States is a constitutional republic," he said. "We don't have a monarch, and one of the best features of our system is that presidents are people just like everyone else."

Mayor Pete Muldoon's decision to remove President Trump's portrait illustrates the Left's complete and utter disregard for tradition, decorum, and basic social graces.

Ultimately, the mayor will have to answer to the good and patriotic people of Jackson, Wyoming.

Until that happens, perhaps someone could inform Mayor Muldoon that Donald J. Trump is the president of the United States, not the manager of a Piggly Wiggly.

MEET THE SCHOOL MOST LIKELY TO VIOLATE THE FIRST AMENDMENT

The yearbook class at Wall Township High School may need to create a new senior superlative: "Most Likely to Violate the First Amendment." And the first inductee might just be the school's yearbook adviser.[45]

Cheryl Dyer, the superintendent of Wall Township Public Schools, told me the yearbook adviser has been suspended amid an investigation into the alteration of photos and the omission of text from students who support President Trump.[46]

"The Board of Education president authorized me to suspend the yearbook adviser. I cannot comment further on personnel matters at this time," Dyer told me.

---

45   Davis, Mike. "Wall HS teacher suspended over Trump yearbook censorship." *App*. Last modified June 13, 2017. https://www.app.com/story/news/education/in-our-schools/2017/06/12/wall-donald-trump-shirt-yearbook-censored/389314001/.

46   Starnes, Todd. "After Pro-Trump photos in high school yearbook are altered, teacher is suspended." Fox News. June 12, 2017. https://www.foxnews.com/opinion/after-pro-trump-photos-in-high-school-yearbook-are-altered-teacher-is-suspended.

In an earlier statement, Dyer said the school district values free speech and said the allegations of censorship were disturbing.

"Any inappropriate challenge to these principles will be rectified as swiftly and thoroughly as possible," she said.

She went on to say "the administration does not condone any censorship of political views on the part of our students."

However, at least three students who support President Trump have reported instances of censorship in the student yearbook.

Junior Grant Berardo could not believe it when he discovered his yearbook photo had been digitally altered. His "Make America Great Again" shirt had been covered up by a black T-shirt.

"It was Photoshopped," he told *Asbury Park Press*. "I like Trump, but it's history, too. Wearing that shirt memorializes the time."

Siblings Wyatt and Montana Debrovich-Fago also reported being censored. The words "Trump-Pence" were digitally removed from his sweater.

Montana, the school's freshman class president, reported that her Trump quote had been taken out of the yearbook. The quote read, "I like thinking big. If you are going to be thinking anything, you might as well think big."

Their mother is demanding answers.

"I'm disappointed and angry," Janet Dobrovich-Fago told me. "The [censorship] leads me to believe it's definitely against President Trump."

Mrs. Dobrovich-Fago said it's hard to believe something like this could happen.

"I don't know how somebody could have done that and thought it was okay to do," she told me.

She said Wyatt is a passionate supporter of the president.

"He went to the inauguration. He went to rallies," she said. "He has a voice and he wants to be heard. He is so upset with what's going on in our country."

Unfortunately, the youngster has been receiving quite a bit of hate mail from the anti-Trump crowd—some of it quite disturbing and vile, his mother said.

"He said, 'Mom, it's so sad to think that people would do this. He is our president. You may not like him, but you should show respect to him because he is our president,'" she said.

HOLLYWOOD HATES THE DONALD

Hollywood wants President Trump to sleep with the fishes. They want him dead—decapitated—and his bloody entrails splayed across the Rose Garden for all of the world to see.

A who's who of actors and directors and musicians want him to suffer the most agonizingly brutal and gory death in the history of assassinations.

Johnny Depp is the latest star of stage and screen to flirt with the idea of murdering President Trump.[47]

"When was the last time an actor assassinated a president? I want to clarify: I'm not an actor. I lie for a living. However, it's been a while and maybe it's time," he told an audience at the Glastonbury arts festival in England.

The crowd erupted in cheers and applause at the idea of someone murdering our commander in chief. Mr. Depp, of course, was referring to John Wilkes Booth, the actor who assassinated Abraham Lincoln, a Republican president.

His remarks were especially offensive considering the timing—just a week after a gunman opened fire on a Republican congressional baseball team. The *New York Times* reported the attacker was upset about President Trump's election.

---

47   Stedman, Alex. "Johnny Depp Apologizes for Donald Trump Assassination Joke." *Variety*, June 23, 2017. https://variety.com/2017/film/news/johnny-depp-trump-assassination-apology-1202477242/.

And how can we forget Nasty Woman Madonna wanting to blow up the White House or that wretched Kathy Griffin's faux decapitation of the president?[48,49] And there was also an incident in Central Park, with a bunch of liberal thespians.[50]

The lead character in the New York Theater production of *Julius Caesar* bore a striking resemblance to Donald Trump. Jack Posobiec was one of several conservative activists who disrupted the show.

"This play was savage and brutal. He is stabbed multiple times, running around stage, crawling through blood," he told me. "It made my blood run cold seeing Americans cheering a depiction of their president being stabbed 100 times with 100 blades."[51]

He said it turned his stomach.

"This Manhattan Central Park crowd was on their feet cheering - they were cheering as an actor dressed as the president was stabbed to death," he told me.

Is this what we've become—a nation that celebrates savagery, a nation that celebrates the silencing and the slaughter of dissent?

---

48   Bernstein, Sharon. "Singer Madonna defends 'blowing up the White House' remark." *Reuters.* January 22, 2017. https://www.reuters.com/article/us-usa-trump-women-madonna/singer-madonna-defends-blowing-up-the-white-house-remark-idUSKBN15704A.

49   "Death threats, cancellations, investigations: Kathy Griffin says she would do it all again." *Sunday Morning.* March 24, 2019. https://www.cbsnews.com/news/kathy-griffin-on-death-threats-cancellations-investigations-over-trump-severed-head-photo/.

50   Andrews, Travis M. "Trump-like 'Julius Caesar' assassinated in New York play. Delta, Bank of America pull funding." *The Washington Post* (Washington, D.C.), June 12, 2017. https://www.washingtonpost.com/news/morning-mix/wp/2017/06/12/trump-like-julius-caesar-assassinated-in-new-york-play-delta-bank-of-america-pull-funding/?noredirect=on&utm_term=.bb37bb3df625.

51   Starnes, Todd. "'Blood of Steve Scalise is on your hands!' Protesters disrupt 'Julius Caesar.'" Fox News. June 17, 2017. https://www.foxnews.com/politics/blood-of-steve-scalise-is-on-your-hands-protesters-disrupt-julius-caesar

Far too many conservatives have been bloodied and beaten for their political beliefs. From May to late June 2017, at least thirty Republican lawmakers were attacked or threatened, Free Beacon reported.[52]

The instigators and fomenters of this anti-Trump, anti-conservative scourge must be held accountable.

The entertainment industry needs to start policing its actors and playwrights and producers and musicians. Perhaps they could encourage the starlets to embrace tolerance and diversity?

And "We the People" have a responsibility as entertainment consumers. We are the ones purchasing theater tickets and downloading music. We need to send a clear message to the entertainment industry that we will not tolerate this kind of hatred.

Maybe we should consider boycotting movie theaters and Broadway musical shows. Maybe we should stop downloading music from those spewing the violent rhetoric? Or maybe we should just hit them where it hurts the most. The most productive protests usually involve a punch to the pocketbook instead of a punch to the face.

It would be easy to dismiss Mr. Depp as a cowardly man whose only discernible skill is to play make-believe for a living—but we live in dangerous days. And his remarks must be given serious consideration.

Considering the unhinged rage in Hollywood toward President Trump and his family, it's quite possible that a star of stage or screen just might try to make good on their threats.

Just ask Abraham Lincoln.

---

52   Griswold, Alex. "30 GOP Congressm3en Have Been Attacked or Threatened Since May." *The Washington Free Beacon*. June 22, 2017. https://freebeacon.com/ issues/30-gop-congressmen-attacked-threatened-since-may/.

SCHOOL SAYS MAGA HAT IS MODERN-DAY SWASTIKA

A Georgia high school teacher compared the "Make America Great Again" slogan to a swastika and ordered students wearing T-shirts supporting President Trump to leave her classroom.[53]

The incident happened at River Ridge High School in Cherokee County, north of Atlanta, and it was all captured on video.

Turning Point News first obtained the exclusive video and it shows the teacher explaining to students that they cannot wear pro-Trump clothing "just like you cannot wear a swastika to school."[54]

The video also shows the teacher doubling down on her argument that the kids have to leave the classroom because the shirts say "Make America Great Again."

"The Neo-Nazis…I'm not saying about Trump, but the slogan," the teacher says.

I warned you that our public schools have been overrun by liberals who are more interested in indoctrinating our children than educating our children. And the only way to restore sanity to our local public schools is for parents and students to stand up and fight back. And that's exactly what happened in Cherokee County, Georgia.

"It's ironic to me that the political left claims to promote free speech, but then attempts to silence conservative free speech," State Representative John Carson told AJC.com.[55]

---

53   Wang, Amy B. "School district apologizes after students told
      'Make America Great Again' shorts not allowed in class." *The
      Washington Post* (Washington, D.C.), September 5, 2017. https://
      www.washingtonpost.com/news/education/wp/2017/09/04/
      school-district-apologizes-after-students-told-make-america-great-again-
      shirts-not-allowed-in-class/?utm_term=.69cb0a3a9a6e.

54   Starnes, Todd. "Teacher compares Trump's 'Make America
      Great Again' slogan to swastikas." Fox News. Last modified
      September 17, 2017. https://www.foxnews.com/opinion/
      teacher-compares-trumps-make-america-great-again-slogan-to-swastikas.

55   Eldridge, Ellen. "Superintendent: Teacher 'wrong' to tell student he can't
      wear Trump shirt." *The Atlanta Journal-Constitution* (Atlanta), September
      3, 2017. https://www.ajc.com/news/local/superintendent-teacher-wrong-
      tell-student-can-wear-trump-shirt/6Cwku3Zuw6QRdswZvcJQfM/.

Parents reached out to local news reporters and local lawmakers, and the school district had no choice but to apologize. The school district said the unidentified math teacher "erroneously" told the students that shirts with campaign slogans were not permitted in class.

"Her actions were wrong, as the 'Make America Great Again' shirts worn by the students are not a violation of our school district dress code," the statement read. "The teacher additionally - and inappropriately - shared her personal opinion about the campaign slogan during class."

The district went on to say that the students involved would not be punished and that the superintendent was "deeply sorry that this incident happened in one of our schools."

"It does not reflect [the superintendent's] expectation that all students be treated equally and respectfully by our employees," the district said.

State Representative Earl Ehrhart told AJC.com he was shocked by the classroom censorship.

"That individual doesn't need to be anywhere near a classroom ever again," he told the *Atlanta-Journal Constitution*.

I concur. The teacher/propagandist compared the atrocities committed by the Nazis to the patriotism of young Americans. That means she is either woefully ignorant of World War II history or she perpetrated what she knew to be a lie on her young students.

Either way, the math teacher at River Ridge High School is unfit to teach in a public school classroom.

MAGA HAT IS WHITE SUPREMACIST SYMBOL, SCHOOL SAYS

A North Carolina teacher displayed a poster in her classroom that described the phrase "Make America Great Again" as an example of white supremacy.[56]

Parents were furious over what they called overt and extreme political indoctrination inside a French class at Franklin Academy High School. The poster featured a "White Supremacy Pyramid" that provided examples of overt and covert white supremacy. It was first reported by American Lens.

Among the examples given of overt white supremacy—deemed socially unacceptable—were hate crimes, racial slurs, cross-burning, and the KKK.

Among the examples of covert white supremacy were Eurocentric curricula, English-only initiatives, police brutality, and police murdering people of color.

Other examples of covert white supremacy included the denial of white privilege, denial of racism, claiming reverse racism, celebrating Columbus Day, and cultural appropriation.

In other words, if you are a white person who marches in a Columbus Day parade, eats a taco on Cinco de Mayo, or picks yourself up by your bootstraps—well, you could be a flaming white supremacist.

The phrase "Make America Great Again" is also listed on the poster.

Parents and students told American Lens the French teacher, Franca Gilbert, warned students that anyone who uttered the words "Make America Great Again" would be sent to the principal's office.

"One family tells American Lens that Gilbert has recently been wearing a T-shirt to class that reads, 'Immigrants are what make America great,'" the online website reported.

---

56   Starnes, Todd. "Teacher: "Make America Great Again" Is Example of White Supremacy." *Todd Starnes* (blog). September 30, 2017. https://www.toddstarnes.com/uncategorized/ teacher-make-america-great-again-is-example-of-white-supremacy/.

I reached out to Franklin Academy High School administrator James Kornegay via telephone and email. I asked a series of questions:

1. Was the white supremacy pyramid part of an official school curriculum?
2. Why was the pyramid posted inside the classroom?
3. Has the pyramid been removed?
4. Was the teacher reprimanded?

I received a one-sentence reply from Mr. Kornegay:

"Per our policy, we are unable to comment on personnel matters at our school. Our administration is appropriately addressing any issues that may arise," he wrote.

It's unfortunate that a taxpayer-funded school has been turned into an anti-Trump indoctrination camp. I'm glad that parents and students have chosen to speak out—and hopefully this teacher has been removed from the classroom.

I do have one more question for the folks who run the Franklin Academy Indoctrination Camp. Could someone explain what white supremacy has to do with teaching kids to speak French, *s'il vous plaît*?

MULTIPLE CHOICE QUIZ THAT REFERENCED SHOOTING PRESIDENT TRUMP[57]

The online quiz was based on George Orwell's novel, *Animal Farm*, according to the Jackson Hole News and Guide.[58]

---

57 Starnes, Todd. "Teacher: "Parent Furious Over Teacher's 'Shooting at Trump' Quiz Answer." *Todd Starnes* (blog). October 7, 2017. https://www.toddstarnes.com/uncategorized/parent-furious-over-teachers-shooting-at-trump-quiz-answer/.

58 Mohr, Kylie. "Parents upset by multiple choice answer: 'shooting at Trump.'" *Jackson Hole News & Guide*. October 6, 2017. https://www.jhnewsandguide.com/news/schools/parents-upset-by-multiple-choice-answer-shooting-at-trump/article_7da8a197-187c-5b06-b731-bc546b054836.html.

The full question read:

Napoleon has the gun fired for a new occasion. What is the new occasion?

* He was shooting at Trump

* His birthday

* For completion of the windmill

* To scare off the attackers of Animal Farm.

Parent Jim McCollum told me he was furious about the question—especially since the quiz was administered four days after the Las Vegas massacre.

"This is not right. You don't do that to a sitting president—you respect the office," McCollum told me in a telephone interview. "They used Trump's name—insinuating gun violence and shooting the president."

"As torn apart as the country is right now, I could not tolerate that and let that go without saying something," he said.

The Teton County School District (TCSD) admitted the quiz contained an inappropriate answer.[59]

"TCSD #1 takes seriously threats of any kind, regardless of intent," the district wrote. "We apologize to the students, families and community for this incident and will be addressing the issue with personnel."

McCollum told me his sixteen-year-old son is a big Trump supporter.

"He admires the man," he said. "He thinks the president is a cross between John Wayne and Clint Eastwood—swagger and grit."

His son is considering enlisting in the Marines after high school—and Trump's affirmative position on the military was a key factor.

---

59   "TCSD Investigating Incident." *Teton County School District*. Accessed May 24, 2019. http://www.tcsd.org/News/33#sthash.3ow4hvDX.dpbs.

"He loves the president's position—to have the biggest, baddest military on the planet," McCollum told me. "That inspired him. He wants to be a part of that."

Here's a thought for teachers across the fruited plain—instead of indoctrinating kids with your far-left political ideology, how about teach them how to parse participles and do long-form division?

And you educators who share your Trump assassination dreams with your students, you might want to put on a pot of coffee and open a package of Pepperidge Farm cookies. You're about to get a visit from the Secret Service.

A POETRY SLAM NAILS THE PRESIDENT

Students at Grand County High School in Utah were supposed to attend poetry slam workshops on tolerance and acceptance. Instead, students were subjected to political rhetoric, LGBT propaganda, and something called "identity mapping."[60]

Parents alerted my radio producers that one of the workshop leaders announced to the children, "I'm queer and I'm Trump's worst enemy."

An untold number of students were directed by workshop leaders to separate themselves into groups based on their sexual identity and their religious preference.

"I'm sending my daughter to school to get an education, not to learn about the LGBTQ community," one parent said.

Superintendent J. T. Stroder told the *Todd Starnes Show* the presentations were made to the entire student body during English class by poets connected to Moab Pride, a local LGBT organization.

---

60   Starnes, Todd. "Guest speaker tells Utah students:
      'I'm queer and I'm Trump's worst enemy.'" Fox News.
      October 18, 2017. https://www.foxnews.com/opinion/
      guest-speaker-tells-utah-students-im-queer-and-im-trumps-worst-enemy.

"There were some inappropriate examples used in those presentations—asking students to identify certain things about themselves that is protected by law," the superintendent admitted.

He sent a letter to parents detailing his concerns about what happened at the high school.

"I would not expect an exercise in which individual students are asked to reveal their sexual orientation and gender identity to be part of the English curriculum," he wrote. "In this case, there was no parent notification that topics relating to sexuality would be discussed outside the approved health curriculum, which was not acceptable."

Parents want to know why the Moab Pride group was allowed inside the high school and why teachers did not intervene when the group began to solicit personal information from the children.

"I really don't have an explanation," the superintendent said. "It caught the school off guard."

One parent, who asked not to be identified, told me students were divided up by religion, sexual preference, and political views.

"Their intention was to plant seeds in the high school. They were trying to indoctrinate the kids. When you have people saying 'I'm a queer and it's okay. I'm a lesbian and it's okay'—I mean—that's indoctrination," the parent told me.

As for the workshop where kids were forced to engage in identity mapping?

"I don't know what that means," the superintendent said.

Regardless, the school district said the presenters will not be invited back to the school.

"Every child that walks into that school has to feel safe no matter what their religious views are or their sexual preference," a parent said. "Instead of it being anti-bullying, the workshops directly pointed them out."

PROFESSOR SAYS REPUBLICANS SHOULD BE EXECUTED

The folks in Grand County, Utah just learned a very important lesson about the sex and gender revolutionaries. They preach tolerance and acceptance, but the revolutionaries don't practice what they preach.

Fresno State University said they would fully cooperate with any federal investigation after a professor posted a series of Twitter messages calling for President Trump to be hanged and for Republicans to be executed.[61]

"To save American democracy, Trump must hang," Professor Lars Maischak wrote on his Twitter account in February. "The sooner and the higher, the better."

"Has anyone started soliciting money and design drafts for a monument honoring the Trump assassin, yet?" the professor asked in an earlier tweet.

Maischak, a history lecturer, also went after Republicans, tweeting, "Justice = The execution of two Republicans for each deported immigrant."[62]

Apparently, the tweets went unnoticed and unreported until Breitbart News broke the story on April 8, 2017.[63]

The university initially launched an investigation to determine that the professor's statements were made as a private citizen and

---

61 Associated Press. "Fresno State professor won't be returning to classroom after 'Trump must hang' tweet." *Los Angeles Times* (Los Angeles), August 5, 2017. https://www.latimes.com/local/lanow/la-me-ln-fresno-state-trump-20170805-story.html.

62 Shimshock, Rob. "'Trump Must Hang' Prof: Trump Supporters 'Believe They Are Better by Virtue of Their Race.'" *The Daily Caller*. November 1, 2017. https://dailycaller.com/2017/11/01/trump-must-hang-prof-trump-supporters-believe-they-are-better-by-virtue-of-their-race/.

63 Hawkins, Awr. "Fresno State Lecturer: 'Trump Must Hang' to Save Democracy." *Breitbart*. April 8, 2017. https://www.breitbart.com/big-government/2017/04/08/fresno-state-lecturer-trump-must-hang-save-democracy/.

not as a representative of the school. However, in the face of massive national outrage, it appeared they were going to revisit the situation.

At the time, Fresno State President Joseph Castro said the professor's comments "warrant further review and consideration."

"Professor Maischak's personal views and commentary, with its inclusion of violent and threatening language, is obviously inconsistent with the core values of our University," Castro wrote on the university's website.

"The review of these and any other statements will be conducted in the context of rights of free expression, but also for potential direct threats of violence that may violate the law," he added.

Maischak told television station KSEE he was "appalled that the president of the university is allowing himself to be instrumentalized for a right-wing smear campaign."

"Specifically, the suggestion that I had made 'potential direct threats of violence that may violate the law' is unwarranted," he said. "It constitutes an embrace by the university of the claims made by right-wing propaganda outlets."

The professor was not a big fan of the "right-wing" media.

"The function of articles like the one produced by Breitbart and affiliates is to whip up a digital lynch-mob of people sending threats and insults to my email and Twitter accounts, with the ultimate goal of silencing dissenters," he told the *Fresno Bee*.

He went on to say he did not condone violence even though that's exactly what he advocated in his Twitter feed.

"From the context of the entirety of my tweets, this should be evident to anyone reading them in good faith (as opposed to malicious intent)," he said.

In other words, he took the "It all depends on what the definition of hang is" defense.

To say the professor was a prolific tweeter might be an understatement. Consider these gems:

"What would you do if your country has been hijacked by a gang of crazed homicidal fanatics? You storm the cockpit #Flight93."

"Mercy towards racists was always the fatal weakness of good Americans. 1865, 1965, they left too many of them alive."

"If only Mary had had an abortion! We would have been spared this Clerical-Fascist crap. #His Glory my ass!"

"You Fascist Trump-voting white trash scum can wallow in your filthy hell-holes of flyover states. Enjoy."

Republican students at Fresno State had every right to be deeply concerned about their safety and well-being inside that man's classroom.

The university decided not to renew Professor Maischak's contract, but he should've been fired—immediately.

Had Fresno State University decided to retain his services, the federal government should have been called on to defund the school. There's no good reason for our tax dollars to pay the salary of a man who wants to execute the president.

Class dismissed, professor.

PRESIDENT TRUMP IS WORSE THAN 9/11 TERRORISTS

The principal of a fancy New York City private school said the election of President Trump was worse than the September 11, 2001 terrorist attacks.[64]

Steve Nelson, principal of the Calhoun School, fired off a hate-filled email to parents blasting the president. He also said Trump's election would be more devastating than Vietnam, Watergate, and the assassination of Rev. Martin Luther King, Jr.

"I walked the complex inner-city streets of Cleveland during the racial unrest of the 60's," he wrote in an email obtained by the *New*

---

64   Rosner, Elizabeth. "Principal says Trump presidency is 'more troubling' than 9/11." *New York Post* (New York), February 8, 2017. https://nypost.com/2017/02/08/principal-says-trump-presidency-is-more-troubling-than-911/.

York Post. "I was in rural Georgia when Martin Luther King Junior was assassinated in Tennessee. I watched every moment of the Watergate hearings that led to the resignation of Richard M. Nixon. I watched soot-covered New Yorkers grimly trudging north on West End Avenue on September 11, 2001. I am more troubled now."

Just to put this in perspective, the principal believes President Trump is worse than the Muslim hijackers who flew jetliners into buildings and slaughtered thousands of Americans.

The principal would have us believe that he was more disturbed by Trump's election than the sight of New Yorkers falling from the sky or the Twin Towers collapsing onto the streets of lower Manhattan.

I do not know Principal Nelson, but he sounds like a deeply disturbed educator who should not be around impressionable school children. I'm rather surprised the principal did not blame Trump for sinking the *Titanic* or causing the Black Plague.

As repulsive as his comments might have been, I believe the principal's beliefs are rather mainstream among liberals. During the 2016 presidential campaign, Hillary Clinton labeled many of President Trump's supporters as a basket of "irredeemable deplorables."

In the liberal mindset, conservatives who support traditional marriage and securing the border and gun rights are not just deplorable. They believe we are *irredeemable* deplorables. In other words, our beliefs make us beyond redemption.

That's why so many parents and teachers defended Principal Nelson's hate speech.

"I've been at the school for 19 years and there was not a message that got a more positive response than this one," he told the *Post.* "If this upset a few people I understand. But you can't make everyone happy all the time."

What a steaming pile of compost.

The Calhoun School's only redeeming quality is that taxpayers are not forced to pay for this dumpster fire of a school.

So, let's set the record straight.

President Trump has never waged jihad against Americans, nor has he assassinated a Civil Rights leader or napalmed a jungle in Vietnam. And to compare those horrific atrocities with the president's desire to make our nation great again is not just offensive—it's downright evil.

KATHY GRIFFIN LOSES HER HEAD

One of the most egregious acts of Trump Derangement Syndrome happened early on in the Trump Administration when Kathy Griffin, the D-List celebrity, held a bloody replica of the president's severed head.[65]

Like many Americans, Barron Trump saw the image of his father's decapitated head. And as you might imagine—the eleven-year-old boy was traumatized by what he saw. It was gruesome, gory, and despicable.

"Kathy Griffin should be ashamed of herself," President Trump wrote in a Twitter message. "My children, especially my 11-year-old son, Barron, are having a hard time with this. Sick!"

Controversial photographer Tyler Shields said he and Miss Griffin were hoping to create a bold message.

"That's what art is meant to do," he told Fox News. "Some people look at it and they love it. Some people look at it and they hate it…I understand there are going to be people that hate this. It's a very touchy subject…but this is not real. We didn't kill anybody nor do I feel anybody should be killed."

Cable Newsers seemed to shrug it off. MSNBC's *Morning Joe* said it was not a story worth covering. I wonder if they would've said

---

65   Starnes, Todd. "Kathy Griffin Represents the Left's Visceral Hatred of Trump, Deplorables." *Todd Starnes* (blog). May 31, 2017. https://www.toddstarnes.com/uncategorized/ kathy-griffin-represents-the-lefts-visceral-hatred-of-trump-deplorables/.

the same if Miss Griffin had been holding President Obama's severed head? It's cliché, I know. But it needed to be said. The hypocrisy of the Left needs to be exposed—it must be exposed.

Miss Griffin is no stranger to the cable news landscape. Since 2007, she has co-hosted CNN's New Year's Eve coverage with Anderson Cooper. The show is known for its vulgar content and sexually charged innuendo.

Mr. Cooper denounced the faux-beheading, calling it "clearly disgusting and completely inappropriate."

Miss Griffin has since apologized for the act of artistic savagery, but I sincerely question her sincerity. I will give her credit, though. That one photograph encapsulates the unbridled fury and visceral hatred of the progressive Left towards those on the Right—the disease we now call Trump Derangement Syndrome.

It was photographic evidence of the political and cultural jihad the Left is waging, not just on President Trump, but on all of us gun-toting, Bible-clinging Deplorables. As they say, a picture is worth a thousand words.

CHAPTER 4

PENNSYLVANIA DEMOCRATS: ALLAH IS FINE, JESUS IS NOT

WILLIAM PENN ESTABLISHED a colony where people of faith could practice whatever religion they desired. Pennsylvania became the only colony without a state-run church.

The Charter of Privileges declared, "That no Person or Persons, inhabiting in this Province or Territories, who shall confess and acknowledge One almighty God, the Creator, Upholder and Ruler of the World; and profess him or themselves obliged to live quietly under the Civil government, shall be in any Case molested or prejudiced, in his or their Person or Estate, because of his or their conscientious Persuasion or Practice, not be compelled to frequent or maintain any religious Worship, Place or Ministry contrary to his or their Mind, or to do or super any Act or Thing, contrary to their religious Persuasion."[66]

William Penn's gift to America was freedom of religion, the right to practice one's faith in the public marketplace.

"All Persons who also profess to believe in Jesus Christ, the Savior of the World, shall be capable...to serve this Government in any Capacity," the Charter of Privileges declared.

---

66   Pennsylvania Charter of Privileges. http://www.ushistory.org/documents/charter.htm.

Nearly 318 years later, that fundamental bedrock of the Commonwealth of Pennsylvania has all but crumbled. And the state-house has now become a place where those who profess Jesus Christ face public rebuke.

In 2019, State Representative Stephanie Borowicz was invited to deliver a prayer at the beginning of the legislative day. Mrs. Borowicz, a freshman lawmaker and the wife of a Christian minister, gladly accepted the invitation.[67]

By chance, the state's first female Muslim lawmaker was scheduled to be sworn into office on the same day. There were many Muslim visitors in attendance. Also on the agenda was a prayer that was delivered by a Muslim cleric.

But it was Mrs. Borowicz's prayer that made national headlines when she invoked the name of Jesus Christ.

"Jesus, you are our only hope," she prayed. "At the name of Jesus, every knee will bow and every tongue will confess Jesus, that you are Lord."[68]

Movita Johnson-Harrell, who was sworn into office after the prayer, and her fellow Democrats were enraged, calling the prayer demeaning, degrading, and Islamophobic.

Now, before I continue, I want to share with you the entirety of Mrs. Borowicz's prayer. It's important for you to understand what the Democrats and Muslims considered to be offensive.

---

67   Starnes, Todd. "Todd Starnes: Pennsylvania Democrats: Allah is fine, Jesus is not." Fox News. Accessed May 29, 2019. https://www.foxnews.com/opinion/todd-starnes-pennsylvania-democrats-allah-is-fine-jesus-is-not.

68   CBS/AP. "First female Muslim member of Pennsylvania House offended by GOP member's praryer before swearing-in." *CBS News*. March 27, 2019. https://www.cbsnews.com/news/pennsylvania-state-rep-stephanie-borowicz-prayer-muslim-offended-gop-swearing-in/.

Jesus, I thank you for this privilege Lord of letting me pray God. That, I, Jesus am your ambassador today. Standing here representing you - the King of Kings, the Lord of Lords, the Great I Am, the One who is coming back again, the one who came, died and rose again on the third day. I'm so privileged to stand here today. So thank you for this honor, Jesus.

God, for those that came before us like George Washington in Valley Forge and Abraham Lincoln who sought after you in Gettysburg and the Founding Fathers in Independence Hall - Jesus - that sought after you and fasted and prayed for this nation to be founded on your principles and your words and your truths.

God forgive us. Jesus we've lost sight of you. We've forgotten you, God, in our country. And we are asking you to forgive us, Jesus. Your promise in your word says if my people who are called by name will humble themselves and pray and seek your face and turn from their wicked ways that you'll heal our land. Jesus, you are our only hope.

God, I pray for our leaders - Speaker Turzi, Leader Culter, Governor Wolf, President Trump. Lord, thank you that he stands beside Israel unequivocally Lord. Thank you that - Jesus—that we are blessed because we stand by Israel and we ask for the peace of Jerusalem as your word says God.

We ask that we not be overcome by evil and that we overcome evil with good in this land once again. I claim all these things in the powerful, mighty name of Jesus, at the name of Jesus every knee will bow and every tongue will confess that you Jesus are lord. In Jesus name, Amen.

In other words, Borowicz prayed the way the Bible commands us to pray for the peace of Jerusalem, for our elected leaders, and in the name of Jesus. And I suspect many of you have heard similar prayers in your houses of worship.

But Pennsylvania Democrats were clearly triggered by the name of the King of Kings and Lord of Lords.

Gov. Tom Wolf, also a Democrat, said he was "horrified" by Borowicz's invocation.

"It blatantly represented the Islamophobia that exists among some leaders—leaders that are supposed to represent the people," Johnson-Harrell said in a statement published by the Pennsylvania Capital-Star. "I came to the Capitol to help build bipartisanship and collaborations regardless of race or religion to enhance the quality of life for everyone in the Commonwealth."[69]

Democrat Representative Margo Davidson shouted "objection" near the end of the lawmaker's prayer.

"As an evangelical Christian, I was offended by [the prayer's] lack of humility or care or, dare I say, love for a human being duly elected by [her] district," Davidson said in remarks reported by the Pennsylvania Capital-Star. "It was mean spirited."

House Democratic Leader Frank Dermody said the prayer should've been more inclusive and inspirational.

"This morning on a very important day, on a day when we're swearing in a new member, the first woman Muslim serving in the Pennsylvania House of Representatives in history, there was a prayer that was not meant to inspire us," he told PennLive.com.[70]

He went on to tell a local television station that the prayer was "beneath the dignity of this House."

---

69   Caruso, Stephen. "Pa. Legislature's first Muslim woman calls prayer delivered by fellow House member blatant 'Islamophobia.'" *Pennsylvania Capital-Star*. March 25, 2019. https://www.penncapital-star.com/government-politics/pa-legislatures-first-muslim-woman-calls-prayer-delivered-by-fellow-house-member-blatant-islamophobia/.

70   "'Divisive' opening prayer given as first Muslim woman is sworn into Pa. House." *PennLive*. March 25, 2019. https://www.pennlive.com/news/2019/03/opening-prayer-sparks-controversy-in-pa-house-of-representative-on-day-it-swore-in-its-first-muslim-member.html.

It's hard to imagine that praying in the name of the Almighty is beneath the dignity of anyone, much less a bunch of Jesus-hating Democrats.

I invited Mrs. Borowicz to appear on my radio program so she could provide some context for the prayer. She told me she considered it a great honor to stand before her fellow lawmakers inside the ornate House chamber and deliver a prayer upon the assembled.

"You can see the Scripture as you stand up there and pray, that we all know the truth and the truth shall set you free," she said, referring to an inscription of John 8:32 in the House chamber.

I have to imagine the Democrats were equally troubled by the fact that their government buildings are inscribed with numerous Bible verses and religious references.

A kind and gracious woman, Borowicz is nevertheless steadfast in her faith and she flat-out refused to apologize to anyone who took offense at the name of Jesus.

"I don't apologize for it because that's how I pray almost every day," she said. "It doesn't matter who I'm standing in front of - I'm standing for Jesus no matter what."

Mrs. Borowicz faced a national firestorm of hate fomented by the mainstream media and Democrats. But their outrage was rather selective. Just a few minutes after the Christian prayer, a Muslim cleric delivered a prayer in Arabic and reportedly quoted from the Koran.

There was no condemnation from Democrats or the mainstream media even though the Muslim cleric prayed to a higher power.

So, if a Muslim can pray to Allah in the Pennsylvania statehouse, why can't a Christian pray in the name of Jesus?

"That's what my 15-year-old son said last night," Borowicz told me. "There's a double-standard."

And it's important to note that no one complained or objected to the cleric's prayer. No one held a press conference and condemned the Muslim as being anti-Christian. And why is that? I would like to think it's because Pennsylvania Republicans are guardians of William Penn's dream of religious freedom.

The freshman lawmaker said she prays to Jesus every day and reads her Bible and quotes Scripture.

"As Christians we don't pray differently based on who we're standing in front of," she said. "So whether that would have been in front of a crowd at my church and Christians or before Muslims or before Hindus I stand for Jesus no matter what and no matter who I'm in front of."

Borowicz dismissed accusations that praying in the name of Christ is somehow Islamophobic.

"That's ridiculous. I said I'd pray to Jesus. It's not directed towards anyone," she said. "But Todd, we know that there's power in the name of Jesus and so I think that it becomes offensive because there's power behind it."

Instead of capitulating to the godless mob of Democrats, the state lawmaker stood her ground.

"It's time for Christians and other people to start standing up and speaking out," she said. "I think we've been silent for too long."

I would imagine a group of Americans who died in a Pennsylvania field in Somerset County on September 11, 2001 would agree. Let's roll.

CHAPTER 5

A WARNING FROM DR. JAMES DOBSON

BACK IN 1977, Jimmy Carter was president, I was in grade school, and Hall & Oates was on the radio. And a Christian radio program started in Arcadia, California. It was called Focus on the Family.

Dr. James Dobson, the host of that program, would go on to have a profound impact on millions of Christian families around the world.

In 2017, National Religious Broadcasters asked me to interview Dr. Dobson for a fortieth anniversary celebration of his ministry. I was honored and also terrified. I mean, this wasn't a president or a congressman. This was Dr. Dobson.

I had grown up listening to this man on the radio. He was an icon, a hero to those of us of the Christian faith. My parents had read his books, especially the ones on discipline. What business did I have interviewing such a great man?

Well, Dr. Dobson and his wife could not have been more gracious on that day and, over the past years, he's become a regular fixture on my radio program. And after forty years of ministry, he has become a prophetic voice for our nation.

His message back in the 1970s still holds true today. There is a tremendous assault on what it means to be married and to raise godly children.

"Everything that matters, everything of value, sits on the foundation of the family," Dobson said. "The institution of marriage and parenthood underlies everything that is good about what we believe in, yet since the '70s, and certainly up to now, there is this effort to redefine marriage and to undermine what it means to raise children."

Dobson said that while he was a professor of pediatrics at the USC School of Medicine, he saw "the roots of a movement to undermine the institution of the family, and nearly everything else I cared about."

The aggressors "came from liberal ideology" and although it can be traced as far back as the '70s and '80s, the left-wing movement has "reached a fever pitch that has brought hatred for everything that made this country great."

"I am deeply concerned about it," he said.

In 2018, he penned a letter to the nation, warning his fellow countrymen that socialism was creeping into our political discourse. We discussed the dispatch at length on my radio program.

"You can't have a socialistic country and have a respect for the Constitution and the rule of law because we're given rights in there that socialistic leaders will undermine," Dobson said. "If you take out the Constitution, there's not a whole lot left. That takes my breath away that there are people out there that are really serious about making this a socialistic country."

His concerns were providential. As we enter the early days of the 2020 presidential contest, a number of the Democratic candidates are pledging allegiance to a socialist agenda. And Senator Bernie Sanders became the early front-runner.

In light of the looming election, Dr. Dobson was kind enough to allow me to reprint the letter he published back in 2018.

Dear Friends,

I would like to tell you about an experience Shirley and I had while visiting the cultural centers of Europe about 20 years ago. One of the cities that we toured was Berlin, Germany. I have been fascinated since I was a child with World War II and what made the adults around me so fearful. I have wondered in the ensuing years how highly educated and intelligent Germans could have been so corrupted and deceived by the propaganda that lay the foundation for tyranny. It is still difficult to comprehend how so many Christian churches with their good people fell prey to the lies screamed by Adolf Hitler and his evil cohorts. Even before he revealed his murderous intentions, they stood with their arms and hands extended, cheering rabidly for a man who was to become one of the most ruthless dictators in world history.

I searched for an understanding of the processes that led to torchlight parades, book burning, racial hatred, mass killings of Jews, Gypsies, Poles, homosexuals, and pitifully disabled and mentally ill people. While most Germans didn't know about the extermination camps, the majority favored his preparations for war. Many books have been written on that subject, but I needed to see it for myself. I found an explanation, at least partially, on the streets of Berlin.

One morning, I paid a small fee to be included in a "walkabout" tour of the important buildings and sites from the Nazi era. An articulate professor led our group and recounted what happened before and during the war. I was taking notes furiously as he spoke. First, we stood outside Herman Goring's headquarters. He was second in command after Hitler. Then we walked past Goebbel's propaganda ministry from which he spread lies and "fake news" during the 1930s and 1940s. Our group then stopped outside Gestapo headquarters where so many people were tortured and murdered for daring to oppose the regime. Demons seemed to leer from the windows and rooftops. The tour ended at the parking lot that now sits over the bunkers where Hitler spent his last days and eventually committed suicide with his wife of less than 40 hours, Eva Braun. Most of the city was demolished by Allied bombing, but these historic locations remain intact because they were reinforced by steel and concrete.

The tour lasted two hours, during which I learned how the Nazis managed to enslave the German people and then molded them into a force that devastated and conquered almost every country in Europe. Millions of people around the world held their breath as destiny hung in the balance.

What the professor told us remains in my memory today. He said the Nazi success was made possible by one primary factor. It was their complete and utter control of the means of communication. There was no Internet or television at that time, of course, but what did exist reached every dimension of the nation. Radio was highly effective in those days, as were newspapers, films, speeches, books and magazines, posters, rallies, and yes, public schools and universities. Every word spoken in Germany was scrutinized, and those who rejected Nazi lies publicly were often murdered or sent to concentration camps from which most didn't return. Terror was the stock and trade of the Gestapo. It was a common occurrence for secret police to knock on the doors of anyone who didn't conform to the party line. An offender would be dragged outside and shot, leaving terrifying images and warnings for the neighbors to see. It told them what would happen if they also got out of line. Even children were urged to report the activities and private conversations of their parents who talked at home about their opposition to the gangsters in government. They were tortured or murdered too. What a ghastly period in human history.

Speaking of children, one of the most wretched elements of the dictatorship was the complete domination of public schools. Parents had no influence on how their boys and girls were educated. In fact, all schools became training centers for Nazi propaganda. The boys were prepared for war, and girls in their mid-teens were actually sent to camps where they were expected to get pregnant from sexual contact with nearby boys. Babies born out of wedlock from these encounters became wards of the state to replace men likely to be killed in battle.

Here's how Adolf Hitler viewed public schools. He said, "Your child belongs to us already . . . what are you? You will pass on. Your descendants, however, now stand in the new camp. In a short time, they will know nothing but this new community." Later, as war approached, he said, "This new Reich will give its youth to no one."

If you want to know more about this tragic era, read The Rise and Fall of the Third Reich, by William Shirer.[3]

WHY AM I RECALLING THESE BITTER MEMORIES?

This historical account is relevant today because America and other Western nations have for decades been losing their God-given rights that define us as a free people. We are not experiencing Nazi-like tyranny yet, but we are steadily being expected to think, speak, write, and act in a prescribed manner in conformity with what is now called "political correctness." The mainstream media has become a tool to influence elections and spread this belief system. Sadly, the rights handed down to us by our forefathers more than 200 years ago are gradually being overridden, ignored, contradicted, or disregarded by the courts and legislatures. Alas, we are less free now than we were even five years ago.

As I hope you learned in school, although it is unlikely, the principles on which our freedom was built are spelled out in the first ten amendments to our Constitution. They are called the Bill of Rights. The first among them addresses the most important guarantee. It promises religious liberty and includes these words: "Congress shall make no law respecting the establishment of religion or prohibiting the free exercise thereof." Despite what you may have heard, nothing within the Constitution mentions the separation of church and state. To paraphrase the First

Amendment, it not only offers an ironclad guarantee that we will enjoy freedom of religion, but also promises freedom of speech, a free press, protects the rights of the people to assemble peacefully and to petition the government when citizens are aggrieved. These rights are fundamental for a liberated people.

The other nine amendments within the Bill of Rights enumerate additional assurances to the people that their government will have restricted authority over them. Alexander Hamilton wrote in Federalist Paper 84 that the Constitution tells Congress what limited powers it has to make law, and the Bill of Rights reiterates to Congress what powers it does not have to infringe on our rights.

Reflecting this affirmation, Abraham Lincoln said in his Gettysburg Address that ours is a government "of the people, by the people, and for the people." These assurances are precious to us today, and I thank God for the dedicated men who inspired and fought for them. We dare not let officious justices, judges, legislators, or politicians take even one of them away from us. But some liberals today are diligently trying to do just that. We must stop them, but how? Our rights are being trampled every day. The only way to defend our liberties is at the ballot box.

Unfortunately, more than half of Americans, including the majority of Christians, don't even bother to vote. Shame on them all! Don't they know that tyranny for us and our children is only one generation, or even one election, away? We must vote, vote, vote to elect leaders who will defend what has been purchased with the blood of patriots who died to protect our liberty. We owe it to the memory of their sacrifice to preserve what they did for us. We must not fritter it away on our watch! If any politician tells you he will "fundamentally change" this nation, what he means is that he plans to undermine our Constitution and take away our heritage of freedom. Run from him or her!

Let me illustrate what can happen in a country that doesn't respect basic human rights as they have been understood historically.

The Parliament of Canada, our neighbor to the north, passed an act into law on June 19, 2017. It is called the Transgender Rights Bill, and it imposes jail time and fines on anyone who uses inappropriate pronouns with regard to gender identity, gender expression, race, national or ethnic origin, color, religion, age, sex, sexual orientation, marital status, family status, genetic characteristics, disability or conviction of an offense for which a pardon has been granted. Forget laws protecting freedom of speech. Violations of this act are considered to be hate crimes in Canada's Criminal Code. Its passage has been lauded by Prime Minister Justin Trudeau as "another step toward equality." No! It is a step toward tyranny for our Canadian friends.

So much for free speech and thought. How about here in America? In my lifetime, I have witnessed the steady erosion of the principles that made this country great. Here are a few examples of what the judiciary has done, or attempted to do, in this great land of the free.

The Ninth Circuit Court of Appeals in California has done more to unhinge liberty than any other court. Some call it "The Ninth Circus." In 2015, for example, it upheld an outrageous legislative measure that forced prolife clinics, which are dedicated to the sanctity of human life, to promote abortions with their patients, and to place posters on the walls telling them where they can go to kill their babies. That became the law of the land in nine Western states for 32 months.

Thanks to President Trump's nomination and the Senate's subsequent confirmation of Neil Gorsuch to the Supreme Court, that ruling was overturned this past June by a vote of 5 to 4. How close the Court came to decimating freedom of speech in those clinics. So many other critical issues related to the Bill of Rights have been decided by a single vote.

Here's another. In Obergefell v Hodges, 2015, the Supreme Court redefined marriage as it had been protected in law and celebrated internationally for more than 5,000 years. The decision was 5 to 4, and it eliminated the exclusivity of marriage between a man and woman in 31 states. Five Justices imposed that cultural earthquake on America. Let me describe that ruling in another way. The laws protecting traditional marriage in 31 states were summarily invalidated. The citizens in those 31 states had recently gone to their polling places and voted to define marriage as being exclusively between one man and one woman. By a single vote, an arrogant, imperious, unelected Justice and four colleagues on the Supreme Court overrode the will of the people and swept away collective decisions of the populous.

These five unelected and imperious Justices imposed a cultural disaster on America. Some court-watchers say it was tantamount to the Roe v Wade decision in 1973, because it helped to undermine the institution of marriage. The family will never be the same. Lincoln's words at Gettysburg became hollow. Whatever happened to the promise that ours is a government of, by, and for the people? What hubris those pious Justices demonstrated with their votes!

In my opinion, this next example stands as one of the most outrageous assaults on parental rights in American history. Children attending Mesquite Elementary School in Palmdale, California, came home one afternoon and told their parents what had happened to them in class. It was a shocker. One of their teachers, with administrative approval, sat for hours with students, aged seven to ten, to ensure that each of them completed 79 items on a questionnaire. The kids, barely out of babyhood, were required to respond to highly personal questions about their private thoughts, including 10 items about their sexuality. Permission was neither requested nor discussed with parents. The children were asked about such topics as frequency of thinking about having sex, and thinking about touching other peoples' private parts, among many others.

The parents were incensed, (wouldn't you be?) and filed suit in both federal and district courts against the school district for invading their children's privacy and the parents' rights to control the upbringing of their children. They were desperately trying to defend the innocence of their children, but to no avail. The courts ruled that there is no fundamental right of parents to be the exclusive provider of information regarding sexuality or education of their children. Both the district and federal courts dismissed the case. One of them asserted that parents have no right to determine what their sons and daughters will be exposed to while enrolled in California's public schools.

When the parents appealed their case it went (where else?) to the Ninth Circuit Court of Appeals in California. You can guess what happened there. The Judges upheld the lower court ruling in favor of the school district and concluded that education is not merely about teaching reading, writing, and arithmetic. Education, they said, serves higher civil and social functions, including the rearing of children into healthy and responsible adults. In other words, "Parents, get lost."

I screamed to the high heavens when this ruling came down, but most residents in California yawned and accepted the invasion with a whimper. What a tragedy! I can envision the founding fathers rolling in their graves, and if they were alive today, thinking, "Is this what we fought the American Revolution for?"

Time and space will not permit me to cite similar horrendous rulings from unelected and imperious judges. Instead, I am excited to end my letter with some encouraging news. For the first time since the courts began to run things in the 1960s, the judiciary is changing dramatically. It is true! Some good things are starting to happen.

In June, the Court overturned a ruling against Jack Phillips, whose beliefs would not allow him to bake a wedding cake for homosexual activists. That assault on religious liberty failed by a 5 to 4 decision.

You can understand why the far left is in a state of panic today. It is looking for anything on which to hang its opposition to Judge Kavanaugh. One of their criticisms is that while in college, he put ketchup on his pizza. Are you kidding me? Does anyone else see the evidences of desperation here?

So far, President Donald Trump has nominated 44 judges who have been confirmed to the bench, and there are many others (88) in the pipeline. There is hope for additional conservative and common-sense decisions to be handed down in the future. This is a matter for sincere prayer among those of us who have longed for relief from judicial tyranny.

Thanks for letting me speak from my heart this month. The newly established Dr. James Dobson Family Institute, which consists of Family Talk, the Policy Center, the Education Center, and the Digital Library, is working hard to defend righteousness and family values on the home front. We will continue to speak for those of you who agree. Please join us as we do. Ours can be a lonely vigil unless defenders of the Constitution, and particularly conservative Christians, stand shoulder to shoulder with us in this struggle. We and other conservative organizations are winning in the public square. This is no time to go wobbly.

Dr. Dobson is absolutely right. We are facing a clear and present danger to our families, our churches, and the Republic. This is no time to go wobbly.

CHAPTER 6

WHY DOES THE LEFT HATE JESUS?

It's HARD TO believe American teenagers could be arrested for delivering a prayer, but that's the kind of nation we live in—a nation that was fundamentally transformed by the Obama administration.[71]

In 2011, the class president at Hampton High School in Tennessee wanted to deliver a prayer at graduation. The principal issued an edict that any child who attempted to pray would be stopped, escorted from the building by police, and arrested.

That incident was one of dozens included in a stunning Family Research Council report documenting a significant upsurge in government hostility to religion. From 2014 to 2017, there was a 76 percent increase in religious freedom violations, according to *Hostility to Religion: The Growing Threat to Religious Liberty in America*.[72]

71 "Hampton High School Graduates Choose Prayer at Ceremony." *Liberty Counsel*. May 24, 2011. https://www.lc.org/newsroom/details/hampton-high-school-graduates-choose-prayer-at-ceremony-1.

72 "Documented Incidents of Hostility to Religion in America Show 76 Percent Increase Within Past 3 Years According to New Report." *Family Research Council*. June 29, 2017. https://www.frc.org/newsroom/documented-incidents-of-hostility-to-religion-in-america-show-76-percent-increase-within-past-3-years-according-to-new-report.

"The recent spike in government driven religious hostility is sad, but not surprising, especially considering the Obama administration's antagonism toward biblical Christianity," Family Research Council president Tony Perkins said.

Perkins said the sixty-six-page report underscores the legitimacy of the actions taken by President Trump to end policies in federal agencies that "fan the flames of this religious intolerance."

"This report is designed to quantify the threat to our First freedom and to challenge Americans to use their God-given freedoms to protect these freedoms we enjoy as Americans," Perkins said.

In Florida, Pace high school Principal Frank Lay and Athletic Director Robert Freeman were charged with criminal contempt because they prayed over a meal. The pair was later found not guilty of violating an injunction banning the promotion of religious events at school.[73]

A Christian a capella group at James Madison University was told they could not perform "Mary, Did You Know?" because it was religious. They were directed to sing only secular songs.[74]

Allstate Insurance Company fired a staffer for allegedly using a company laptop to write a column against homosexuality. The company alleged said the column violated its diversity standards.[75]

---

73   Duin, Julia. "School prayer charges stir protests." *The Washington Times* (Washington, D.C.), August 14, 2009. https://www.washingtontimes.com/news/2009/aug/14/criminal-prayer-case-stirs-protests/?feat=home_headlines.

74   Thompson, Grace. "Christian a cappella group's song request for tree lighting ceremony denied." *The Breeze. December 6, 2015.* http//www.breezejmu.org/news/christian-a-cappella-group-s-song-request-for-tree-lighting/article_36ff7660-9c83-11e5-8bbd-d3f67d3a24ab.html.

75   Higgins, Michael. "Allstate and ex-worker settle online-essay suit." *Chicago Tribune (Chicago), February 17, 2016.* http://articles.chicagotribune.com/2006-02-17/news/0602170193_1_allstate-same-sex-spokesman-michael-trevino.

San Diego firefighters were threatened with disciplinary action if they refused to participate in a gay pride parade. The firefighters were subjected to verbal abuse and sexual gestures during the parade.[76]

A woman who rented out rooms in her home was sued after she refused to rent to a same-sex couple.[77]

An Oklahoma bank was forced to remove religious Christmas decorations under orders from the Federal Reserve.[78]

Travis Weber, FRC's director of the Center for Religious Liberty, said he hopes the report will be a wakeup call for people of faith.

"In a society like ours, we must be the guardians of our own freedom," he said. "Anyone who desires freedom in the future must take note of what these trends tell us about our freedom right now—relative to where we have come from—in order to protect freedom from going forward."

I've compiled a collection of stories that illustrate the grave dangers facing religious liberty. Much like the Islamic radicals, the atheists and secularists want to erase Christianity from the public marketplace. And they are waging their cultural jihad not with bombs—but with lawsuits.

---

76   Gilbert, Kathleen. "San Diego firefighters victorious in suit against forced participation in gay pride parade." *LifeSite. January 29, 2011.* http://www.lifesitenews.com/news/san-diego-firefighters-victorious-in-suit-against-forced-participation-in-g.

77   Andersen, Kirsten. "Judge rules against Christian innkeeper who refused to rent bedroom to lesbian couple." *LifeSite. April 16, 2016.* https://www.lifesitenews.com/news/judge-rules-against-christian-innkeeper-who-refused-to-rent-bedroom-to-lesb.

78   Matthews, Steve. "Fed Reverses Bann on Christian Symbols, Verses at Oklahoma Bank." *Bloomberg.* December 17, 2010. http://www.bloomberg.com/news/2010-12-17/fed-s-hoenig-reverses-ban-on-christian-symbols-verses-at-oklahoma-bank.html.

JOY BEHAR QUESTIONS A CHRISTIAN'S SANITY

Evangelical leader Franklin Graham said on the *Todd Starnes Radio Show* that every Christian in the nation should be offended and alarmed by anti-Christian rhetoric that was broadcast on ABC's *The View*.

Joy Behar, one of the co-hosts of *The View*, suggested in February 2018 that Christians who listen to the voice of God may be mentally ill.[79]

Graham, the president of Samaritan's Purse and the Billy Graham Evangelistic Association, said he could not believe ABC News would permit such dangerous rhetoric to be broadcast on national television.

"Every Christian who is listening right now—whether you are a Catholic, whether you are a Protestant, Baptist, Evangelical—whatever you may be…Pentecostal…this should scare the socks off of you," Graham said.

"For Joy Behar to say that all Christians are mentally ill is like suggesting we need to lock them up. They need to be taken out of society because these people are a danger," he added.

Behar's remarks were in response to a segment on Omarosa Manigault Newman, the reality television star turned White House staffer turned reality television star.

"As bad as y'all think Trump is, you would be worried about Pence. So everybody that's wishing for impeachment, might want to reconsider their life," Omarosa said in a clip from *Celebrity Big Brother*.

"I am Christian. I love Jesus, but [Pence] thinks Jesus tells him to say things," Omarosa told her fellow contestants.

---

79   Eltagouri, Marwa. "Joy Behar called Mike Pence's faith a 'mental illness.'
      Then she called to apologize." *The Washington Post* (Washington, D.C.),
      March 8, 2018. https://www.washingtonpost.com/news/acts-of-faith/
      wp/2018/03/08/joy-behar-called-mike-pences-faith-a-mental-illness-then-
      she-called-to-apologize/?utm_term=.eab30ea45202.

Behar was stunned by the revelation that Vice President Mike Pence would listen to the voice of God.

"It's one thing to talk to Jesus. It's another thing when Jesus talks to you. That's called mental illness, if I'm not correct, hearing voices," Behar declared.

"We are mentally ill because we believe in God and we believe in his son Jesus Christ? I'm offended by what she said," Graham told me.

Vice President Pence responded to Behar's vile claims during an interview broadcast on C-SPAN.

"To have ABC maintain a broadcast forum that compared Christianity to mental illness is just wrong," Pence said on C-SPAN. "It is simply wrong for ABC to have a television program that expresses that kind of religious intolerance."

The View co-host Sunny Hostin called the vice president's Christianity "dangerous."

"When you have a Mike Pence who now puts this religious veneer on things and who calls people 'values voters,' I think we're in a dangerous situation. Look I'm Catholic. I'm a faithful person, but I don't know that I want my vice president, um, speaking in tongues and having Jesus speak to him," she said.

Brent Bozell, the founder and president of Media Research Center, called on ABC News to apologize for what he called a "deplorable episode."

"Make no mistake, the slurs against the Vice President's faith insult millions of Christians and are unacceptable," Bozell wrote in a letter to the network.

Behar offered a half-hearted apology amid a grassroots uprising that targeted the network's sponsors.

"I think Mike Pence, say what you want about him and his religiosity. I don't think he's mentally ill. Even though he is saying he hears voices I don't think he's that crazy," she said.

Whatever.

If ABC News wants to employ a zealous anti-Christian, that is their business.

But let's be honest, had Joy Behar said about gay people what she said about Christians, she would've been fired on the spot.

MSNBC TAKES A CHEAP SHOT AT JERRY'S KIDS

MSNBC host Rachel Maddow took a cheap shot at Liberty University in a podcast interview with her leftist colleague Chris Hayes.[80]

Maddow bemoaned Christian universities like Liberty as representing "this anti-intellectual, anti-elite line of argument that we've seen from right-wing populists since the beginning of time."

Maddow then attempted to prove her point by attacking Kerri Kupec, the new spokesperson for the Justice Department. The story was first reported by Newsbusters.

"We've got a new Justice Department spokesperson who's from Liberty University, and Liberty University was founded by a televangelist so that your Christian child wouldn't be corrupted by actual higher education. And now that's the spokesperson for the Justice Department," she said.

Ms. Kupec was the former communications director for Alliance Defending Freedom, an organization that has argued a number of religious liberty cases before the Supreme Court. She was also a law clerk for Judge William Petty on the Court of Appeals of Virginia.

Ms. Kupec earned an undergraduate degree at Queens College and she studied at the graduate level at Fordham. She graduated from Liberty University School of Law in 2011.

---

80   Ellis, Christian. "'Liberty Is Not a Real University': MSNBC's Rachel Maddow Disses Christians, Falwell's Response Is Priceless." *CBN News*. December 20, 2018. https://www1.cbn.com/cbnnews/us/2018/december/liberty-is-not-a-real-university-msnbcs-rachel-maddow-disses-christians-falwells-response-is-priceless.

"These things add up," Ms. Maddow said. "They have real results in the world. Is there going to be a backlash to that? Is there going to be a resurgent intellectualism in hard line conservatism that isn't the kind of white supremacist stuff that we're seeing, which is the pseudo-intellectual stuff, right? I don't know, but it adds up. It adds up over time."

In other words, liberals like Ms. Maddow think all of us church-going folks are a bunch of ignorant hillbilly Klansmen who worship at the cross on Sunday and then burn the cross on Sunday night.

Liberty University President Jerry Falwell, Jr., whose father founded the school, told me Ms. Maddow demonstrated her religious bigotry. Not only that, he said her comments were stupid and ignorant.

"She needs to study her history. Harvard, Yale, Princeton, Brown—most of the Ivy league schools were founded by preachers and evangelists," Falwell said on my nationally syndicated radio show. "That's a long tradition in this country. She just shows her ignorance when she makes comments like that."

In addition to a law school, Liberty University has a medical school and a school of engineering. The university's students are sought-after in the workforce because of their work ethic and servant hearts.

Several years ago, I was privileged to have a Liberty University student as a college associate at Fox News. He was one of the hardest-working college students I've known.

"They don't have an entitlement attitude," Falwell said. "They go out with the idea of serving people and earning their way."

In reality, Liberty University is a school that thrives on debate and free speech, unlike many government-run schools.

The university has introduced students to a diverse group of speakers, from former President Jimmy Carter and Sen. Bernie Sanders to President Trump and even yours truly.[81]

---

81   Starnes, Todd. "Todd Starnes - Liberty University." *YouTube*. Video File. March 3, 2017. https://www.youtube.com/watch?v=PlAHXAqKCDs.

Compare that to places like the Ivy League, where conservatives are treated like enemy invaders and evangelical speakers are persona non grata.

"Those universities founded by good Christian people centuries ago are now places of liberal indoctrination," Falwell told me. "They are intolerant. They've become fascists. They want to shut you up. They don't want any other viewpoint but theirs in the classroom."

It's true that Liberty University is firmly rooted in Judeo-Christian philosophy—the same philosophy that is the foundation for our nation.

I'd say we are better off with a private Christian university that affirms the teachings of Jesus Christ than a government-run university that affirms the teachings of Karl Marx.

GOD AND GRIDIRON, GOOD GRAVY!

In the South, faith and football go together like biscuits and gravy. And that's especially true in a place like Laurens County, Georgia, where faith flavors everyday living far beyond the walls of the church house.

Those traditions were especially evident at West Laurens High School, where the marching band performed great songs of the faith and folks bowed their heads to pray before Friday night football games.

But those traditions are a problem, according to Americans United for Separation of Church and State, a Washington, D.C.-based group that loves to put its nose in other people's business—especially when it comes to public displays of the Christian faith.

They fired off a letter after someone complained about a pre-game prayer and the marching band's performance of the Christian hymn "How Great Thou Art," which was "timed to accentuate the prayer."[82]

---

82   Royals, Kate. "Brandon band reportedly not allowed to perform Christian hymn." *Clarion Ledger*. Modified August 22, 2015. https://www.clarionledger.com/story/news/2015/08/21/brandon-high-school-how-great-thou-art/32143307/.

"The opening prayer and religious hymn at the football game were plainly unconstitutional," Americans United wrote to the school district. "The presentation of prayers at school sporting events violates the Establishment Clause of the First Amendment to the U.S. Constitution."

Now we don't know who complained, but I'd be willing to bet a bucket of chicken that we're dealing with one of those long-haired, hummus-eating, godless pedagogues who smell of patchouli. The offended party probably doesn't eat meat, either.

After consulting with their legal counsel, the school board decided to replace the prayers with a "moment of silence," according to *The Courier Herald*, the local newspaper of record.

(It should be noted that there have been no reported instances of football fans converting to Christianity as a result of the prayers or the playing of "How Great Thou Art.")

Dr. Juliann Alligood is the school superintendent. She flat-out told me the decision to drop the prayers was made before she got hired. She also informed me in short order that she is a good Christian lady and a church pianist.

That being said...

"I believe we should follow the law," she said. "And the moment of silence probably protects everyone's religious interests. We're doing what we have to do."

Dr. Alligood said the now-banned invocations were just a part of the fabric of the community.

"We're the Bible Belt," she said. "It wasn't something we were doing belligerently or to thumb our nose at anybody. It had been common practice."

But a common practice no more. They decided to follow the demands of Americans United.

So, when the West Laurens Raiders started their season, instead of one person leading the invocation, the entire stadium led the invocation. Hundreds stood on their feet and recited The Lord's Prayer.

And the marching band also complied with the demands of Americans United. They did not follow the prayer with a rendition of "How Great Thou Art." Instead, they played "Amazing Grace."

Will Americans United perceive that as a musical act of civil disobedience? Will they fire off another cease-and-desist letter?

If Americans United wants to ban "Amazing Grace," so be it. There are plenty more songs in the hymnal, songs like "All Hail the Power of Jesus' Name" and "When the Roll is Called up Yonder I'll be There."

So give it your best shot, Americans United. The rest of us are ready for a toe-tapping, hand-waving, all-night singing—armed with the Baptist Hymnal in one hand and the Church of God Red-Back hymnal in the other.

Finally, a word of advice to the hummus-eating, hymn-hating culprit who caused this kerfuffle. I sincerely doubt that our Lord appreciates you picking on a bunch of teenagers. So knock it off. Otherwise, when the roll is called up yonder, you may not be there.

CHRISTIAN MUSIC BANNED IN SENIOR HOUSING CONDO

The sign was not very hard to miss: "ANY AND ALL CHRISTIAN MUSIC IS BANNED."

That message was posted on an organ located in a commons area of Cambridge House, a condo building in Port Charlotte, Florida. Residents could belt out the theme song to *Frozen* or Kelly Clarkson's "Stronger," but they were not permitted to sing "Amazing Grace."[83]

Residents were also allegedly told they could no longer host a weekly Bible study in the commons area, according to a Fair

---

83　Smith, Samnual. "Residents Banned From Holding Bible Study, Praying in Condo's Common Area." *The Christian Post.* March 12, 2018. https://www.christianpost.com/news/residents-banned-from-holding-bible-study-praying-in-condos-common-area.html.

Housing complaint filed with the Department of Housing and Urban Development.

Cambridge House passed a resolution "regarding religious observances on the common elements."

"Prayers and other religious services, observations, or meetings of any nature shall not occur at meetings of the Association (Owner meetings, member meetings, committee meetings, or, otherwise) and shall not occur in or upon any of the common elements," the resolution read.

According to First Liberty Institute, a law firm that specializes in religious liberty cases, the resolution led to a religious cleansing of the entire condo association. Residents removed decorative crosses from their doors and a decorative angel fountain was removed from a courtyard—along with a statue of St. Francis of Assisi.

The statue had been donated by a resident in memory of a deceased family member, First Liberty Institute noted.

But perhaps the most egregious allegation involved Donna Dunbar, a devout Christian and a lay minister in the Seventh Day Adventist Church.

First Liberty Institute filed the Fair Housing Act complaint on her behalf. They told me residents were not given a reason for the crackdown.

Dunbar hosted a weekly Bible study for ladies in the condo's social room. They sang songs, prayed, and studied a book called *Experiencing God* by Henry Blackaby.

Other groups of similar size used the room for thrice-weekly card games and movie nights.

However, Dunbar was ordered by the condo association's treasurer to obtain insurance in order to continue her meetings, the complaint alleged.

Nevertheless, Dunbar obtained the insurance policy and continued the Bible study meetings.

But all that changed in early February when the condo association passed what First Liberty Institute called a "discriminatory resolution" without prior notice.

If true, that would constitute a violation of Florida law.

Dunbar and her husband received a letter from Gateway Management ordering them to cease and desist the Bible study.

"The result of this resolution prohibits Bible Study meetings in the Social Room effective February 16, 2018," the letter read.

So why not just host the Bible study in her home?

According to First Liberty Institute, the participants would not be able to fit comfortably in Mrs. Dunbar's 919-square-foot condo.

Regardless, First Liberty Institute and Greenberg Traurig, P.A. contended that the Bible study group had every right to use the social room for their weekly gathering.

"The Cambridge House Resolution, both in text and in application, is discriminatory and violates the Fair Housing Act because it prohibits Mrs. Dunbar and other Christian residents from accessing common condominium areas for any religious activity, while allowing other residents to use those same facilities for similar non-secular purposes," attorney Adam Foslid wrote in the complaint.

Neither the condo association nor its management company responded to my telephone calls.

It seems like a slam dunk case for the religious residents. If management allows residents to play poker in the social room, they should also allow folks to hold a Bible study.

I'm putting my money on the church ladies.

TOWN BANS CATHOLIC FARMER
FROM SELLING BLUEBERRIES

The Tennes family has been farming in Michigan for generations. They grow all sorts of crops at the Country Mill Farm: organic apples, blueberries, pumpkins, sweet corn.[84]

Steve Tennes and his family sold their produce at the farmer's market owned by the city of East Lansing. But in 2017, city officials told the devout Catholic family that their blueberries and sweet corn were not welcome at the farmer's market—and neither were they.

Someone posted a message on Country Mill's Facebook page inquiring whether they hosted same-sex weddings at the farm.

Tennes told the individual they did not permit same-sex marriages on the farm because of the family's Catholic belief that marriage is a sacramental union between one man and one woman.

City officials later discovered the Facebook posting and began immediate action to remove Country Mill from the Farmer's Market, alleging the family had violated the city's discrimination ordinance.

"It was brought to our attention that The Country Mill's general business practices do not comply with East Lansing's Civil Rights ordinances and public policy against discrimination as set forth in Chapter 22 of the City Code and outlined in the 2017 Market Vendor Guidelines, as such, The Country Mill's presence as a vendor is prohibited by the City's Farmer's Market Vendor Guidelines," read a letter the city sent to the family.

It also did not seem to matter to city leaders that the farm is located twenty-two miles outside the city limits, and that their decision had absolutely nothing to do with the business of selling blueberries at the farmer's market.

---

84   "Catholic Family Fights for Freedom of Speech Over Gay Weddings on Their Farm." *The Epoch Times.* April 13, 2019. https://www.theepochtimes. com/catholic-family-fights-for-freedom-of-speech-over-gay-weddings-on-their-farm_2878333.html.

"We were surprised and we were shocked," Steve told me. "My wife and I both volunteered to serve in the military—to protect freedom. Now we come home and the freedom that we worked to protect—we have to defend in our own backyard."

"Whether you are a Jew, Muslim, or Christian—people of faith should not be eradicated from the marketplace simply because they don't share the same thoughts and ideas that the government is choosing to promote," Steve told me.

So, they decided to fight for their constitutional rights.

Alliance Defending Freedom (ADF) filed a federal lawsuit alleging East Lansing violated the constitutional rights of the Tennes family.

"All Steve wants to do is sell his food to anyone who wants to buy it, but the city isn't letting him," said ADF Legal Counsel Kate Anderson. "People of faith, like the Tennes family, should be free to live and work according to their deeply held beliefs without fear of losing their livelihood. If the government can shut down a family farmer just because of the religious views he expresses on Facebook—by denying him a license to do business and serve fresh produce to all people—then no American is free."

But this story has a very happy ending. In 2017, a federal judge sided with the Tennes family, ruling that the city had discriminated against the farmers because of their views on marriage.

There is a concerted effort by the Left to silence free speech and eradicate Christianity from the public marketplace. The only course of action is to stand and fight.

I commend the Tennes family and Alliance Defending Freedom for filing a lawsuit. They did not let up until every last kernel of sweet corn had been restored to its rightful place in the farmer's market. They shucked it to the cob.

TEENAGER BANNED FROM DELIVERING
GRADUATION PRAYER

Moriah Bridges wanted to thank God for His immeasurable blessings on Beaver High School's graduating class. But she could not because it was against the law.[85]

The Pennsylvania teenager wanted to offer thanksgiving to the Almighty for parents and coaches and teachers. But, again, she could not because it was against the law.

"Make us selfless. Make us just. Make us successful people, but more than that, make us good people," Moriah wanted to pray. But that, too, was determined to be unlawful.

This is America, the land of the free, the home of the brave. But it is also a place where a young teenager girl is not permitted to mention the name of Jesus Christ or anything remotely religious in a graduation speech at a public high school.

Moriah Bridges, a member of the 2017 graduating class, was asked to provide what they call the closing exercise at Beaver High School's graduation. She crafted a lovely prayer that mentioned her "Heavenly Father" and her "Lord."

"Lord, surround us with grace and favor everywhere we go," she prayed. "Soften our hearts to teach us love and compassion, to show mercy and grace to others the way that you showed mercy and grace to us, even to the ultimate sacrifice. Help us love our brothers and our sisters deeply. Lead us to bless them."

Unfortunately, Moriah was not permitted to deliver that prayer, thanks to the Beaver Area School District. They notified the teenager that her prepared remarks were unlawful, unconstitutional, and therefore, impermissible.

---

85   "Moriah Bridges Case: High school senior instructed to censor graduation remarks." *First Liberty*. Accessed May 24, 2019. https://firstliberty.org/cases/moriah-bridges/.

"The selected students may still address their class and indicate the things that they wish/hope for their class, but they may not do it in the style of a prayer and most certainly may not recite a prayer that excludes other religions (by ending 'in the name of our Lord and Savior, Jesus Christ' or 'in the matchless name of Jesus')," principal Steven Wellendorf wrote to Moriah in a letter.

The principal flat-out told the young lady that prayer—even student-led prayer—is not permissible by federal law.

"I was shocked that the school said my personal remarks broke the law and I was saddened that I could not draw upon my Christian identity to express my best wishes for my classmates on what should've been the happiest day of high school," Moriah said.

"The last lesson this school district taught its students is that they should hide their religious beliefs from public view," said Jeremy Dys, of First Liberty Institute. "That fails the test of the First Amendment."

It wasn't Moriah who broke the law; it was the school district, Dys said.

"In short, school officials—in violation of the First Amendment—forced Moriah to censor her personal remarks during the closing exercise of her commencement ceremony merely because of the religious viewpoint of her remarks," the attorney said. "Moriah was muzzled and restrained by school officials on the penultimate day of her high school career."

The U.S. Department of Education has a long-standing policy regarding student speech, a policy that covers graduation ceremonies.

"Where students or other private graduation speakers are selected on the basis of genuinely neutral, evenhanded criteria and retain primary control over the content of their expression; however, that expression is not attributable to the school and therefore may not be restricted because of its religious (or anti-religious) content," the policy reads.

The school district's suggestion that Moriah should offer wishes or hopes for her fellow graduates is ludicrous. Moriah was not praying to some sort of fairy godmother. She was praying to Almighty God.

Ironically, by refusing to allow a student to pray in the name of Jesus Christ, the school district excluded the Christian religion. But these days, excluding Christianity to achieve inclusiveness is a standard operating procedure on high school campuses.

In Oklahoma, East Central University said they would remove crosses, Bibles, and other religious symbols from a campus chapel to appease a bunch of out-of-town agitators. The Kathryn P. Boswell Memorial Chapel opened in 1957.[86]

"We will continue to use the building as we always have, for all faiths," ECU President Katricia Pierson said in a statement to *The Ada News*. "We do not want to presume to embrace one faith over another. We support all cultures and attempt to make them comfortable when they are here."

The university's president went on to say they were "looking at the feasibility of removing the cross on the steeple, but need to respond to the request for removal of religious icons from the chapel."

"We are exploring options for preserving the items," she said.

So, on the bright side, East Central University did not burn the Bibles or toss the crosses into a wood chipper.

Americans United for the Separation of Church and State was responsible for the Christian cleansing at ECU. They fired off a terse letter accusing the school of displaying "religious iconography." That letter was obtained by *The Ada News*.

"These displays include Latin crosses on the top of and inside the building, Bibles and a Christian altar," the letter stated. "While it is legal for a public university to have a space that can be used by students for religious worship so long as that space is not dedicated

---

86   Franklin, Dallas. "Oklahoma Attorney General fires back at Washington, D.C. group that is demanding ECU remove cross from chapel." *Oklahoma's News*. August 30, 2017. https://kfor.com/2017/08/30/oklahoma-attorney-general-fires-back-at-washington-d-c-group-that-is-demanding-ecu-remove-cross-from-chapel/.

solely to that purpose, it is a violation of the Establishment Clause of the First Amendment to the U.S. Constitution to display religious iconography on government property."

That's a great big load of legal malarkey.

Hiram Sasser, director of litigation for First Liberty Institute, said there is federal precedent to maintain chapels in taxpayer-funded facilities.

"We have a Congressional Prayer Room in the Capitol, we have chapels in government-owned airports and many other government owned chapels," Sasser told me.

Sasser suspected that Americans United was just testing Oklahoma's new attorney general, Mike Hunter.

"They want to see if he backs down or stands up to their ridiculous claims and I predict Mike Hunter will fight hard to preserve this historic chapel," Sasser said.

Meanwhile, many Oklahomans were furious over the university's decision to capitulate to those who want to eradicate Christianity from the public marketplace.

"I feel betrayed by our own country, upset that this could take place in America," alum Jill Tucker Brown told me. "We are a nation founded on Christianity."

Ms. Brown believes the university should have stood up to the atheist and secularist bullies.

"I think it is absurd that anyone would go to this length (to remove the cross)," she told me. "If this university does not stand up for their rights, this will not be their only fight."

Anita Thomas, also a graduate of East Central University, was heartbroken over the news.

"I am heartbroken because our country has become a place where things like this can happen," she told me.

STUDENT BOOTED FROM CLASSROOM
FOR READING BIBLE

It's apparently okay to read history books at Northern Arizona University, but not the Good Book.

Early in 2017, Mark Holden, a twenty-two-year-old history major, was ordered to leave a lecture hall after his professor objected to him reading the Bible before the start of the class.[87]

Holden alleged that Professor Heather Martel ordered him to put away the Good Book around six minutes before a scheduled history class. It's unclear why she objected to the reading of God's Word. She declined to talk to me for this book.

According to her biography, Professor Martel is a noted scholar who is working on an essay titled, "The Gender Amazon: Indigenous Female Masculinity in Early Modern European Representations of Contact." She also teaches classes on Global Queer History and Feminist Theory.

When Holden declined to stop reading his Bible, the professor summoned Derek Heng, the chairman of the department. Heng then proceeded to explain the situation.

Holden recorded the conversation and turned it over to congressional candidate Kevin Cavanaugh. In turn, Cavanaugh provided me with a copy of the audio.

"So Professor Martel says that she doesn't want you sitting in front of her because you put, you know, a Bible out, right?" Heng said.

"So she doesn't want me in the front because I have my Bible out," Holden replied.

"No, I think she, I mean, well why do you have your Bible out anyway," Heng asked.

---

87   Gockowski, Anthony. "A Northern Arizona University student was recently asked to stop reading his Bible prior to the start of one of his classes." *Campus Reform*. April 27, 2017. https://www.campusreform. org/?ID=9114.

After a bit more back and forth regarding the dynamics in the classroom, the chairman of the department got to the heart of the issue.

"So, will you, will you, will you, put your Bible away," Heng asked.

The incident occurred in February 2017, but only became public after Campus Reform reported on the controversy.

Holden had previously drawn the ire of his professor during a classroom discussion on assimilation.

"All the students agreed with her that assimilation is oppressive and evil," Holden said. "I suggested there are both positive and negative aspects to assimilation."

As an example, he referenced a report about two Muslim men in California who reportedly said the Koran justified doing terrible things to women.

"She told me I was a racist and she would not tolerate that kind of racism in the class," Holden said. "I told her Islam was not a race and I was only talking about what the two Muslim men as individuals said—I was not making broad claims about Islam or my interpretation of the Koran."

After a bit of back and forth, Holden said the professor told the class, "Welcome to Trump's new America—where straight white males can say prejudicial things without being reprimanded for it."

I reached out to Holden and university officials for their side of the story, but so far, they have not returned my calls.

However, I did obtain an email Martel sent to Holden warning him about "disruptive behavior."

"For the remainder of the class, I will ask you to move to one of the desks along the wall by the door," she wrote. "The roll sheet will be passed to you. You will make sure that students who come in late sign in. I will also require that you respect me and the other students in the class by acting in a civil manner."

In a separate email addressed to the entire class, Martel vowed to "re-instate civility" in the classroom.

"I want this to be clear: hate speech does not meet the definition of respectful discussion and will not be tolerated," she wrote. "In law, hate speech is any speech, gesture or conduct, writing, or display which is forbidden because it may incite violence or prejudicial action against or by a protected individual or group, or because it disparages or intimidates a protected individual or group."

Something tells me Christians and Conservatives are not considered to be a protected group at Northern Arizona University.

"If you are a Christian, you are being targeted," Cavanaugh told me. "Christians are being silenced."

Cavanaugh said he got involved in Holden's case because stopping the radicalization of public universities is a part of his campaign platform.

"If free speech is not permitted on a public university campus, federal funding should be refused," he told me. "If you want to limit free speech, don't take federal money."

"We have seen on this campus and across the nation that people are being punished for their Christian views," Cavanaugh said.

That may or may not be the case here, but based on that audio recording, there's not much wiggle room.

The cold hard reality is that a student was yanked out of a classroom for reading the Bible. Woe be unto us, America.

ATHEISTS RAGE AGAINST THE HALLELUJAH CHORUS

A gaggle of disgruntled atheists did a whole lot of hollering about the "Hallelujah Chorus" in Oak Ridge, Tennessee.[88]

The Freedom From Religion Foundation's local chapter was angry after a teacher at Linden Elementary School played a portion of the "Hallelujah Chorus" during morning announcements.

88   Pounds, Ben. "Dispute over 'Hallelujah Chorus.'" *OakRidger*.
      September 11, 2017. https://www.oakridger.com/news/20170911/
      dispute-over-hallelujah-chorus.

"While this music may be beautiful and even inspirational for Christians, it is not acceptable for broadcasting to the entire student body at Linden Elementary," Aleta Ledendecker wrote in a letter to the school district that was obtained by the *Oak Ridger*.

The aggrieved atheist group said they were acting on behalf of two parents who had children enrolled in the school.

"In consideration of all the possible choices of music, this piece with its distinctly religious content can be interpreted as proselytizing," Ledendecker wrote.

For the record, there have not been any reports of children spontaneously converting to the Christian faith as a result of George Frideric Handel's beautiful song.

"This is the litmus test I use: if I were a Christian parent walking in the school, and I heard over the PA system during morning announcements music with the words 'Praise Allah. Allah is king on high. Bow down to Allah,' how would I feel as a Christian parent with that being broadcast to all the children in the schools," Ledendecker told the *Oak Ridger*.

The school district told *The Todd Starnes Show* that a teacher had a good reason for playing a twenty-second excerpt from Handel's *Messiah*.

"The passage was selected to correspond with the school's overall music curriculum that, for that particular week, featured the musical works of George Handel," the school spokesperson told me.

Long story, short—Handel is not going anywhere.

"The school system strongly disagreed with her position and, through our school board's attorney, we responded promptly to the writer suggesting that she was in error," the spokesperson told me.

"The criticisms articulated by Ms. Ledendecker appear to have been based upon insufficient information taken entirely out of context, incorrect assumptions about the school's music curriculum and a fundamental misunderstanding of the First Amendment's relationship with historically sacred classical music compositions being taught in a public school music curriculum," the spokesperson added.

Yeah, that's probably going to jingle the atheists' bells.

It's about time a school district stood up to those godless bullies and politely told them to blow it out their piccolo.

As George Handel would say, "Hallelujah!"

ALABAMA SCHOOL STOPS PRE-GAME PRAYERS

Faith and football go hand in hand across the fruited plain, especially in the great state of Alabama.

It's not all that unusual for high school football games to start with a moment of prayer, an invocation.

The game announcer will ask folks to stand and remove their hats as the marching band belts out "The Star-Spangled Banner." Then, he'll hand the press box microphone to a student who will thank God and ask for His blessings upon the evening's game.

It's a longtime tradition—a beloved tradition where folks of all colors and backgrounds unite as one people, in public—before all you-know-what breaks loose on the field.

But in 2017, that tradition came to an abrupt end in Lee County, Alabama, when the school district announced that student-led prayers would no longer be permitted before high school football games.[89]

"That is a violation of the Constitution," Supt. James McCoy told me during a telephone interview. "Students and adults are not allowed to pray over the public address system."

The public prayer ban was the result of a complaint letter filed by the Freedom From Religion Foundation (FFRF), a notorious group of atheists, agnostics, and free-thinkers based in Wisconsin.

Apparently, a local parent got triggered by the name of Jesus and suffered a raging micro-aggression.

---

89   "Threats of lawsuit leads to Lee County Schools banning pre-game prayer tradition." *WTXL.com*. Modified September 21, 2017. https://www.wtxl.com/news/threats-of-lawsuit-leads-to-lee-county-schools-banning-pre/article_39994e20-9ee6-11e7-af6c-b7660abb0c87.html.

"It is illegal for a public school to sponsor religious messages at school athletic events," FFRF's Christopher Line wrote in a letter to the district.

"Even if student-led, the Court said prayers at a regularly scheduled school-sponsored function conducted on school property would lead an objective observer to perceive it as state endorsement of religion," Line added.

The Freedom From Religion Foundation said football games must be secular to "protect the freedom of conscience of all students."

Oh, good grief. It's a pre-game prayer—not a Sunday morning revival service.

To the best of his knowledge, Supt. McCoy said no one had ever complained about the prayer before FFRF filed their letter.

Supt. McCoy said the public prayer would be replaced with a moment of silence.

"In our business—it's not a problem until it becomes an issue," he said. "I understand the decision. I don't necessarily agree with it. I am bound to follow the law and uphold what is supposed to be done."

So what happens if someone in the stadium on Friday night decides to recite The Lord's Prayer? Will they be kicked off school property? Will they be tossed in jail?

The superintendent said spontaneous recitation of The Lord's Prayer would be permissible.

"That has not been banned," he said.

Well, if that's the case, the student who was previously assigned the prayer should pull out a megaphone and in a very subtle way holler, "Hey y'all—hush up. We're about to spontaneously recite The Lord's Prayer."

And if I know the folks in Alabama, I reckon those godforsaken atheists will be able to hear that prayer all the way back in Wisconsin.

LEFTISTS SAY JUDGE'S CHRISTIAN BELIEFS
DISQUALIFY HIM FROM OFFICE

A Wisconsin Supreme Court candidate is facing an onslaught from radical leftist groups who contend his religious beliefs should disqualify him from serving as a judge.[90]

Brian Hagedorn, who currently sits on the Wisconsin Court of Appeals, has been accused of being anti-gay because he helped launch a Christian grade school that requires students, faculty, and parents to follow Christian teachings.

The Augustine Academy bars students, parents, and teachers from "participating in immoral sexual activity." The school also defines marriage as a union between one man and one woman.

In other words, the Christian school adheres to orthodox Christian teachings that Christians have been following for more than two thousand years.

The state chapter of the Human Rights Campaign said Judge Hagedorn's involvement with the school should disqualify him from the bench, Wisconsin Public Radio reported.

"Judges are tasked with a sacred duty to uphold equal treatment for all people under the law," said Wendy Strout, state director for the pro-LGBTQ organization. "As someone who has publicly and unabashedly voiced contempt for LGBTQ equality, Brian Hagedorn's record is disqualifying."

Statewide media also accused Hagedorn of comparing homosexuality to bestiality in a blog post he wrote during law school.

Judge Hagedorn told the *Todd Starnes Radio Show* that the attacks by leftist groups are "an effort to silence people and push people out of public life if they are people of faith."

---

90   Glauber, Bill, Patrick Marley, and Molly Beck. "'We made history.' Brian Hagedorn declares victory in Wisconsin Supreme court race." *Journal Sentinel,* Last modified April 4, 2019. https:// www.jsonline.com/story/news/politics/elections/2019/04/03/ wisconsin-supreme-court-brian-hagedorn-declares-victory/3352041002/.

"If you volunteer at the local parish council or v
local Catholic school or orthodox Jewish school, Musl
school you may not be qualified for public office or p
public life, according to my opponents," Hagedorn told
a dangerous development, it's wrong and we need to call t

He blasted critics and rightly accused them of religious i

"Hopefully, we are going to send a message and sa
wrong,'" he told me. "People of faith can participate in pu
They should not be relegated to the sidelines. It's okay to be
your church. It's okay to practice your faith and to live it out
life and still be an excellent judge."

Unfortunately, a good many leftist groups, along with
anti-Christian cronies in the Wisconsin media, don't agree
the judge. And they have piled on by publishing all sorts of
news stories.

The *Milwaukee Journal Sentinel* accused Hagedorn of deliver
a speech to an anti-gay legal group. That legal group turned out
be Alliance Defending Freedom, one of the most respected religiou
liberty law firms in the nation.

Alliance Defending Freedom has argued a number of cases before
the Supreme Court, including the high-profile Masterpiece Cake
Shop case. The Supreme Court sided with the Christian baker in that
particular case.

The most scurrilous charge came from the far-left website Think-
Progress. They accused Judge Hagedorn of comparing homosexuality
to bestiality in a 2005 blog post he wrote in law school.

He simply paraphrased Supreme Court Justice Antonin Scal-
ia's dissent on a case about Texas sodomy laws. And Hagedorn
wrote that his argument was from a legal perspective, not a moral
perspective. Regardless, the Human Rights Campaign condemned
Hagedorn's "horrific and outdated comments."

"Judges are tasked with a sacred duty to uphold equal treatment
for all people under the law," Strout said in a statement. "Hagedorn's

ti-LGBTQ rhetoric is deeply disturbing, and as someone who has
ublicly and unabashedly voiced contempt for LGBTQ equality he
as no place on the bench or in public office. If elected, Wisconsin-
tes could not count on him to uphold their civil rights."

Joy Pullmann, writing in *The Federalist*, correctly surmised that
leftists are sending a message that Christians cannot be good judges
because of their faith.

"These smears against Hagedorn and others like him nominated
or running for public office hang a 'No Christians need apply' sign
on not only public offices but entire professions, such as law, health,
and education," she wrote. "In all of these domains, and more, Christians are increasingly told to check their convictions at the door."

Judge Hagedorn is just the latest public official who has faced a
public inquisition because of his religious beliefs. In recent months,
federal nominees have been interrogated over their Catholic dogma
and their involvement in the Knights of Columbus.

The Human Rights Campaign wants you to believe the crusade
against Judge Hagedorn is about tolerance. In reality, it's about
shoving Christians into the closet.

FAITH-BASED POSTERS REMOVED FROM AIR FORCE BASE

The Air Force has removed several "faith-based" posters from a
display at Langley Air Force Base to appease a group of hysterical
feminists who got their pantyhose in a twist over what they called
"sexist, male-supremacist language."

Before we go any further, it's important to understand that the
offending passage on the poster was first published in a 1955 Air
Force manual.[91]

---

91   Vergakis, Brock. "Air Force Removes Posters at Langley AFB Following
       Sexism Complaints." *Military.com*. Accessed May 24, 2019. https://www.
       military.com/daily-news/2017/02/28/air-force-removes-posters-langley-afb-
       sexism-complaints.html.

"Men cannot live without faith except for brief moments of anarchy or despair," one poster read. "Faith leads to conviction— and convictions lead to actions. It is only a man of deep convictions, a man of deep faith, who will make the sacrifices needed to save his manhood.... It is obvious that our enemy will attack us at our weakest spot. The hole in our armor is our lack of faith. We need to revive a fighting faith by which we can live, and for which we would be willing even to die."

The words the National Organization for Women (NOW) found most egregious were "man," "men," and "manhood."

"The passages glorify the military's reliance on male dominance, stating without equivocation that 'It is only a man of deep convictions, a man of deep faith, who will make the sacrifices needed to save his manhood,'" wrote NOW president Terry O'Neill in a letter to Gen. Herbert Carlisle.

"What message does that send to young women who currently serve, or want to serve, in the military? What do you say to the women in your command who make the same sacrifices to protect their country as do men? Is the purpose of the U.S. armed forces really to assist 'only' men to make sacrifices necessary to save their 'manhood?'" she added.

The Military Religious Freedom Foundation (MRFF) fired the first shot on the "faith-based" poster, demanding it be removed because it was an endorsement of religion.

"This message undoubtedly expresses a preference for airmen of religious faith over those who practice no religion," MRFF founder Mikey Weinstein wrote to General Carlisle. "It not only states that men cannot even LIVE without faith, it questions the loyalty, strength, and sacrifice of non-religious airmen by stating that only men of faith are willing to make necessary sacrifices, as well as that faith is 'our only safety.'"

But the Air Force dismissed the MRFF's concerns—and that's when the feminists got involved.

"This offensive propaganda must NOT be allowed to continue on display at ACC Headquarters," O'Neill wrote.

The Air Force surrendered to the feminists faster than you could put on a pair of Birkenstocks.

"With additional time to review all seven posters outside the narrower, primarily religious context of the original complaint about two of them, we concluded the gendered language used in the display interfered with intended messages about personal integrity," an Air Force spokesperson told *The Virginian-Pilot.*

The posters, which had been on display for at least six years, have been removed.

It's time for the Trump administration to crack down on the man-haters and Jesus-haters that have infested the greatest fighting force on the planet.

The Military Religious Freedom Foundation once bragged about having a hotline to the Pentagon. Well, it's time for the Defense Secretary to disconnect the number.

As for the overly sensitive gals at the National Organization for Women, they need to ease up on the politically correct hysterics.

It's time to man up, ladies.

UNIVERSITY: CARDBOARD VAGINAS ARE APPROPRIATE, NOAH'S ARK IS NOT

The University of Central Oklahoma has opened its arms to drag queen shows and safe sex carnivals, but they draw the line at Christians who believe God created the Heavens and the Earth in six days.[92]

The university apparently has no problem with students tossing dildos through cardboard vaginas, but they draw the line at exposing impressionable young minds to the teachings of a creationist.

---

92   "Public Outcry Forces University to Re-Invite Creationist Speaker. *CBN News.* February 16, 2018. https://www1.cbn.com/cbnnews/us/2018/february/public-outcry-forces-university-to-re-invite-creationist-speaker.

Ken Ham, president of Answers in Genesis and founder of the popular Creation Museum and Ark Encounter, was disinvited from speaking on the public university campus after an ugly campaign of bullying by LGBT activists.

The *Todd Starnes Radio Show* obtained exclusive emails between the UCO Student Association and Answers in Genesis explaining why they had to rescind the invitation and opt out of a signed and legally binding contract.

"We are currently getting bombarded with complaints from our LGBT community about Ken Ham speaking on our campus," student body president Stockton Duvall wrote.

Ham was scheduled to deliver his remarks in the university's Constitution Hall.

"I find it highly ironic that after being booked to speak in the school's Constitution Hall, our constitutional right to free speech and the exercise of religion, guaranteed under the First Amendment, have been denied," Ham said.

"While I know this looks awful censoring certain parts of Mr. Ham's views, I want to ensure that we stay on topic of the research Mr. Ham and his team have done over creationism," Duvall wrote.

For the record, Ham's university lecture was titled, "Genesis and the State of the Culture."

Paul Blair, the pastor of a local church that sponsors a student ministry called "Valid Worldview," told me Ham's speech had nothing to do with LGBT issues.

"The backlash we are already receiving is quite immense and I do not want this event to be spoiled due to a topic that isn't relative to Mr. Ham's research of creationism," Duvall wrote.

Not too long after that, the university's student government group canceled the speaking engagement.

"A small but vocal group on campus put up a fuss about my talk and the university caved in, tearing up the contract and contradicting its policies of promoting 'free inquiry' and 'inclusiveness' on campus," Ham said.

Pastor Blair told me he does not fault the student government association president for caving in to the LGBT mob.

"I think this young man was bullied and intimidated," Blair said. "I think he succumbed to the bullying that these LGBTQ groups are known for. Those that scream out and demand tolerance are in actuality the least tolerant group of individuals on the planet."

A university spokesman told me there had been no complaints of LGBT bullying.

"The UCO community is an inclusive environment that encourages the civil expression of diverse thoughts and ideas, while also keeping the safety of our students a top priority," the spokesman said.

Blair, the pastor of Fairview Baptist Church, pointed out the university's blatant hypocrisy and what he called "the obvious discrimination against Christianity on campus."

"I am beside myself with frustration that our tax dollars go to promote a drag queen show and safe sex events with carnival games that are obscene and graphic," he said. "Yet when it comes to something like debating Darwinian evolution or talking about the literal Creation account of Genesis—well that kind of speech must be censored."

The pastor has a valid point.

If the University of Central Oklahoma expects Christian students to be tolerant of LGBT-themed events, why aren't they demanding that same expectation from LGBT students when it comes to Christian events?

ATHEISTS: ANIMALS MAY NOT BE BLESSED

A bunch of bird-brained atheists sued a New Jersey animal shelter for holding a blessing of the animals.[93]

American Atheists filed the lawsuit in federal court against the Bergen County Animal Shelter, claiming the law was broken when a Franciscan bishop conducted a "blessing of the animals" ceremony.

According to the lawsuit, Candice Yaacobi dropped by the shelter in search of a Chihuahua. Instead, she stumbled upon the animal blessing ceremony and the bishop dressed "in full religious vestments."

American Atheists described the event as a "ritual performed by Franciscan clergy annually on October 4th in honor of the Catholic saint, Francis of Assissi [sic]."

The atheists may not be aware, but many Protestant denominations host animal blessing ceremonies, too, from pot-bellied pigs to exotic birds.

My denomination, Southern Baptists, normally bless our animals after they're slathered in barbecue sauce.

They claim the animal shelter violated the Establishment Clause of the First Amendment by forcing a religious viewpoint on people like their client.

"Religion is a suspect class and governmental policies which classify individuals based on their religion are subject to strict scrutiny," the lawsuit states.

Religion is a suspect class? Now, wait just one doggone minute…

"The government established one religious sect, Catholicism, over all others," the lawsuit further states.

The animal shelter did not respond to the lawsuit.

---

93   Kanzler, Kaitlyn. "Animal shelter operated by Bergen County sued by atheists over pet blessings." *NorthJersey.com*. Last modified November 2, 2017. https://www.northjersey.com/story/news/bergen/2017/11/21/animal-shelter-operated-bergen-county-sued-atheists-over-pet-blessings/884146001/.

"This is a suit that we shouldn't have had to file," American Atheists attorney Geoffrey Blackwell told Atheists.org. "We warned the shelter that using government resources to promote a religious event was unconstitutional, but they chose to ignore our claims."

The shelter had been holding the annual blessing for the previous two years without a whisper of a complaint—from human or animal.

"I've lived in New Jersey for more than twenty years," American Atheists president David Silverman said in a statement. "When I walk into a government building to use government services, the government should be absolutely neutral on religious matters. Allowing a Franciscan friar to conduct religious services with staff is the antithesis of neutrality."

Well, I can't imagine the puppies or the kittens or any other furry critter having any objections to receiving a blessing from the One who made the fish of the sea and the fowl of the air and the beasts of the field.

That being said, I suspect the real reason for the atheistic angst had more to do with concerns that the Chihuahua was going to convert.

They say that all dogs go to heaven, but as for unrepentant atheists, well, that's a different story.

SCHOOL WORKER ORDERED TO CEASE PRAYER WITHOUT CEASING

A school worker in Augusta, Maine was ordered to stop using religious phrases like "I will pray for you" and "You were in my prayers" because such language is not allowed inside a public school building—even in private conversations with coworkers.[94]

---

94   "The Maine Character in Prayer Suit Wins!" *Family Research Council.* November 13, 2017. https://www.frc.org/updatearticle/20171113/maine-character.

The Augusta School Department launched an investigation of Toni Richardson after they alleged she "imposed some strong religious/spiritual belief systems" on a coworker.

Now, imposing your religion on someone is a serious allegation. Was Ms. Richardson forcing her coworker to convert to Christianity? Did she attempt to baptize him against his will?

It turned out to be nothing of the sort.

According to an official memorandum from the school district, Ms. Richardson had told a colleague that she was going to pray for him. It just so happens that Ms. Richardson and the colleague attended the same church.

Back in 2016, the colleague had been having a difficult time adjusting to his new job and Ms. Richardson did what most Christians would do—she told him that she would be praying for him.

Months later, the colleague and Ms. Richardson had a falling out, leading to the complaint about the prayers.

The district sent Ms. Richardson a "coaching memorandum," warning her that such language is not acceptable "even if that other person attends the same church as you."

She was not even allowed to use the word "blessing."

"In the context of the 'separation of church and state,' this case prohibits public school-sponsored religious expression," the memo read. "Therefore, in the future, it is imperative that you do not use phrases that integrate public and private belief systems when in the public schools."

She was also specifically ordered not to make any "reference to your spiritual or religious beliefs."

The district warned her that any additional infractions could lead to disciplinary action or dismissal.

"I was shocked that my employer punished me for privately telling a coworker, 'I will pray for you,'" Ms. Richardson said. "I'm afraid I will lose my job if someone hears me privately discussing my faith with a coworker."

Sweet Lord Almighty, America!

Fortunately, Ms. Richardson had the good sense to contact First Liberty Institute, one of the nation's most prominent religious liberty law firms.

"No one should be threatened with losing their job for privately telling a coworker that they are going to pray for them," First Liberty attorney Jeremy Dys told me. "School employees are not required to hide their faith from each other while on campus."

First Liberty Institute and the Eaton Peabody law firm filed a formal complaint with the Equal Employment Opportunity Commission, alleging religious discrimination and retaliation.

"What August Public Schools did by punishing Toni for discussing her faith in a private conversation with a coworker is unconscionable," attorney Timothy Woodcock said. "The law is clear: employers cannot discriminate against employees who privately discuss their faith while at work."

When it comes to defending religious liberty, First Liberty is like a pit bull going after a pork chop—they are relentless.

DEPUTIES TOLD THEY CANNOT BE PEACEMAKERS

The peacemakers are not allowed to be blessed in Montgomery County, Virginia.

On May 17, 2017, the sheriff was ordered to remove decals bearing a portion of a well-known Bible verse from patrol cars.[95]

The decal, which had been posted on vehicles in March, bore the words, "Blessed are the peacemakers...Matthew 5:9."

---

95   Gangloff, Mike. "Bible verse decals to come off patrol cars immediately, Montgomery County sheriff says." *The Roanoke Times* (Roanoke), May 17, 2017. https://www.roanoke.com/news/local/montgomery_county/ bible-verse-decals-to-come-off-patrol-cars-immediately-montgomery/ article_2c4f208b-4a5e-55a0-b98e-8a5eaaa6d5c8.html.

"Our intent was, and still is, to honor our fellow brothers and sisters in law enforcement," Sheriff C. H. Partin wrote in a statement to Fox News.

The sheriff said the decals were removed at the request of the county's board of supervisors.

"In the midst of National Police Week, we want to focus on those who have paid the ultimate sacrifice while serving their communities," the sheriff said. "The last thing that I want is for this to become a distraction to the men and women who serve their communities selflessly every day."

I could not imagine any elected leaders giving such a detestable order, so I reached out to the board of supervisors to verify the report. It turns out that they really gave that detestable order.

"In my mind, there's nothing wrong with the statement itself," supervisor Chris Tuck told me. "Any individual can put that on your car however they would like. However, based on our legal advice, when you put, 'Blessed are the peacemakers' and make the reference to Matthew 5:9, there are some serious concerns about the Establishment Clause and Separation of Church and State and the First Amendment."

Mr. Tuck told me the board made its decision after first consulting with their attorney.

Their attorney told them "the decals would be a violation of the First Amendment based on the current case law because of the reference to Matthew 5:9."

It sounds to me like the Montgomery County Board of Supervisors is in desperate need of an attorney who understands the law.

Mr. Tuck told me they could've ignored their attorney's advice, but that would've put the county at risk for hundreds of thousands of dollars in legal fees.

"I don't believe the citizens of Montgomery County want me to get into a situation where hundreds of thousands of dollars of tax money may end up having to be given to the ACLU," he said.

Blessed are the attorneys for they shall inherit everyone's money…

I was curious, though: who raised a complaint about the decals in the first place?

"The first notice we had was an inquiry by the Roanoke Times," Mr. Tuck told me. "That was the first that the board received."

Well, there you have it, folks. This is why people don't like newspaper reporters. They stir up a stink when there's no stink to stir.

Perhaps the readers of the *Roanoke Times* might want to keep that in mind when their subscription comes up for renewal.

LGBT ACTIVISTS WANT CHURCH BANNED FROM RENTING SCHOOL BUILDINGS

The Texas Attorney General's office is warning the Austin Independent School District not to ban churches from renting facilities because their views might conflict with LGBT groups.[96]

"The District should not make any changes to its facilities use policy that would prevent churches from renting those facilities on the same terms as other community organizations, lest it violate state and federal law," First Assistant Attorney General Jeff Mateer wrote in a letter obtained by *The Todd Starnes Radio Show*.

In August 2018, Celebration Church began holding services at a performing arts facility owned by the school district. The so-called mega-church is a well-respected and long-established congregation in the Austin area.

The church also holds to traditional and biblical views on issues regarding marriage and homosexuality.

---

96   Platoff, Emma. "Texas Ag warns Austin ISD: Don't stop
      churches from renting school facilities." *CBS Austin*.
      September 21, 2018. https://cbsaustin.com/news/local/
      texas-ag-warns-austin-isd-dont-stop-churches-from-renting-school-facilities.

"We believe that marriage is a lifelong covenant between a man and a woman, god-designed—and do not endorse or condone it in any other context," Pastor Joe Champion told me.

In other words, the church holds to a belief shared by thousands of other churches across the nation.

"Our focus is and has always been as what we do as a church—serving the community—spreading the word of God based on the Bible. And we continue to do that," the pastor said.

Stonewall Militant Front-ATX, a self-described militant LGBT group, declared war on the church and demanded that the school district sever its contract. And they made no secret that their number one goal was to run the church out of town.

"They think they can use their money to spread their hate in our city and our halls—we are going to run them out," the organization wrote on its Facebook page.

The group has already protested and picketed the church during Sunday worship services, calling congregants "anti-LGBT bigots."

"If bigoted churches come to town opposing the existence of LGBTQ people, the masses must organize and take the fight to the church doors and oppose their existence in Austin," they wrote.

As a result of the LGBT group's campaign, the school district has decided to reconsider its rental policies.

"I'm not in favor of renting to any entity that doesn't support our values…and that's full inclusion of our LGBTQ community," school board trustee Ann Teich told the *Statesman-American*.

And trustee Jayme Mathias offered up a similar assessment, saying the church had "values that did not align with those of the district."

Mateer said Celebration Church and other congregations have every right to rent school facilities.

"Excluding churches from a government forum or program due to their religious nature is odious to our Constitution," Mateer wrote in his letter to the school district.

The attorney general's office said the school district is "targeting Celebration Church for discriminatory treatment."

"The District's proposal to exclude churches with traditional beliefs about marriage, while allowing churches that agree with same-sex marriage to continue renting its facility smacks of denominational preference, and is unconstitutional," he wrote.

Pastor Champion said the focus of their church is to share the love of Jesus Christ with their community. And he rejected any accusations that the mega-church is homophobic.

"God called us to love everyone and we welcome everyone in the community to attend our church," he told me.

And yet the militant LGBT mob wants to run this precious church out of town. The war on religious liberty wages on, friends. They say everything is bigger in Texas—and I reckon that includes hate and bigotry too.

CHAPTER 7

LESSONS FROM A SALTINE-AMERICAN

WELL, I RECKON I'd best address the big elephant in the room. I'm a white guy. Yes, the rumors of my pigmentation are true. Your friendly neighborhood commentator is about a shade lighter than a sack of Martha White Self-Rising Flour.

I am also a Christian man and I am a son of the South. My detractors might call me a cracker, but I prefer to be called a Saltine-American.

Truth be told, I love NASCAR and the Grand Ole Opry and vacations in Branson, Missouri. I'm also particular to *Gone with the Wind* and tomato biscuit sandwiches slathered in Duke's Mayonnaise.

But I also enjoy Tyler Perry movies and collard greens with cornbread baked in a cast iron skillet. And I'm partial to the late Aretha Franklin, the Queen of Soul. Sadly, I don't have any rhythm, but it's not because I'm white. It's because I'm a Baptist.

That being said, all this talk about identity politics and cultural appropriation and white privilege has really gotten the nation riled up. The culture jihadists have really stirred up a hornet's nest. Honestly, it's all a great big steaming pile of fertilizer.

We didn't have much money when I was growing up. My dad was an electrician and there were stretches of time when he could not find work. But there was always food on the table and we had a roof over our heads.

My dad taught me at a young age to judge a man by the content of his character, not the color of his skin. He taught me that all men are created equal. And that was that.

Dad was also a musician and our home was always filled with an assortment of characters from around Memphis—white and black. Looking back to those times, I never once thought of anyone as a black person or a white person. They were just friends of my parents—they were grown-ups.

My dad could tear up a guitar singing the blues, and my mother could fry up a chicken so crispy on the outside and juicy on the inside that you'd be speaking in tongues.

Nowadays, they would've been accused of cultural appropriation. How dare a white man sing the blues. Who does that white woman think she is, appropriating our poultry?

It's really sad that a segment of the population wants America to segregate itself from music, food, clothing, hair styles, and culture based on one's ethnicity. America is a melting pot. Immigrants from all over the globe came to this country legally, bringing the best of their traditions from the Old Country.

Cultural appropriation used to be a sign of respect and appreciation. If you wanted a mess of greens with a turkey neck, you'd go to Sylvia's in Harlem. If you wanted to experience the finest Latin cuisine, you'd go to Washington Heights. If you wanted to scarf down sausage and peppers, you'd go to Defontes in Brooklyn. And if you wanted to enjoy overpriced roast beef and shrimp cocktail, you'd dine with the rich WASPs at the Waldorf. But these days, cultural appropriation is an egregious sin and that's really a shame because what used to unite us, is now being used to divide us.

"I'M WATCHING YOU, WHITE BOY"

It's open season on white males at Yale University. In February, the student newspaper published a disturbing column that called for the targeting of white students—specifically white male students.

"I'm watching you, white boy," Isis Davis-Marks wrote in an op-ed published in the *Yale Daily News*.[97]

She called for her fellow students to keep copious notes about the behavior of campus white guys so that the evidence might be used against them in future government confirmation hearings.

"Everyone knows a white boy with shiny brown hair and a saccharine smile that conceals his great ambitions," Davis-Marks added.

"When I'm watching the white boy, I'll remember a racist remark that he said, an unintentional utterance that he made when he had one drink too many at a frat party during sophomore year," she wrote.

It's not just a Yale problem.

At Pennsylvania's Dickinson College, students are debating whether or not white male students should even be allowed to talk. That was the focus of an op-ed titled, "Should White Boys Still Be Allowed to Talk?"[98]

"I am so g****mned tired of listening to white boys," wrote Leda Fisher. "I cannot describe to you how frustrating it is to be forced to listen to a white boy explain his take on the Black experience in the Obama-era."

She went on to explain that guys named "Jake, Chad, or Alex" really don't have First Amendment rights.

"American society tells men, but especially white men, that their opinions have merit and that their voice is valuable, but after four

---

97 Davis-Marks, Isis. "Davis-Marks: Evil is banal." *Yale News.* February 7, 2019. https://yaledailynews.com/blog/2019/02/07/davis-marks-evil-is-banal/.

98 Fisher, Leda. "Should White Boys Still Be Allowed to Talk?" *The Dickinsonian. May 24, 2019.* https://thedickinsonian.com/opinion/2019/02/07/should-white-boys-still-be-allowed-to-talk/.

years of listening to white boys in college, I am not so convinced," she wrote. "There is an endless line of white boys waiting to share their opinions on the state of feminism in America, whether the LGBTQ+ population finally has enough rights, the merits of capitalism, etc. The list of what white boys think they are qualified to talk about is endless."

It would be simple to dismiss the bigoted columns as the misinformed rantings of youngsters. However, the idea that white students should be stripped of their Constitutional rights and targeted by baseless accusations should alarm every freedom-loving American.

So what's behind this new brand of bold-faced bigotry? It's something that leftists call white privilege. But it's nothing more than old-fashioned identity politics. And it has infected many universities across the fruited plain.

Professors have poisoned the minds of a generation, convincing minorities to embrace victimhood, while brainwashing white young people into believing any success they achieve is due only to their skin color.

Sadly, the society dreamed of by the late Rev. Martin Luther King, Jr. has become a nightmare where academic radicals are judging everyone by the color of their skin instead of the content of their character.

Here are some other shocking examples of campus bigotry directed at white students:

In 2016, Drexel University Professor George Ciccariello-Maher advocated on social media for the mass extermination of white people.[99]

"All I want for Christmas is white genocide," the white professor wrote on Twitter.

---

99   Butterworth, Courtney. "The Drexel professor who tweeted, 'All I want for Christmas is white genocide' resigned." *The Daily Pennsylvanian.* January 10, 2018. https://www.thedp.com/article/2018/01/drexel-professor-controversial-christmas-tweet-resignation-philadelphia-upenn.

Drexel condemned the tweet, but took no further action. The professor resigned a year later citing death threats. The university called him an outstanding classroom teacher.[100]

During Supreme Court Justice Brett Kavanaugh's confirmation hearing, Georgetown Professor Christine Fair called for the castration and execution of white men.

"All of them deserve miserable deaths while feminists laugh as they take their last gasps," she wrote on Twitter. "BONUS: we castrate their corpses and feed them to swine? Yes."[101]

In January, a teaching assistant at the University of Georgia declared that "some white people may have to die" for black people to advance.[102]

Irami Osei-Frimpong wrote that "we have made a national project out of coddling White people about Whiteness, and we are living the consequences."[103]

The teaching assistant, who still works for the University of Georgia, is no stranger to anti-white rhetoric. He wrote in 2017 in Medium, "We had to kill some white people to get out of slavery.

100   Eltagouri, Marwa. "Professor who tweeted, 'All I want for
        Christmas is white genocide,' resigns after year of threats." *The
        Washington Post* (Washington, D.C.), December 29, 2017. https://
        www.washingtonpost.com/news/grade-point/wp/2017/12/29/
        professor-who-tweeted-all-i-want-for-christmas-is-white-genocide-resigns-
        after-year-of-threats/?utm_term=.0f7fe3dfe499.
101   Parke, Caleb. "Georgetown professor says white GOP senators 'deserve
        miserable deaths' after Kavanaugh hearing." Fox News. Accessed May 29,
        2019. https://www.foxnews.com/us/georgetown-professor-says-white-gop-
        senators-deserve-miserable-deaths-after-kavanaugh-hearing.
102   Thomas, Tony. "'Some white people may have to die': UGA teaching
        assistant under fire for post." *WSB-TV*. Last modified January 22, 2019.
        https://www.wsbtv.com/news/local/-some-white-people-may-have-to-die-
        uga-teaching-assistant-under-fire-for-facebook-post/908340952.
103   Chasmar, Jessica. "University of Georgia TA: 'Some white people may have
        to die' for blacks to advance." *The Washington Times* (Washington, D.C.),
        January 18, 2019. https://www.washingtontimes.com/news/2019/jan/18/
        university-georgia-ta-some-white-people-may-have-d/.

Maybe if we'd killed more during the 20th century we still wouldn't talk about racialized voter disenfranchisement and housing, education, and employment discrimination."[104]

We should all be horrified that our tax dollars are funding the salaries of bigots and racists who have weaponized their classrooms. There should be no place in higher education for academic-sanctioned hate lessons.

And any university that continues to advance the white privilege theory should be stripped of its taxpayer-funded support. I don't want a single penny of my tax money funding identity politics.

CHILDREN LECTURED ABOUT WHITE PRIVILEGE

Children at a Raleigh, North Carolina grade school were given lessons on white privilege that left at least one parent demanding to know why eight-year-olds were being exposed to such radical concepts.

Amber Pabon told television station ABC 11 that her son came home from Hunter Magnet Elementary School with one of the lessons in his folder.[105]

"He's eight years old. What does he need to know about racism or white privilege?" Pabon said.

"11-Step Guide to Understanding Race, Racism, and White Privilege" was sent to every parent and child at the school. It was part of an initiative led by the PTA, not the school.[106]

---

104 "Some White People May Have to Die?" *95.3 WBCKFM*. January 24, 2019. https://wbckfm.com/some-white-people-may-have-to-die/.

105 Perchick, Michael. "Raleigh parent upset about 'white privelege' paper sent home with student." *ABC11 Eyewitness News*. April 3, 2018. https://abc11.com/education/raleigh-parent-upset-about-white-privilege-paper-sent-home-with-student/3297299/.

106 Greenberg, Jon. "11-Step Guide to Understanding Race, Racism, and White Privilege." *Citizen & Social Justice* (blog). October 14, 2017. http://citizenshipandsocialjustice.com/2017/10/14/11-step-guide-to-understanding-race-racism-and-white-privilege/.

"I think the message itself is inappropriate because yes there is racism out here, and they need to learn about it. But let the parents do that," Pabon told the television station.

"Because, like I said, if she's teaching him the way she knows, it could be completely different from the way I know. And me being part of the black community, I know different from how the white community sees it."

The lessons, compiled by Jon Greenberg, were downright sickening. Consider this item pulled from the original lesson:

"Since Trump's rise has emboldened racists across the country, we don't hear much about this country being 'post-racial' anymore, a concept that dominated the media during the Obama administration," the lesson states.

And check out some of the other lessons:

"White dominates the culture, from our government leaders to our professors to our media stars," the lesson read. "Yet—for the most part, for too many White Americans—whiteness remains unexamined. What does it mean to be white?" The lessons also urged students to eradicate the "idea of colorblindness."

"The idea of 'colorblindness'—that being color conscious is problematic, that you 'don't see race'—has been prevalent among white circles for decades," the lesson states. "For people of color, it's pretty tough to disregard the concept of race when you are reminded of your race regularly."

They also gave the students data to back up their argument:

1. Congress: 90% white

2. Governors: 96% white

3. Top military advisers: 100% white

4. President and Vice President: 100% white

5. Current POTUS cabinet: 91% white

6. People who decide which TV shows we see: 93% white

7. Owners of men's pro-football teams: 97% white[107]

The white privilege propaganda being distributed at Hunter Magnet Elementary School is disgusting. To shame children and their parents based on the color of their skin is simply unthinkable in this day and age.[108]

"DON'T TREAD ON ME" IS RACIST

The "Don't Tread on Me" Flag just got trod upon by the Equal Employment Opportunity Commission (EEOC).

The EEOC is investigating whether the Revolutionary War-era Gadsden Flag could be considered a racist symbol in the workplace. In recent years, the yellow flag with its coiled snake has also become a symbol of the Tea Party.[109]

"Whatever historic origins and meaning of the symbol, it also has since been sometimes interpreted to convey racially-tinged messages in some contexts," the EEOC report states.

The distinguished scholar Eugene Volokh first exposed this absurd story in the pages of the *Washington Post*. Here's the back story:[110]

107   Starnes, Todd. "Second Graders Exposed to 'White Privilege' Lessons." *Todd Starnes (blog). April 4, 2018.* https://www.toddstarnes.com/show/second-graders-exposed-to-white-privilege-lessons/.

108   Hui, T. Keung. "Rush Limbaugh, other conservatives attack NC school over white privilege handout." *The News & Observer* (Raleigh), Last modified April 6, 2018. https://www.newsobserver.com/news/local/education/article208140689.html.

109   U.S. Equal Employment Opportunity Commission. *What You Should Know about EEOC and Shelton D. v. U.S. Postal Service (Gadsden Flag case).* Washington, D.C. https://www.eeoc.gov/eeoc/newsroom/wysk/gadsden-flag.cfm.

110   Volokh, Eugene. "Wearing 'Don't Tread on Me' insignia could be punishable racial harassment." *The Washington* Post (Washington, D.C.), August 3, 2016. https://www.washingtonpost.com/news/volokh-conspiracy/wp/2016/08/03/wearing-dont-tread-on-me-insignia-could-be-punishable-racial-harassment/?utm_term=.43fc5b68d3a1.

In 2014, a black government worker filed a complaint alleging he had been discriminated against by a coworker who wore a ball cap that bore an insignia of the Gadsden Flag.

The aggrieved government snowflake "found the cap to be racially offensive to African Americans because the flag was designed by Christopher Gadsden."

The EEOC report goes on to identify Gadsden as a "slave trader and owner of slaves."

The overly sensitive employee "maintains that the Gadsden Flag is a 'historical indicator of white resentment against blacks stemming largely from the Tea Party.'"

The EEOC conducted a "thorough review" and found there was no evidence that the flag was created in a racial context.

"Moreover, it is clear that the flag and its slogan have been used to express various non-racial sentiments, such as when it is used in the modern Tea Party political movement, gun rights activism, patriotic displays, and by the military," the EEOC report states.

You can almost feel the "but" coming, can't you, good readers?

"However, whatever the historic origins and meanings of the symbol, it also has since been sometimes interpreted to convey racially-tinged messages in some contexts," they declared.

Citing the "ambiguity in the current meaning" of the Gadsden Flag, the EEOC decided to investigate to "determine the specific context."

The government's ruling is going to open up a great big can of worms, folks. They are basically suggesting that if an item is used in a racially-tinged context or if a worker thinks something may be racist—it is therefore racist.

What happens if a white guy shows up to work with fried chicken and collard greens in his lunch pail? Could he be accused of cultural appropriation, even if he simply enjoys finger-licking good cuisine?

As Mr. Volokh pointed out, there was no evidence the gentleman who wore the Gadsden Flag cap said or did anything racist to his coworker.

The worker's sole objection "was apparently just to the wearing of the flag, and the ideology that he thinks has become associated with the flag," Mr. Volokh surmised.

Well, using the government's logic, they could very well ban white bed sheets and reruns of the "Dukes of Hazzard."

IF YOU'RE A WHITE GUY YOU MIGHT BE PRIVILEGED

If you are a white, heterosexual, Evangelical Christian male whose parents are still married and can afford to send you to summer camp—then you may be privileged, according to the West Bend School District in Wisconsin.

As many as 150 students at Badger Middle School were given an optional "privilege test." The fifty-five questions covered a wide range of topics from sexuality and race to religion and economics.[111]

Among the items on the questionnaire:

- I am white

- I have never tried to hide my sexuality

- I feel comfortable in the gender I was born in

- I have never been called a derogatory term for a homosexual

- I never doubted my parents' acceptance of my sexuality

- My parents are heterosexual

- My family can afford a therapist

- I have never been called a terrorist

- Nobody has tried to "save me" from my religious beliefs

---

111   Spencer, Suzanne. "Questionnaire called 'the privilege test' sparking controversy in West Bend." Fox6Now. December 21, 2017. https://fox6now.com/2017/12/21/questionnaire-called-the-privilege-test-sparking-controversy-in-west-bend/.

- I feel privileged because of the identities I was born with
- I have never been mocked for my accent
- I have never been told that I "sound white"
- I am a man
- I went to summer camp
- I have never been catcalled

The school district said teachers wanted to spark a conversation on privilege after reading *To Kill a Mockingbird*.

"If we want our students to be successful when they go out into their careers in the future, they have to understand that not everyone is like them," Assistant Superintendent Laura Jackson said.

However, parents who contacted Fox 6 in Milwaukee said the school crossed the line.

"As a parent, it's my responsibility to teach my children the difference between right and wrong," parent Kim Goldman told the television station.

"Some of the language in the questionnaire I can see why, as a part of a 13-, 14-year-old eighth grader, some people may feel as though those are topics that should be discussed in the home and not the classroom," principal Dave Uelman told the television station.

But in reality, there's no such thing as privilege—it's a left-wing fallacy.

The truth is that if a young person works hard and takes personal responsibility for their actions, they can be anything they want and they can do anything they want in life.

The "privilege test" is a classic example of a public school that has been turned into an indoctrination center for the Left. They want the children to believe there's something wrong with white, heterosexual, middle-class Christians. That's not privilege—that's discrimination.

HELP WANTED: WHITE PEOPLE NEED NOT APPLY

Imagine that you are an out-of-work performer—looking for a job.

You discover an advertisement for *Hamilton*—the hottest show on Broadway. The producers are searching for cast members for nationwide productions.

You can sing. You can act. You can dance. You're a triple threat. But there's just one problem—you are also black. And the casting notice stipulates the producers are hiring only "WHITE ACTORS."

Now, let's imagine the cries of injustice. Al Sharpton would lead marches through Times Square. Civil Rights groups would stage boycotts. #ThespianLivesMatter would trend online.

I could imagine former President Obama stepping into the national firestorm. He would remind us of the teachings of Dr. Martin Luther King, Jr. He would tell us: judge people on the content of their character, not the color of their skin.

But, in reality, the producers of *Hamilton,* a rap musical that offers a fresh take on the Founding Fathers, put out the following casting call: "Seeking NON-WHITE men and women, ages 20s to 30s, for Broadway and upcoming Tours!" The NON-WHITE part was in all caps.[112]

Oh, they also needed singers who could rap. Sorry, Vanilla Ice. I'm afraid you might be a bit too…vanilla.

CBS 2 News in New York City reported that *Hamilton*'s casting notice for "NON-WHITE" performers may violate the city's human rights law.[113]

---

112   Concha, Joe. "Flashback: 'Hamilton' once had casting notice seeking 'non-white' performers." *The Hill* (Washington, D.C.), November 19, 2016. https://thehill.com/pundits-blog-author/306907-flashback-hamilton-once-had-casting-notice-seeking-non-white-performers.

113   Aiello, Tony. "Broadway Union Takes Issue With 'Hamilton' Casting Call for 'Non-White' Performers." *CBS New York*. March 29, 2016. https://newyork.cbslocal.com/2016/03/29/hamilton-casting-call-non-white/.

"You cannot advertise showing that you have a preference for one racial group over another," civil rights attorney Randolph McLaughlin told the television station. "As an artistic question—sure, he can cast whomever he wants to cast, but he has to give every actor eligible for the role an opportunity to try."

Actors' Equity, the Broadway union, told me the *Hamilton* casting notices were not in compliance with their policies. They said that all casting notices are supposed to be open to performers of all races and ethnicities.

And while the show has earned national praise for casting minority performers to portray our Founding Fathers, it's not the first time *Hamilton* has courted controversy.

They actually posted a casting call for actors to portray Aaron Burr and George Washington, the *New York Daily News* reported.

Here's the actual casting call:

"George Washington: Males & Females, 30-49, African American, Hispanic, Asian, South Asian, Native American, Middle Eastern, Southeast Asian/Pacific Islander, Ethnically Ambiguous/Mixed Race, African Descent. Non-White, tenor/baritone."

In other words, no white folks need apply.

After a bit of online outrage, the producers changed their minds and decided to open the auditions to the pigmentationally-challenged.

But don't expect too much diversity. As the *Daily News* pointed out, none of the lead roles are currently played by a Caucasian.[114]

And by the way, what in the world does "ethnically ambiguous" mean—Canadian?

---

114   Alcorn, Chauncy. "'Hamilton' hiring practices under fire after casting call solicits non-white actors only." *Daily News* (New York), March 30, 2016. https://www.nydailynews.com/entertainment/theater-arts/hamilton-hiring-practices-fire-due-discrimination-article-1.2582555.

Ironically, opinion seems to be on the side of the producers.

"NON-WHITE in all caps and bold is my favorite part," one Broadway fan wrote on Facebook. "It's just so unapologetic and something we're all not used to seeing. The great white way is finally getting revamped."

"Caucasian actors are way at the front of the line when it comes to casting so give other ethnicities a chance to catch up," another wrote.

And then there's this item: "For all the white people complaining about the NON-WHITE part of this ad, just go audition for the 98.9 percent of the other roles that are out there for you."

There were some critics, though. One Broadway fan said they understand that *Hamilton* was trying to make a point by using ethnic actors to play our white Founding Fathers, but "do they really have to exclude ALL whites to make that point?"

"That would be considered racism if the tables were turned," wrote one reader. "It should be called out for what it is—racism."

Hamilton producer Jeffrey Seller told CBS his casting call for NON-WHITE performers is on the up and up.

"I stand by it and believe it to be legal," he told the television station.

That may be true, Mr. Sellers. But discrimination is discrimination, no matter which way you color it.

IF YOUR NAME IS ROBERT E. LEE, YOU MIGHT BE A RACIST

ESPN pulled a veteran college football announcer from the season-opener between the University of Virginia and William and Mary because of the announcer's name—Robert Lee.[115]

---

115   Haag, Matthew. "ESPN Pulls Announcer Robert Lee From Virginia Game Because of His Name." *The New York Times* (New York); August 23, 2017. https://www.nytimes.com/2017/08/23/business/media/robert-lee-university-virginia-charlottesville.html.

One of the perpetually offended snowflakes at ESPN apparently thought Lee's name might offend some viewers because of similarities to namesake Civil War General Robert E. Lee.

OutkicktheCoverage.com was the first to report on this politically correct nonsense.[116]

It is highly doubtful he is a descendant of the Civil War general. And to our knowledge, there are no monuments or statues in his honor posted anywhere in Charlottesville.

Oh, and Mr. Lee happens to be Asian-American.

An ESPN spokesperson confirmed to me they made the decision to remove Mr. Lee from the broadcasting booth and dispatch him to the Youngstown State vs. Pittsburgh game.

"We collectively made the decision with Robert to switch games as the tragic events in Charlottesville were unfolding, simply because of the coincidence of his name," ESPN told me.

I asked the network's spokesperson if they would implement a similar ban on broadcasters named Jefferson Davis or Stonewall Jackson, but they did not return my call.

So let's review the facts. Robert Lee (the broadcaster) is not a descendant of a Civil War general. He did not own slaves. He did not fight in the War of Northern Aggression.

He is not a neo-Nazi. He is not a member of Antifa. And he had absolutely nothing to do with the violent protests in Charlottesville.

But that did not matter to the emotionally stunted morons who run ESPN.

"In that moment it felt right to all parties," ESPN said. "It's a shame that this is even a topic of conversation and we regret that who calls play-by-play for a football game has become an issue."

---

116 Travis, Clay. "MSESPN Pulls Asian Announcer Named Robert Lee Off UVa Game To Avoid Offending Idiots." *Outkick the Coverage*. August 22, 2017. https://www.outkickthecoverage.com/msespn-pulls-asian-announcer-named-robert-lee-off-uva-game-avoid-offending-idiots/.

Well, it's only an issue because the politically correct pinheads at ESPN made it an issue.

Sadly, this great nation is being wussified by the Left. Our cultures and traditions are being turned into a steaming pile of rubble by a rampaging mob of cultural jihadists.

So, don't be surprised if the human resources department at ESPN announces one day soon that they are firing employees who are descendants of Civil War veterans.

You say, "Todd, that's outrageous."

Well, you know what else is outrageous—dumping a broadcaster just because his name is Robert Lee.

SKIN COLOR TRUMPS GRADES

A Virginia high school sent a disturbing letter to parents and students announcing they would be selecting students for Advanced Placement and honors classes at least partly based on skin color, **a** concerned parent told Fox News.[117]

Martin Luther King, Jr. must be turning over in his grave.

A parent forwarded me a copy of the letter sent from John Handley High School in Winchester.

"Through our collective work, advanced classes such as AP and Honors will have proportional representation," read the letter. "Proportional representation is 40% White, 35% Hispanic, 12% African American, 10% mixed race."

The letter went on to explain that public schools across the country "continue to see outcomes that are disproportionate by race and social class."

---

117   Starnes, Todd. "School: Honors Classes Will be Decided by Skin Color." *Todd Starnes* (blog). August 8, 2017. https://www.toddstarnes.com/ uncategorized/school-honors-classes-will-be-decided-by-skin- color-not-intelligence/.

"American demographic trends indicate that America will be a majority minority nation in the next 25 years," the letter read. "Therefore, the new work of American public schools is to develop systems to address disparate outcomes."

Interesting—I thought the work of American public schools was to teach kids how to read, write, multiply, and divide.

A school district spokesperson reached out to me and strongly denied that they have any policies dictating racial quotas for advanced courses.

"Our school division does not have, nor has it ever had, any policy that utilizes race for enrollment into honors or AP courses. All students, regardless of race, must meet academic criteria to enroll in advanced level coursework. Over the past years, the School Board has continued its focus on providing advanced level coursework as well as increasing advanced course offerings across a variety of disciplines. The School Board has not contemplated, nor adopted, any policy or practice that utilizes race in determining which students can or cannot take such courses, or any other courses for that matter," the spokesperson said.[118]

However, the letter clearly states that is their goal.

"I disagree that those statements mean that students will be placed in classes based on race," said school board chairman Erica Truban.

Her comment strains credulity.

Eric Sitton, father of a rising sophomore honors student at the high school, was one of the parents who received the letter.

"I was taken aback. I couldn't believe someone would put words like that in print to send around to the homes of students," he told me.

---

118   "AP and honor Classes Awarded by Race?" *95.3 WBCK*. August 10, 2017. https://wbckfm.com/ap-and-honor-classes-awarded-by-race/.

He said he was especially distressed when his teenage son read the rules governing honors classes.

"I felt powerless to help my child," he said. "Seeing the look on his face when he realized that he was being judged by the color of his skin was agonizing."

So how does a public school district explain judging children based on their pigmentation?

"My son asked me, 'Am I not going to be able to be in an AP class because I'm white?' And I didn't know what to tell him," Mr. Sitton said.

Last year, he said one of his son's teachers told students she could not believe anyone would vote for Donald Trump. She attempted to influence students with her political ideology.

"It is honestly like trying to run a marathon in mud—trying to deal with the school system," Mr. Sitton told me.

Hopefully, Mr. Sitton's son will be among the 40 percent of white people permitted to enroll in honors classes.

"I told my son to just do the best you can do, show your aptitude and hopefully you will get the classes you want," he said.

IT'S A SHOELACE—A SHOELACE

A leather shoelace mistaken for a noose triggered a massive microaggression at Michigan State University, leading to public denunciations by university officials and at least two investigations.[119]

MSU President Lou Anna Simon issued a statement alerting students of what she called a "racial incident" in one of the university's residence halls.

---

119   Starnes, Todd. "Maybe Michigan State Students Should Wear Penny Loafers." *Todd Starnes* (blog). October 6, 2017. https://www.toddstarnes.com/uncategorized/university-panic-stricken-over-shoelace/.

"A student reported a noose was hung outside of her room," President Simon breathlessly declared.

She announced that investigations had been commenced by MSU police and the Office of Institutional Equity (no idea what that is, but it's probably funded by your tax dollars).

"A noose is a symbol of intimidation and threat that has a horrendous history in America," the president said.

She said such behavior would not be tolerated on the campus.

"No Spartan should ever feel targeted based on their race, or other ways in which they identify," President Simon said.

I completely agree.

But there's just one glaring problem—the piece of leather turned out not to be a noose. It was a packaged shoelace.

In case President Simon is not aware, a shoelace is a cord or leather strip passed through eyelets or hooks on opposite sides of a shoe and pulled tight and fastened.

"The matching packaged shoelace was found outside of the residence hall," a university spokesperson said. "Officers located and spoke to the student who lost both of the shoelaces, which are packaged in a way that someone could perceive them to look similar to a noose."

I sincerely doubt the last part of that flaccid explanation. It turns out the student who filed the original complaint exaggerated her perceived microaggression.

"The original shoelace found inside the residence hall was not directed at any individual," the university admitted. "It was originally seen on a hallway floor and later on a stairwell door handle where officers believe someone put it after picking it up."

So, it was a fake "racial incident."

Instead of apologizing for scaring the living daylights out of the campus, the university seemed to double down on its handling of the matter.

"The university takes any reported racial incident very seriously," they said. Apparently, they also take fake racial incidents seriously.

President Simon stressed that no student should ever feel targeted based on their race—and I echo her belief. However, I also believe that no student should be targeted for their selection of footwear.

That being said, I would recommend that Michigan State students might want to consider trading in their sneakers for a pair of penny loafers—or Uggs.

YOUR BREAKFAST CEREAL COULD BE RACIALLY OFFENSIVE

Prepare to have your Lucky Charms curdled, America.

Kellogg's apologized after a member of the Social Justice Breakfast Brigade complained about racially insensitive artwork on a package of Corn Pops.[120]

The artwork included cartoon characters shaped like corn kernels frolicking about in a shopping mall. All but one of the kernels was yellow. The lone brown kernel was working as a janitor.

Well, faster than you could say snap, crackle, pop, a customer raised a stink on social media.[121]

"Why is literally the only brown corn pop on the whole cereal box the janitor? This is teaching kids racism," aggrieved cereal-eater Saladin Ahmed wrote on Twitter.

USA Today reported that Ahmed is a writer for the Marvel Comics' Black Bolt series and a fantasy novel author.

---

120   Starnes, Todd. "Maybe Michigan State Students Should Wear Penny Loafers." *Todd Starnes* (blog). October 6, 2017. https://www.toddstarnes.com/uncategorized/university-panic-stricken-over-shoelace/

121   Snider, Mike. "Kellogg's to replace racially insensitive Corn Pops boxes following Twitter call out." *USA Today* (McLean), Last modified October 26, 2017. https://www.usatoday.com/story/money/business/2017/10/25/kelloggs-replace-racially-insensitive-corn-pops-boxes-following-twitter-rant/797911001/.

A number of folks observed that the brown kernel was the only one actually doing something, putting in a hard day's work while other corn kernels goofed off. I contend it's just a cartoon on a cereal box, so why is this even a "thing?" But my opinion seems to be in the minority (no pun intended).

Kellogg's dutifully responded on Twitter, reaffirming its commitment to diversity and inclusion. In other words, they respect corn kernels of all colors and socioeconomic backgrounds.

"Kellogg is committed to diversity & inclusion. We did not intend to offend - we apologize. The artwork is updated & will be in stores soon," the company stated.

And for the sake of inclusivity, I imagine Kellogg's would affirm vegetables that identify as corn kernels, or corn kernels that might be yellow but identify as brown. I mean, who are we to judge if a head of lettuce identifies as a corn kernel?

Folks, the country has gone plumb nuts.

The notion that a major American company was forced to apologize after somebody got their flakes frosted by a cartoon corn kernel demonstrates just how perpetually offended and overly sensitive we've become.

I can only imagine what the Social Justice Breakfast Brigade will do when they discover Cocoa Puffs or—heaven forbid—Fruity Pebbles.

TRICK OR TREAT AT YOUR OWN RISK, AMERICA

Trick-or-treaters are having a difficult time finding Halloween costumes that won't get them in trouble with the identity politics and social justice crowd.[122]

Folks can deal with flesh-eating zombies and demon-possessed children. But accusations of cultural appropriation? Well, that's a whole different story.

Let's be honest—nobody wants to tangle with a bunch of perpetually offended liberals who were triggered by a white guy wearing a sombrero. Most folks would rather climb into a storm drain and take their chances with a deranged circus clown.

Two Disney costumes caused quite a bit of "cultural appropriation and white privilege" controversy in 2018: Moana, the Polynesian character, and Elsa, from *Frozen*.[123]

"I had some reservations regarding both costume choices…about cultural appropriation and the power/privilege carried by Whiteness, and about Whiteness and standards of beauty," wrote Sachi Feris on the Raising Race Conscious Children blog.[124]

In their estimation, dressing up like a Polynesian is akin to wearing black face—or calling a white Southerner a "cracker." The blog also posted a guide urging white parents to use Halloween as an opportunity to "dismantle white supremacy."

"White parents who want to dismantle White supremacy have a special burden to check their entitlement on Halloween—and make

---

122   Snider, Mike. "Kellogg's to replace racially insensitive Corn Pops boxes following Twitter call out." *USA Today* (McLean), Last modified October 26, 2017. https://www.usatoday.com/story/money/business/2017/10/25/kelloggs-replace-racially-insensitive-corn-pops-boxes-following-twitter-rant/797911001/.

123   Juneau, Jen. "Parents Are Divided on Whether It's Okay to Let Their Kids Dress as Moana for Halloween." *People*, October 4, 2018. https://people.com/parents/moana-halloween-costume-cultural-appropriation-debate/.

124   *Raising Race Conscious Children* (blog). http://www.raceconscious.org.

sure that their children's costume choices are not reinforcing a culture of racism," the bloggers warned.

In other words, no Colin Kaepernick costumes, kids.

"White people have been dressing up in costumes 'in good fun' with little regard to whom they might be offending," the bloggers wrote.

I think they might be talking about you folks who dressed up as President Trump's border wall.

The Raising Race Conscious Children bloggers also want moms and dads to use Halloween as an educational opportunity. It's not just about candy corn and orange marshmallow circus peanuts.

"Halloween is an opportunity to have a conversation with your child about race, power and privilege," they wrote.

I must confess, it is indeed a burden for us pale faces, celebrating Halloween without culturally appropriating.

But this year, I may have stumbled upon the foolproof costume. I've decided to dress up in a button-down Oxford shirt, with khakis and penny loafers. If anybody asks, I'm a Saltine-American.

CONFESS YOUR SINS, WHITE PEOPLE

Georgia lawmakers are investigating what they call systematic bias against conservative and Christian students at Kennesaw State University.

"They are threatened. They are retaliated against all because of their viewpoint," State Representative Earl Ehrhart told me.[125]

The taxpayer-funded university is already facing two federal lawsuits alleging bias against conservatives.

---

125   Starnes, Todd. "University students in Georgia forced to confess their white privilege." Fox News. Last modified March 29, 2018. https://www.foxnews.com/opinion/university-students-in-georgia-forced-to-confess-their-white-privilege.

Ehrhart went on to say that some students were forced "as a condition of their grades to confess their white privilege in a video."

"That's horrifying," he said.

The *Marietta Daily Journal* reports that college Republicans were unable to bring a GOP gubernatorial candidate to campus because the university charged outrageous security fees. They also force students to get approval from four different departments.

Another student alleged that she was kicked out of class after the professor disagreed with her conservative viewpoint.

"Many of my professors make it a regular habit to push their own political agendas in the classroom, and I fear that if I express my own opinion in opposition, I will receive a poor grade in the class," Victoria Thompson said. "In one of my classes, my professor regularly talks about how stupid Republicans are. He makes fun of us on a regular basis."[126]

The LGBT and social justice warriors are at the top of the food chain, and Christians and conservatives are at the bottom, Ehrhart said.

A caller on my radio program, "Kay from Kennesaw," said her daughter was required to attend a one-man play that included Trump-bashing, profane tirades against Republicans, and explicit sex talk.

"She called me in tears," the caller said. "These teenagers are already subjected to so much."

---

126   Gargis, Jon. "Legislators: 'Systemic' bias within Kennesaw State against conservative viewpoints." *Marietta Daily Journal* (Marietta), March 27, 2018. https://www.mdjonline.com/news/legislators-systemic-bias-within-kennesaw-state-against-conservative-viewpoints/article_c87970dc-3222-11e8-8b0c-77ac09938870.html.

THE HORRORS OF WHITE PEOPLE SHAMPOO

A Grammy-nominated singer-songwriter is on a mission to do something about "white people shampoo" in hotel bathrooms.[127]

Now, before we go any further into the story, it's important to understand what the word "woke" means. It's got nothing to do with getting out of bed in the morning. These days, "woke" refers to raising awareness about social and racial injustice.

And that brings me to the singer-songwriter known as Halsey.

In 2018, she posted a series of messages on social media lamenting the state of affairs regarding hair products provided in hotels and motels.

"I've been traveling for years now and it's been so frustrating that the hotel toiletry industry entirely alienates people of color," Miss Halsey tweeted to her nine million followers.

Ah yes, the notorious hotel toiletry industry. (Actually, I had no idea there was such a thing as the hotel toiletry industry, but apparently there is indeed such a thing).

"I can't use this perfumed watered down white people shampoo. Neither can 50% of ur customers. Annoying," she added.

Miss Halsey's original tweet sparked an online debate that raged for several days. A number of critics wondered why the pop star could not just pack a bottle of her own shampoo?

"I'm fortunate enough to be financially in a position to do so, but POC traveling frequently for work/medical reasons might not be. Just making a point is all!" Halsey replied.

The controversy generated headlines across the nation from the *Washington Post* ("Singer Halsey stirs debate over hotels offering only 'white people shampoo'") to the *New York Daily News* ("Halsey says hotels only provide 'white people shampoo'").

---

127 Ruffo, Jillian. "Halsey Says Hotels Should Provide More Than Just 'White People Shampoo' in Bathrooms." *People*. April 27, 2018. https://people.com/style/halsey-hair-biracial-hotel-products/.

The twenty-three-year-old pop star said the problem is that people of color feel left out.

"It's not just hotels. I stayed in a psychiatric hospital as a teenager and they didn't have hair products for any patients who were POC. It's hard enough being in there as it is, but then ur gonna too feel ugly and dry n frizzy too? Nah. Anyways. Y'all still missing the point lol," she tweeted.

I sincerely doubt the good people who run LaQuinta or Hampton Inn are conspiring to inconvenience hotel guests by stocking their bathrooms with generic shampoo.

But just because you lather up with Pert or Vidal Sassoon does not necessarily make you a racist. Now that's woke, America.

NOW, WAIT A PEA-PICKIN' MINUTE

In 2017, Hobby Lobby, the national arts and crafts chain, was embroiled in a raging controversy over whether cotton is racist.[128]

As absurd as it may sound, a Texas customer wrote a Facebook post blasting Hobby Lobby for selling raw cotton plants.

"Wrong on so many levels," Daniell Rider declared as she described a vase filled with cotton bolls. "There is nothing decorative about raw cotton."

"A commodity which was gained at the expense of African-American slaves," she thundered. "A little sensitivity goes a long way. Please remove this 'décor.'"

More than 200,000 people weighed in—and many agreed with her argument that cotton was a commodity gained at the expense of African-American slaves.

---

128   Starnes, Todd. "Customer Triggered by Hobby Lobby Cotton Décor." *Todd Starnes* (blog). September 19, 2017. https://www.toddstarnes.com/uncategorized/customer-triggered-by-hobby-lobby-cotton-decor/.

To be clear, the same could be said about peanuts and tobacco, but I don't want to give the perpetually offended crowd any ideas.

Cotton is the fabric of our lives, harvested today by both black and white people.

Hobby Lobby did not comment on the faux controversy and, as of this writing, they were still selling cotton-themed decorations on their website.

Meanwhile, African-American students at Lipscomb University in Tennessee became enraged after they were invited to what they described as a racially offensive dinner party at the university president's house.

The ungrateful urchins were angered after they were served collard greens, macaroni and cheese, and cornbread. But the university president's most egregious offensive was to decorate the tables with cotton bolls.[129]

We can only hope the decorations were not purchased at Hobby Lobby.

The president of Lipscomb University issued a public apology after an untold number of African-American students were offended by a dinner table centerpiece made from stalks of cotton.

Yes, good readers—a group of college students was triggered by the fabric of our lives.

Randy Lowry, president of the Christian university based in Nashville, had invited African-American students to his home for dinner.

One student who attended the gathering posted a diatribe on Instagram, along with a photo of the "offensive" centerpiece.

---

129   Bever, Lindsey. "A university president held a dinner for black students—and set the table with cotton stalks and collard greens." *The Washington Post* (Washington, D.C.), September 19, 2017. https://www.washingtonpost.com/news/grade-point/wp/2017/09/19/a-university-president-held-a-dinner-for-black-students-and-set-the-table-with-cotton-stalks-and-collard-greens/?utm_term=.9b500686b9d5.

"We were very offended," the student wrote. "My friend … asked why there was cotton on the table as the centerpiece. His response was that he didn't know, he seen it before we did, he kind of thought it was 'fallish', THEN he said, 'it ISNT INHERENTLY BAD IF WERE ALL WEARING IT.'"

The students were also angered by the home-cooked meal they were served.

"The meals that were provided resembled many 'black meals' they had mac n cheese, collard greens, corn bread, etc.," the student wrote.

President Lowry posted an apology on the university's Facebook page.[130]

"The content of the centerpieces was offensive, and I could have handled the situation with more sensitivity," he wrote. "I sincerely apologize for the discomfort, anger or disappointment we caused and solicit your forgiveness."

Now, wait just one cotton-picking minute.

The university president graciously invited students to his home, had a home-cooked meal prepared in their honor, and lavished them with Southern hospitality.

Instead of a cordial "thank you," the students pitched a public hissy fit.

What a bunch of ingrates.

I know there are many who are confused and amused by the number of Americans who were triggered by cotton and cornbread. But this rabid type of political correctness is a clear and present danger to our nation.

130　Lipscomb University. 2017. "President Randy Lowry just sent the following email to the Lipscomb community." Facebook, September 15, 2017. https://www.facebook.com/lipscombuniversity/posts/president-randy-lowry-just-sent-the-following-email-to-the-lipscomb-community-la/10154953700931662/

We must speak up and call out those who want to silence and eradicate cotton in the name of tolerance and diversity. We must do so for the sake of cotton swabs and Fruit of the Loom.

We must also ensure that those who suffer microaggressions as a result of cotton and collard greens seek the psychological help they so desperately need.

I'm not quite sure where this war on cotton is headed, but don't be surprised if leisure suits come back in style.

By the way, what's wrong with collard greens and cornbread and macaroni and cheese? Back home in the Deep South, we don't call those "black meals" or "white meals." We just call it good eatin'.

IF A WHITE GUY FELL IN THE WOODS, WOULD IT BE PRIVILEGE?

The University of Vermont recently held a retreat exclusively for Caucasian students so they could explore white privilege.

"Examining White Privilege: A Retreat for Undergraduate Students Who Self-Identify as White," was the name of the three-day conference, as first reported by the website Campus Reform.[131]

It's a bit wordy for a T-shirt, in my humble opinion. They should've just called it "Blame the White Guy 2015."

The retreat was sponsored by the university's African, Latino, Asian, Native American, and Bi/Multiracial Student Center, ALANA for short.

"It's a new retreat specifically for white students to engage in building a stronger and inclusive campus community," ALANA stated on its website.

---

131   "Examining White Identity Retreat." *The University of Vermont.*
        Accessed May 29, 2019. https://www.uvm.edu/health/
        examining-white-identity-retreat.

The taxpayer-funded university would not tell me how the "free" retreat was financed. Typically, when you see the word "free," it means "courtesy of the American taxpayer."

ALANA said the purpose of the getaway was for white students to "recognize and understand white privilege from an individual experience as well as the impact of white privilege on the UVM community and beyond."

They also felt it was necessary for the university's white students to "conceptualize and articulate whiteness from a personal and systematic lens."

I have no idea what that means.

I'm also having a difficult time understanding what it means to self-identify as white. Is that someone who belongs to a country club, cuts the crust off his bread, and doesn't have any discernable rhythm?

ALANA provided testimonials from white privilege alumni who gave the retreat a thumbs-up.

It was a "great opportunity to talk about an identity that I had not previously felt equipped to comfortably discuss," said one pale face.

I can only imagine the fun they must've had noshing on salmon and arugula in the mess hall, sitting around a campfire crooning Barry Manilow songs, and sharing scary stories about how their pigmentation oppressed people of color.

As we all know, the only way to build a stronger and inclusive university campus is to shame the white children into acknowledging they are personally responsible for every imaginable evil that has befallen the world—from global warming to that episode of *Happy Days* when Fonzie jumped over the shark.

I was particularly intrigued by one of the questions they asked the campers: what does it mean to be white and how does whiteness impact you? Well, that's a mighty loaded question. But here's how I would've responded had I been seated around the campfire:[132]

Some folks might self-identify as black. Others might self-identify as white. But as for me, I self-identify as an American—a free man. And I think that's a privilege no matter what color you are.

---

132 Starnes, Todd. "Blame the White Guy 2015: University hosts 'White Privilege' retreat." Fox News. November 19, 2015. https://www.foxnews.com/opinion/blame-the-white-guy-2015-university-group-hosts-white-privilege-retreat.

CHAPTER 8

PANDERING POLITICIANS CAN KISS OUR COLLECTIVE GRITS

ALL THIS CULTURAL appropriation nonsense reminded me of a few hilarious incidents back on the 2016 presidential trail.

That was the year Hillary Clinton went down to Dixie and tried to pull off a faux Southern accent. Sweet Lord Almighty, folks, it was pitiful. Miss Hill'ry was drawling and dropping *g*'s all over the stage during a speech to Democrats in South Carolina, the Palmetto State.[133]

I was surprised Miss Hill'ry didn't show up at her campaign rally in bare feet, waving a cast iron skillet and singing Dixie.

"Hillary Clinton's southern twang is back," announced *New York Times* writer Maggie Haberman on Twitter.[134]

The folks over at Hot Air crafted a spot-on analysis of Miss Hill'ry's politically expedient dialect in a story titled "Hillary's Fake Southern Accent is Back."[135]

---

133   Mills, Curt. "Clinton's Southern strategy? Hillary fakes her accent for local crowd." *Washington Examiner*, October 17, 2017. https://www.washingtonexaminer.com/clintons-southern-strategy-hillary-fakes-her-accent-for-local-crowd.

134   Halper, Daniel. "Hillary Brings Back Southern Twang for South Carolina Visit." *The Weekly Standard*, May 27, 2015. https://www.weeklystandard.com/daniel-halper/hillary-brings-back-southern-twang-for-south-carolina-visit.

135   Pundit, Allah. "Campaign Season Now Officially Underway: Hillary's Fake southern Accent Is Back." *HotAir*. May 27, 2015. https://hotair.com/archives/2015/05/27/campaign-season-now-officially-underway-hillarys-fake-southern-accent-is-back/.

The problem is that it's not a very good Southern accent. It's almost as if her linguistic advisors made her watch every episode of *The Beverly Hillbillies*.

"It's ce-ment pond, not cement pond, ma'am. And it's 'pert near' not 'pretty near.'"

Folks, I'm a native of Tennessee, the Volunteer State. And there's nothing more unpleasant to the ear than a phony Southern accent. It's downright disrespectful and a bit condescending. But because she's Miss Hill'ry, the mainstream media laughs off her faux dialect.

The Republican strategist Rick Wilson offered this spot-on analysis via Twitter: "Just for ONE SECOND imagine Ted or Marco or Jeb doing a speech somewhere and speaking in an exaggerated fake accent."[136]

Imagine, indeed.

The truth is, that lady couldn't tell the difference between a collard green and a turnip green. She probably thinks "fat back" is something a personal trainer can help you get rid of. And heaven only knows how she would smoke a pork butt. Rolling papers, anyone?

Clearly, Miss Hill'ry has mastered the art of speaking from both sides of her mouth, but she still needs to work on her drawl.

Therefore, I propose a crash course in Southern Living 101, and there's no better place than Monroe, Louisiana—home of the Duck Commander.

Miss Kay could teach Miss Hill'ry the finer points of frying up a batch of frog legs. Mr. Phil could provide her with a briefing on the moral decline of America. And Uncle Si could regale her with pearls of Southern wisdom.

---

136 Wilson, Rick (@TheRickWilson). 2015. "Just for ONE SECOND imagine Ted or Marco or Jeb doing a speech somewhere and speaking in an exaggerated fake accent." Twitter, May 27, 2015, 11:50 AM. https://twitter.com/therickwilson/status/603629392565248001.

Or I could just brew up a jug of my special recipe sweet tea. One swig is all it would take to put a little drawl in her "y'all."

President Obama behaved just as badly in North Carolina. He was caught dropping his *g*'s and throwing around Southern slang like he was slinging hash browns down at the Waffle House.

He started off by talking about how much he "loves me some North Carolina."

Lord Jesus.

The president tossed out the word "holler" and then said it was time to get down to "bidness." Not business, but "bidness."

The Obama Administration seemed to think all of us Southerners walk around talking like Boss Hogg from the Dukes of Hazzard. There's really nothing worse than a politician pandering for votes down in Dixie. Southern folk may not know our way around a foie gras buffet, but we do know the difference between field peas and fat back.

It's even worse when they commandeer church pulpits and invoke their faux "preacher voice." During her 2016 presidential campaign, I was just waiting for Miss Hillary to do back flips down the center aisle in her Sunday-best pant suit while a church choir sang a spirited worship tune (apologies to the Blues Brothers).

It's cultural appropriation for a political purpose.

Now, cultural appropriation is something the culture jihadists invented to take all the fun out of holidays. It's all the rage on college campuses. For example, you can't wear an Indian costume on Halloween or else you could be accused of appropriating Native American culture.

A number of schools have eliminated traditions that might cause grave offense to overly sensitive millennials. For example, some universities have banned beloved culinary traditions like Taco Tuesdays. Some Latino students came down with a bad case of indigestion at the sight of all those Gringos scarfing down chalupas. And heaven help the poor Anglo kid who gets caught wearing a sombrero on Cinco de Mayo. ¡*Ay caramba!*[137]

And it's not just a Democrat issue. Anybody remember Mitt Romney dishing on "cheesy grits" and trying to say "y'all" back in 2012? Then there was his infamous flip-flop on fried catfish.[138]

He told Alabama voters that he loved catfish, but he told South Carolina voters he was not "a catfish man, or not a fish man so much."[139]

The man was from Massachusetts—what did he know about catfish battered in cornmeal and served with slaw? He probably thought a hush puppy was a comfortable shoe.

Back in 2008, Romney blew his chances at the GOP nomination because of an incident involving the Gospel Bird (as we refer to fried chicken back home in Memphis).

He was caught at a campaign stop in the Deep South at a Kentucky Fried Chicken. As egregious as that might have been, the real sin was when the governor peeled the skin off of the fried chicken. Now, I want to flat-out tell you that ain't right and, in some Southern states, that's the kind of behavior that'll get you put on the church prayer list (normally as an unspoken).[140]

---

137   James, Alexander. "Major college forced to apologize for 'Taco Tuesday' promotion." *Washington Examiner*. January 15, 2019. https://www.washingtonexaminer.com/red-alert-politics/ brigham-young-university-forced-apologize-taco-tuesday-promotion.

138   Saenz, Arlette. "Taste of the South: Mitt Romney Morphs Into Grits Lover." *ABC News*. March 9, 2012. https://abcnews.go.com/blogs/ politics/2012/03/taste-of-the-south-mitt-romney-morphs-into-grits-lover/.

139   Haberman, Maggie. "Romney pro-meat, not a fish man." *Politico*. January 18, 2012. https://www.politico.com/blogs/burns-haberman/2012/01/ romney-pro-meat-not-a-fish-man-111366.

140   "Huckabee challenges Romney over fried chicken." CNN Politics. January 28, 2008. http://politicalticker.blogs.cnn.com/2008/01/28/ huckabee-challenges-romney-over-fried-chicken/.

Arkansas Governor Mike Huckabee, a devout consumer of fried chicken, rightfully called out Romney's peculiar poultry peccadillo.

"I can tell you this—any Southerner knows if you don't eat the skin, don't bother calling it fried chicken," Huckabee said at an impromptu press conference. "So that's good. I'm glad that he did that, because that means I'm going to win Alabama, Georgia, Tennessee, Arkansas, Oklahoma ... all these great Southern states that understand the best part of fried chicken is the skin, if you're going to eat it that way."

You see, Southerners can smell a phony a mile away. And politicians who culturally appropriate, well, that's a mighty big stink. It's unfortunate that so many politicians put on airs instead of just being themselves.

That's why President Trump, a billionaire from Queens, endeared himself to Southerners and Midwesterners. He didn't try to slurp down boiled peanuts or drop his *g*'s. He did something much more effective to endear himself to voters: he kept his campaign promises.

Now, don't get me wrong. I'm not saying that Northern candidates should avoid campaigning in the Southern states. Just be authentic. So before you politicos start dropping *g*'s, consider the following questions:

Have you ever owned a pickup truck or had a Moon Pie or watched the Tennessee Volunteers on a cool October day? Have you ever floated down the Chattahoochee or listened to Merle or Reba or Hank Jr. on the radio? Have you ever been to a Jerry Clower show or read a Lewis Grizzard column or watched the sunset over Talladega?

Have you ever sipped sweet tea from a mason jar? Have you ever spent a warm summer night sitting on your front porch in a rocking chair watching the lightning bugs flitter about the magnolia tree?

We have a saying back home, "Bless your Heart." It can either be used to convey sincere empathy or it means you're an idiot. It takes a true Southerner to know the difference.

So even though Hillary is not running in the 2020 presidential election, don't be surprised if you see a bunch of northern and Midwestern Democrats trying to bond with all of us folks down on the farm. In other words, brace yourself for Instagram videos of Mayor Pete slinging hash browns at the Waffle House and Crazy Bernie Sanders plunking a banjo at the Grand Ole Opry.

So, to all those 2020 presidential candidates who plan to embrace their inner "Beverly Hillbillies" and appropriate our culture, bless your pea-pickin' hearts.

CHAPTER 9

TRUMP JINGLES THE CHRISTMAS HATERS' BELLS

PRESIDENT TRUMP VOWED to put the Christ back into Christmas and that's exactly what he did, delivering on a promise to end the ongoing war on Christmas.

You might recall that during the first year of the Obama administration, the president and first lady considered removing the Nativity from the White House for the sake of inclusivity.

The New York Times buried that yuletide nugget deep inside a story about then-White House Social Secretary Desiree Rogers. Read it for yourself, ladies and gentlemen:[141]

"But Washington is a city that likes its traditions, and Ms. Rogers has raised a few eyebrows by trying to bend them. When former social secretaries gave a luncheon to welcome Ms. Rogers earlier this year, one participant said, she surprised them by suggesting the Obamas were planning a 'non-religious Christmas'—hardly a surprising idea for an administration making a special effort to reach out to other faiths.

"The lunch conversation inevitably turned to whether the White House would display its crèche, customarily placed in a prominent

141   Gay Stolbert, Sheryl. "The Spotlight's Bright Glare." *New York Times* (New York), December 4, 2009. https://www.nytimes.com/2009/12/06/fashion/06desiree.html.

spot in the East Room. Ms. Rogers, this participant said, replied that the Obamas did not intend to put the manger scene on display—a remark that drew an audible gasp from the tight-knit social secretary sisterhood. (A White House official confirmed that there had been internal discussions about making Christmas more inclusive and whether to display the crèche.)

"Yet in the end, tradition won out; the executive mansion is now decorated for the Christmas holiday, and the crèche is in its usual East Room spot."

Yes, good readers, Barack and Michelle Obama wanted to mark their first Christmas in the White House by tossing the Baby Jesus out of the building.

And if you recall, for a number of years, the White House decorations were more pet-centric than Jesus-centric. And of course, there were those infamous "religion-free" holiday cards, featuring the family dogs without the word "Christmas."

It ultimately became an issue in the 2016 presidential campaign—and one that endeared many culture war voters to the Trump campaign.

"We are stopping cold the attacks on Judeo-Christian values," then candidate Trump declared to the attendees at the Values Voter Summit in Washington, D.C. "You know, we're getting near that beautiful Christmas season that people don't talk about anymore. They don't use the word 'Christmas' because it's not politically correct. You go to department stores, and they'll say, 'Happy New Year' and they'll say other things. And it will be red, they'll have it painted, but they don't say it. Well, guess what? We're saying 'Merry Christmas' again."[142]

---

142 Kamisar, Ben. "Trump: 'We're saying merry Christmas again.'" *The Hill* (Washington, D.C.), October 13, 2017. https://thehill.com/homenews/ administration/355303-trump-were-saying-merry-christmas-again.

And sure enough, the Trump family's first presidential holiday card is adorned with the words "Merry Christmas and Happy New Year."[143]

And the Christmas decorations were simply spectacular, the White House decorated with lots of red and green and gold. And yes—there was even a Nativity.

That being said, not everyone in America is thrilled that President Trump is not ashamed to declare the reason for the season. The mainstream media concocted some sort of wild-eyed theory that President Trump's promise to say "Merry Christmas" is some sort of coded language for white nationalism and white supremacy.

CNN host Don Lemon was among the most high-profile mainstream media minions to advance the race-baiting narrative.

"This is a dog whistle to the base because no one has ever stopped using Merry Christmas," the Clinton News Network host said during a broadcast.[144]

In reality, the entire CNN network is a dog whistle for race-baiting, anti-Trump, America-bashing pinheads.

But CNN is not the only mainstream media outlet to get its tinsel in a twist over the president's frequent use of the words, "Merry Christmas."

Consider this headline from *Newsweek*: "How Trump and the Nazis Stole Christmas to Promote White Nationalism."[145]

143 Jacobs, Sarah. "Happy Holidays from the White Hous3e: See 91 years of presidents' Christmas cards, from Trump to JFK to Coolidge." *Business Insider*. December 24, 2018. https://www.businessinsider.com/donald-trump-white-house-christmas-card-2017-12#barack-obama-2011-5.

144 Schwartz, Ian. "Don Lemon: Is Trump's Use of 'Merry Christmas' A Dog Whistle?" *RealClear Politics*. December 21, 2017. https://www.realclearpolitics.com/video/2017/12/21/don_lemon_is_trumps_use_of_merry_christmas_a_dog_whistle.html.

145 Maza, Christina. "How Trump and the Nazis Stole Christmas to Promote White Nationalism." *Newsweek*, December 24, 2017. https://www.newsweek.com/how-trump-nazis-stole-christmas-promote-white-nationalism-755991.

At first glance, I just assumed one of the copy editors had slurped a bit too much eggnog. But it turns out, *Newsweek* was dead serious.

"Trump has been using the so-called war on Christmas to wage a culture war that pits multicultural liberals against Christian conservatives. He began doing this long before Christmas. Meanwhile, some members of the religious right support Trump's most nationalist, race-baiting form of political rhetoric, including his reclaiming of Christmas," *Newsweek* declared.

Newsweek moaned about how the president is "promoting a version of the holidays that excludes members of other religions, and that his crusade to bring back Christmas is part of a larger attempt by the president to define America as a country for white Christians alone."

Apparently, *Newsweek* is unaware that many African Americans and Asian-Americans and Hispanic-Americans celebrate the Christmas season too.

"Wishing people 'merry Christmas' instead of 'happy holidays' is thus in line with Trump's decision to ban citizens of Muslim-majority countries from entering the United States, critics say. It fits neatly with his refusal to condemn white supremacists when they march against diversity, and with his condemnation of athletes who protest police brutality against black men," the magazine noted.

Far be it for me to offer psychological advice, but it sounds to me like *Newsweek* is a few nuts shy of a fruitcake.

However, the mainstream media holds fast to its belief that Christmas is supposed to be some sort of all-inclusive, one-ornament-fits-all, religiously neutral holiday.

And yet they don't seem to have a problem with the exclusivity of other religious holidays, like Ramadan. Why don't we hear Don Lemon demanding that Muslim holidays be inclusive?

I believe I know the answer.

It's because the attacks on President Trump and Christmas have nothing to do with inclusivity. It's about marginalizing people of faith and silencing Christianity in the public square.

In fairness to CNN and *Newsweek*, President Trump is sending the nation a coded message. He's telling us that it's okay to say "Merry Christmas." He's telling us that he understands and recognizes the reason for the season.

And in spite of what Don Lemon or CNN or *Newsweek* say, Christmas will always be an exclusively Christian holiday, a moment for us to celebrate the birth of the newborn king.

Still the attacks on Christmas continue, proving that Christians must be diligent no matter who is in the White House.

Franklin Graham told me that secularists were on a mission last Christmas season to destroy the name of Jesus Christ.

"These are more than just an attack on Christmas. This is an attack on Jesus Christ," Graham said on my Fox Nation television program.[146]

Graham, president of Samaritan's Purse[147] and the Billy Graham Evangelistic Association, is one of the nation's most prominent evangelical Christian leaders.

"The secularists want to do everything they can to take Christ out of everything in this country—even his birthday," he said. "The secularists want to destroy not only the name of Christ but take him out of our society completely."

Graham said he is encouraged that people of faith across the nation are standing up and fighting back against the attempts to take Christ out of Christmas. And he gave some of the credit to President Trump.

"When the president takes a stand, like saying 'Merry Christmas,' this emboldens others to take a stand just like the president—not just to say 'Merry Christmas,' but to fight back," he said.

---

146   Starnes, Todd. "Starnes Country." Fox Nation. 2019. https://nation. foxnews.com/starnes-country/.

147   *Samaritan's Purse*. Access May 29, 2019. https://www.samaritanspurse.org/.

He referenced the incident in Elkhorn, Nebraska where citizens complained after a principal banned anything related to Christmas—including Christmas carols and candy canes.[148]

Jennifer Sinclair, the principal of Manchester Elementary School, sent a letter to teachers explaining that her decision to ban Christmas decorations was for the sake of inclusiveness.

"Please remember that we are not to be doing any Christmas or holiday-specific themed activities with students," she wrote in a letter to faculty. "Santa and Christmas items are not to be on activities or copies. We have varied religious beliefs in our school, and it is our job to be inclusive."

Principal Sinclair banned Christmas trees and Christmas carols, Santa Claus, and Elf on the Shelf. Candy canes were also off limits because the principal said "the shape is 'J' for Jesus."

"The red is for the blood of Christ, and the white is a symbol of his resurrection," she wrote.

Also deemed not acceptable:

o singing Christmas Carols

o playing Christmas music

o making a Christmas ornament as a gift

o Christmas clip art

o reading Christmas-themed books (sorry, Tiny Tim)

o the colors red and green

o reindeer

o Christmas movies (so long, Frosty)

---

148   Dejka, Joe. "An Elkhorn elementary school principal tried to ban Christmas. It didn't go well." *Omaha World-Herald* (Omaha), December 27, 2018. https://www.omaha.com/news/education/primary-secondary/an-elkhorn-elementary-school-principal-tried-to-ban-christmas-it/article_1655103a-673c-5749-a73c-a8155ef89537.html.

Liberty Counsel, a public policy organization dedicated to religious liberty issues, fired off a letter to Elkhorn Public Schools warning them that the principal's Christmas ban was unconstitutional.[149]

"The ban violates the U.S. Constitution by showing hostility toward Christianity," attorney Robert Mast wrote. "The principal appears to have conflated her own values and preferences with the law."

And as Liberty Counsel pointed out, the First Amendment does not require the elimination of all Christmas symbols—religious or secular.

"The effort to comprehensively eliminate Christmas symbols is Orwellian," Mast concluded.

The school district investigated the matter and determined that Principal Sinclair's memorandum to teachers violated district policy. They quickly reversed course, meaning Santa Claus is once again welcome in the classroom.

One final note: the principal had also issued a list of acceptable seasonal decorations, including yetis, penguins, polar bears, and Olaf—a character from the movie *Frozen*.

She also permitted teachers to decorate with "gingerbread people" and "snow people" and snowflakes. That certainly seems to be appropriate—seeing how there appear to be lots of snowflakes in the Elkhorn school system.

After massive national outrage, the school district reversed the ban and placed the principal on administrative leave.

"People rose up and now she's on the naughty list," Graham said. "When the president takes a stand for Christmas others take a stand and I say God bless you."

---

149   "Christmas Goes Back to School." *Liberty Counsel.*
        December 4, 2018. https://www.lc.org/newsroom/
        details/120418-christmas-goes-back-to-school-1.

SCHOOL: CHILDREN MIGHT FEEL UNCOMFORTABLE
AROUND CHRISTMAS ORNAMENTS

In 2018, an Arkansas school district warned teachers not to decorate their classrooms with anything that might make a student feel uncomfortable or not included.

"When we choose to decorate or celebrate any specific tradition, be it the Christian Christmas, Kwanzaa, Hanukkah, or any other tradition, we run the risk of creating an environment where a student does not feel comfortable or included," read a letter written by John Colbert, the superintendent of Fayetteville Public Schools. "This is unacceptable."[150]

I'm sure it was just a coincidence that the Nov. 29th letter was sent to principals and school leaders just before Christmas and not before a Muslim holiday.

Colbert warned teachers in his letter that any decoration that offended a child was a violation of a school board policy that states, "No religious belief or non-belief should be promoted by the school district or its employees, and none shall be disparaged."

A *Starnes Country* viewer in Fayetteville reached out to me, expressing her extreme concerns about what teachers interpreted as a ban on Christmas décor of any kind.

"They are also banning angel trees from all campuses," the viewer said. "Staff are not allowed to help families in need during the Christmas season."

I asked the school district about the alleged ban on angel trees, but they did not respond to my questions.

"While Fayetteville has traditionally been a liberal city, over the past decade there has been even more of a shift toward the PC and liberal culture," the viewer told me.

---

150   Perozek, Dave. "Fayetteville community disputes district's holiday policy." *AP News*. December 30, 2018. https://www.apnews.com/43c3add7418247a8adf2d8a9c80f607a.

The school district's letter to principals was, quite frankly, confusing. On the one hand, they encouraged teachers to celebrate the season with "winter decorations."

But on the other hand, they threatened teachers if they did not provide "an inclusive and safe environment."

According to the district policy, religious holidays may be "taught in the public schools, but they may not be celebrated."

What does that even mean?

It sounds to me like the school district is trying to confuse teachers by parsing the policies. It's as if they are telling teachers, "Go ahead, put up the Christmas tree, but if an atheist complains you'll be looking for a new job."

Mr. Colbert's letter is a classic example of a left-wing educator using his authority to bully and badger Christian teachers.

JUNIOR LEAGUE GETS IN TROUBLE FOR REFERENCE TO BABY JESUS

In 2018, a Louisiana school district did not allow grade schoolers to attend a Christmas play that mentioned Jesus during school hours because it might have violated a federal court order barring the district from promoting religion at school.[151]

For the previous several years, the Minden Junior Service League had performed a free Christmas production during school hours at the local high school.

The half-hour production featured a *Toy Story* theme along with a brief reference to the Baby Jesus.

"Several in attendance felt that it was necessary to report us for the mention of the reason for the season—Jesus," a Junior Service League spokesperson said in a powerful and emotional Facebook video.

---

151 "Christmas play to proceed despite complaints of Jesus' name." *KSLA 12 News*. Last modified November 30, 2018. http://www.ksla.com/2018/11/30/christmas-play-proceed-despite-complaints-jesus-name/.

After the first performance, the Webster Parish School District reached out to the service organization and urged them to remove the reference to Jesus.

The ladies in the Junior Service League flat-out rejected the request—even though it meant that their own children would not be permitted to see the performance.

"When this request was rejected, the school district had no other alternative than to withdraw from participation in the event or otherwise face contempt of court," the district said in a statement.

Now, the local school officials are not the bad guys here, folks. It's the American Civil Liberties Union and the federal court.

Earlier in 2018, the school district was slapped with a federal court order "regulating religious activities in schools."[152]

That order specifically prohibited the school board and its employees from promoting religion at school—and the order also covered events hosted by third parties.

"The Junior Service League of Minden fell victim to the politics of the public school system and the religious debate that is abundantly present in their path," the spokesperson said on Facebook.

The district feared that allowing children to attend the Christmas production would've violated the court order and subjected the district to a contempt of court citation.

"Because of the totality of the circumstances that we are now in, a newfound spotlight is shining upon the Webster Parish School System. No longer is there a gray area associated with this matter in our school system. This federal court order clearly spells out what is allowable and what is not," Supt. Johnny Rowland, Jr. said.

The Junior Service League tearfully apologized to the many boys and girls who will not be able to see the performance.

---

152   Wooten, Nick. "Webster Parish schools settle federal lawsuit alleging promotion of Christianity." *Shreveport Times*. Last modified May 15, 2018. https://www.shreveporttimes.com/story/news/2018/05/15/webster-settles-federal-religion-lawsuit/609396002/.

"We are so very sorry," the spokesperson said. "You are the reason we do this. You are why we do this play."

What happened to the Minden Junior Service League should appall and disgust every freedom-loving American. May God bless those dear, sweet ladies.

We must stand up to the anti-Christian mafia and reject their hatred. We must stand up to the bullies—even if they wear judicial robes.

Now, you understand why President Trump's most important assignment is to fill our federal courts with strict constitutionalists.

FROSTY AND ELSA ARE JUST FINE, BUT JESUS IS NOT

At Robious Middle School, it's okay to sing about Rudolph and Frosty, but it's not okay to sing about the little Lord Jesus.

Parents at the Virginia school received an email alerting them that Christmas songs mentioning Jesus would no longer be permitted.[153]

If that doesn't jingle your bells, I don't know what will, folks.

David Allen told television station WWBT that he received an email from the school's chorus teacher explaining that the school had decided to avoid singing "anything of a direct sacred nature in order to be more sensitive to the increasing diverse population at the school."[154]

"I'm trying to rationalize how you can encourage diversity and yet be exclusionary in one specific area," Allen told the television station.

---

153 "Yes, Virginia, There Is a War on Christmas." *Family Research Council.* November 26, 2018. https://www.frc.org/updatearticle/20181126/war-christmas.

154 Bolster, Karina. "Christmas songs with 'Jesus' excluded from winter concert." *NBC 12.* Last modified October 11, 2018. https://www.nbc12.com/2018/10/10/christmas-songs-with-jesus-excluded-winter-concert/.

First Liberty Institute, one of the nation's top law firms handling religious liberty cases, said it is permissible under the U.S. Constitution for public school choirs to perform sacred music.

"Federal courts have upheld the constitutionality of public school holiday programs that include the use of religious music, art, or drama, so long as the material is presented in an objective manner 'as a traditional part of the cultural and religious heritage of the particular holiday,'" First Liberty attorney Michael Berry wrote in a letter to the Chesterfield County School District.

Berry went on to cite several federal court rulings that indicate warbling "Joy to the World" and "Silent Night" do not violate the Establishment Clause.

Putting legal precedent aside, let's be honest, folks—Jesus *is* the reason for the season.

SENIOR CITIZENS BANNED FROM DECORATING DOORS

Christmas has always been a festive time of year for the residents of Lake Ridge Commons, a senior living community in Wilmington, North Carolina.[155]

"We had door decorating contests, wrapping paper covered doors, festive wreaths," resident Leigh Bowser told television station WECT.

But in 2018, there were no door decorating contests or doors covered in wrapping paper or even Christmas wreaths.[156]

---

155   Starnes, Todd. "Outdoor Christmas Decorations Banned at Senior Living Complex." *Todd Starnes* (blog). December 7, 2017. https://www.toddstarnes. com/faith/outdoor-christmas-decorations-banned-at-senior-living-complex/.

156   Smart, Ben. "Christmas, holiday decorations banned at senior living community." *WECT 6 News*. Last modified August 15, 2018. http://www.wect.com/story/37011410/christmas-holiday-decorations-banned-at-senior-living-community/.

"Now, Christmas is illegal," Bowser said. "Any display of Christmas is banned."

For the record, residents are more than welcome to haul out the holly and hang the tinsel inside their homes, but outside decorating is strictly forbidden.

"During 2017, offensive postings were placed on some doors which were offensive to other resident [*sic*] and other visitors and not of an acceptable nature and some resident's [*sic*] items were removed," Excel Property Management president Ann Hanson wrote in a letter to residents.

She acknowledged that in previous years, the apartment complex had permitted folks to deck the halls with boughs of holly, but in July they advised tenants of a provision in their lease that prohibits placing items outside their apartments in public view.

"Most residents have complied as requested—however recently a season wreath was placed on a door," Hanson wrote (and by "season" wreath I assume she's referring to a Christmas wreath).

Last month, residents organized and sent a letter to the management company urging them to reconsider, the television station reported. But the management company doubled down.

"Moving forward we have been advised by our legal counsel to adhere to our lease to the fullest," the management company informed the senior citizens.

Hanson wrote in her letter to residents that they were welcome to help decorate common areas of the complex "where we can more easily supervise that."

Heaven forbid one of the Golden Girls tries to sneak in Mary, Joseph, and the Baby Jesus.

"That policy is not intended to hurt the Holiday Season, but to preserve it," Hanson wrote.

Ah yes—out of sight, out of mind.

"I think it's a shame because it's holiday time," resident Ann Taylor told the television station. "People are paying their rent. They own that door. To be told we can't put wreaths up is really horrible and a lot of people are upset."

Technically, residents do not own the doors. They rent the doors. And this is a good lesson for renters. Be sure to read the lease before you sign the lease.

Excel Property Management has every right to require residents to follow the terms of their lease. If the management company wants to turn Lake Ridge Commons into a modern-day version of Potterville, that is their prerogative. But just because Excel Property Management has a legal right to be cold-hearted and cruel and Grinch-like, doesn't mean they should.

COLLEGE SNOWFLAKES TRIGGERED BY SANTA

The social justice warriors in charge of The College at Brockport in New York are urging holiday decorators to deck their halls and don their gay apparel with a flair for cultural sensitivity and inclusion.

"When planning holiday displays on campus, please consider an inclusive approach to your creativity," the Office of Diversity and Inclusion wrote on the college's website. "Displays that feature exclusively single-themed decorations may be well intentioned, but they can marginalize those who celebrate other religious and cultural beliefs during this season."[157]

That's a polite way of saying dump the Nativity.

The Office of Diversity and Inclusion, which is typically neither diverse nor inclusive, posted a long list of suggestions designed to take the Christ out of Christmas.

"The holiday season should be considered an opportunity to demonstrate cultural sensitivity and inclusivity by acknowledging multiple cultural traditions rather than imposing or endorsing a

---

157 "Culturally Inclusive Communities All Year Long." *The College at Brockport.* https://brockport.edu/about/diversity/holiday.html.

single tradition on everyone," the Office of Diversity and Inclu=
sion wrote.

I think they're talking about you, Santa Claus. I mean, why *does*
Jolly Old Saint Nick get to decide who's been naughty and who's
been nice?

Culturally sensitive holiday decorations are also a big issue for the
social justice snowflakes.[158]

"Keep decorations general and non-specific to any religion,"
the college recommended. "Create a winter theme with lights and
color rather than religious icons, or include decorations from all the
cultural traditions represented in your department."

In other words, toss the poinsettias and drape a burka over the
Christmas tree—pardon me, holiday tree.

As for holiday parties, well, the college recommends a multicultural, potluck buffet that respects religious dietary restrictions. What
about fruit cake? Is fruit cake still allowed?

The college said their suggestions are meant to "ensure inclusiveness and respect for a wide range of religious and cultural customs all
year long."

The annual Starnes Family Christmas Party is a completely
inclusive affair—we include everyone in our celebration of the birth
of Christ.

The house is decked out in red and green with a beautiful Nativity
scene in the foyer and a Christmas tree (adorned with an angel) in
the living room.

We sing carols like "Joy to the World, the Lord is Come" and we
feast on all sorts of delicious treats like smoked pork butt sliders and
bacon-wrapped shrimp.

---

158   Starnes, Todd. "Outdoor Christmas Decorations Banned at Senior Living
Complex." *Todd Starnes* (blog). December 7, 2017. https://www.toddstarnes.
com/faith/outdoor-christmas-decorations-banned-at-senior-living-complex/.

I can only imagine the raging microaggressions the Starnes Family Christmas Party would trigger among the culturally sensitive snowflakes at The College of Brockport.

DONUT SHOP FORCED TO APOLOGIZE FOR HELPING SALVATION ARMY

What in the sweet name of Santa Claus is wrong with liberals?

A popular donut shop in Portland, Maine, was forced to apologize to the community after it offended customers by working with the Salvation Army to provide Christmas to a needy family.[159]

The Holy Donut had asked customers to help them with a gift drive for a local family with five children. Those customers who participated received free donuts.

The donut shop reached out to the Salvation Army to find the family in need, the *Press-Herald* reports.[160]

Instead of saluting the donut shop for doing a good deed, an online mob stormed their Facebook page. Many accused the Salvation Army of being anti-gay and discriminating against the LGBT community.

It was all untrue, of course, but as we established earlier in this book, truth doesn't really matter these days.

"They proselytize to the people in their programs, they reject LGBT people from their shelters," one outraged customer wrote. "They have tried to scrub their image, but still discriminate."

For the record, the Salvation Army is a well-respected Christian ministry that provides shelter for the homeless, addiction programs, and, of course, the iconic red kettles at Christmas time.

---

159   Starnes, Todd. "Donut Shop Faces Leftist Fury for Helping Christmas Charity." *Todd Starnes* (blog). December 5, 2017. https://www.toddstarnes. com/faith/donut-shop-faces-leftist-fury-for-helping-christmas-charity/.

160   Starnes, Todd. "Donut Shop Faces Leftist Fury for Helping Christmas Charity." *Todd Starnes* (blog). December 5, 2017. https://www.toddstarnes. com/faith/donut-shop-faces-leftist-fury-for-helping-christmas-charity/.

Some freedom-loving donut eaters defended the popular mom-and-pop establishment.

"Going after a donut shop because they don't like their politics is exactly why people voted for Trump," one observer wrote online.

"I don't care if someone is L, G, B or T, but when they stand in the way of people helping people simply because their own personal noses are out of joint, they lose my respect and any sympathy I have for their cause," wrote another.

But the *Press Herald* reports that the anti-donut mob was unrelenting—going so far as to threaten boycotts unless the donut shop renounced its association with the Salvation Army.

"In case you forgot, a solid 70 percent of your clientele is part of the LGBTQ community," one rabble-rouser wrote. "You're making a silent statement that you're completely fine with their choices."

Ah yes, nothing quite like an old-fashioned yuletide public shaming.

"We do not support the Salvation Army or consider them our 'partner' for this project, they simply linked us to a needy family," the store owners wrote on Facebook. "We have nothing to gain here, we just wanted to help a family in need."

As unthinkable as it might be, a good number of the pro-LGBT protesters were upset that the donut shop dared to help a family in need during the Christmas season.

To quell the growing controversy, The Holy Donut threw themselves at the mercy of the surging mob.

"We take this opportunity to sincerely apologize to anyone that we have offended," the store owners wrote on Facebook. "We are an organization which prides itself on our track record of kindness and acceptance of everyone."

The Holy Donut should be commended for helping a family in need and spreading a bit of Christmas cheer.

They should also be commended for making delicious donuts. (I've been privileged to sample their Maple Bacon Maine Potato Donut.)

And shame on all of you folks out there for harassing these good people and spreading outright lies about the Salvation Army. Shame! No donuts for you.

YOU CAN ADVERTISE PORN ON THE BUS, BUT NOT THE NORTH STAR

A federal judge appointed to the bench by President Obama says the public transit authority in Washington, D.C. has the right to ban religious-themed Christmas advertisements.[161]

The Archdiocese of Washington had filed for an emergency injunction after the Washington Metropolitan Area Transit Authority rejected a Christmas ad promoting its annual "Find the Perfect Gift" program.

The advertising banner featured shepherds and sheep walking toward the North Star, along with the words, "Find the perfect gift."

The transit authority argued that the banner was declined because of a ban on religious-themed advertising.

Their attorneys explained in a court filing that Christmas is actually divided into two components, a religious half and a secular half.[162,163]

This idea that Christmas can be divided into a secular side and a religious side is ludicrous. It's like taking Cupid out of Valentine's Day or taking the Irish out of St. Patrick's Day.

---

161   Starnes, Todd. "Obama-appointed Judge says Transit Authority Can Ban Christmas Ads." *Todd Starnes* (blog). December 12, 2017. https://www.toddstarnes.com/faith/obama-appointed-judge-says-transit-authority-can-ban-christmas-ads/.

162   Starnes, Todd. "Obama-appointed Judge says Transit Authority Can Ban Christmas Ads." *Todd Starnes* (blog). December 12, 2017. https://www.toddstarnes.com/faith/obama-appointed-judge-says-transit-authority-can-ban-christmas-ads/.

163   Catholic News Service. "Washington Archdiocese considers next step in lawsuit over transit ad." *National Catholic Reporter*. December 12, 2017. https://www.ncronline.org/news/politics/washington-archdiocese-considers-next-step-lawsuit-over-transit-ad.

"Advertisements involving secular symbols of the holiday—reindeer, the Yule log, the Christmas trees…address the secular half of Christmas," the transit authority argued. "Overtly religious ads, like those featuring religious imagery like a scene of shepherds and the Star of Bethlehem…address the religious half of Christmas."

"Here, WMATA has simply prohibited advertisements related to the subject of the religious half of Christmas, but not the secular half," the transit authority pointed out. "That is not viewpoint discrimination."

Shockingly, Judge Jackson actually bought into that nonsensical argument and rejected the Catholic Church's emergency injunction.[164]

She said the transit authority has the right to ban advertising that either promotes or opposes "any religion, religious practice or belief," Courthouse News reports.

"Given (the transit authority's) concerns about the risks posed by issue-oriented ads, including ads promoting or opposing religion, its decision was reasonable," the Obama-appointed judge ruled. "The regulation is reasonably aligned with WMATA's duty to provide safe, reliable transportation…and it does not violate the First Amendment."[165]

Bah! Humbug!

"We are disappointed," Archdiocese spokesman Ed McFadden said in a prepared statement. "We will continue in the coming days to pursue and defend our right to share the important message of Christmas in the public square."

164　Starnes, Todd. "Obama-appointed Judge says Transit Authority Can Ban Christmas Ads." *Todd Starnes* (blog). December 12, 2017. https://www.toddstarnes.com/faith/obama-appointed-judge-says-transit-authority-can-ban-christmas-ads/.

165　Starnes, Todd. "Obama-appointed Judge says Transit Authority Can Ban Christmas Ads." *Todd Starnes* (blog). December 12, 2017. https://www.toddstarnes.com/faith/obama-appointed-judge-says-transit-authority-can-ban-christmas-ads/.

Jeremy Dys, an attorney with First Liberty Institute, made an interesting observation regarding the Christmas-hating public transportation authority.

"The remarks that President Trump delivered at the lighting of the national Christmas Tree could not be quoted on the side of a DC Metro Bus," he told the Todd Starnes Radio Show.

But they will accept advertising from the "secular" side of Christmas.

"They will take Santa but not Jesus, three French hens, but not the three wise men," Dys noted.

The birth of Christ is the reason for the season. As Linus so eloquently said, "That's what Christmas is all about."

HALLMARK TARGETED FOR CELEBRATING CHRISTMAS

The Hallmark Channel is a throwback to an age when Hollywood produced family-friendly films and love stories that did *not involve leather and whips.*[166]

The network has earned millions of loyal fans for broadcasting movies that promote the virtues of faith and family—stories that tug at your heartstrings.

"We are a place you can go and feel good," Bill Abbott, the chief executive of Crown Media, told the *Washington Post.* "We intentionally branded ourselves as the happy place."

Abbott said, "Hallmark's tagline is 'the heart of TV.'"[167]

166 Starnes, Todd. "Hallmark Christmas Movies Under Fire for Spreading 'Caucasian Cheer.'" *Todd Starnes* (blog). December 13, 2017. https://www.toddstarnes.com/faith/hallmark-channel-christmas-movies-fire-caucasian-cheer/.

167 Long, Heather. "The feel-good Hallmark Channel is booming in the age of Trump." *The Washington Post* (Washington, D.C.), August 21, 2018. https://www.washingtonpost.com/news/wonk/wp/2017/08/21/the-feel-good-hallmark-channel-is-booming-in-the-age-of-trump/?noredirect=on&utm_term=.f12b0842ed8b

And viewership has skyrocketed since President Trump promised to make America great again—making Hallmark one of the most-watched cable television networks in the nation.

For the sake of full disclosure, I'm a fan of *When Calls The Heart*, produced by my good friend, Brian Bird. It's a great place to escape from the unhinged rantings of Rachel Maddow and Don Lemon.

But it turns out not everyone is a fan of Hallmark. Slate published a scathing review of the network—complaining about its around-the-clock Christmas movies.

"They brim with white heterosexuals who exclusively, emphatically, and endlessly bellow 'Merry Christmas' to every lumberjack and labradoodle they pass. They're centered on beauty-pageant heroines and strong-jawed heroes with white-nationalist haircuts," the Slate writer declared.[168]

There were complaints about the lack of gay people and feminists and Muslims in Hallmark Channel's movies. Slate also whined about what it called the network's "42 hours of sugary, sexist, preposterously plotted, plot hole-festooned, belligerently traditional, ecstatically Caucasian cheer."

It's true that most of the stars in Hallmark's Christmas movies have a fair complexion—but to say it's a holiday white-out would be inaccurate.

Would Slate be just as indignant about the ethnic casting habits of BET or Univision or the LGBT-friendly Bravo television network?

"The Christmas-down-your-throat bombast, holly-jolly sexism, the characters' zaniness and unyielding impulsiveness—it's all very Trumpian behavior," the Slate writer said.

I say better that than the run-of-the mill pornographic debauchery that normally spews out of Hollywood.

---

168   Jason, Zachary. "The Hallmark Channel's 21-movie fusillade in the War on Christmas is a ratings sensation. I'm watching it all to find out why." *Slate*. December 12, 2017. https://slate.com/arts/2017/12/hallmarks-21-movie-christmas-countdown-reviewed.html.

Fortunately, for the folks over at Slate, there is a perfect solution to their television viewing dilemma—just change the channel.

As for me and my house, we're going to put an extra log on the fire, pour a cup of hot cocoa, and enjoy a very Hallmark Christmas.

LAWMAKERS BATTLE ATHEISTS OVER RED KETTLES

A group of Republican lawmakers in Connecticut said they would not allow themselves to be bullied by a bunch of angry, out-of-town atheists.

The Freedom From Religion Foundation, a Wisconsin-based horde of atheists, agnostics, and free-thinkers, were outraged after they learned that Republican lawmakers were raising money for the Salvation Army.[169]

"I received a letter from the group and they suggested quite strongly that I should refrain from volunteering from any organization or charity that is religious based," State Sen. George Logan told the *Todd Starnes Radio Show*.

For the past several years, Republicans in the Connecticut house and senate have volunteered their time to ring bells during the Salvation Army's red kettle drive.

But the Freedom From Religion Foundation pitched a hissy fit and fired off a nasty letter to Sen. Logan, obtained by the Connecticut Post.[170,171]

---

169   Starnes, Todd. "Lawmakers Vow to Ring Salvation Army Bells in Defiance of Atheists." *Todd Starnes* (blog). December 16, 2017. https://www.toddstarnes.com/show/lawmakers-vow-ring-salvation-army-bells-defiance-atheists/.

170   Vigdor, Neil. "Group Opposes State Lawmaker's Salvation Army Volunteering." *U.S. News & World Report*, December 11, 2017. https://www.usnews.com/news/best-states/connecticut/articles/2017-12-11/group-opposes-state-lawmakers-salvation-army-volunteering.

171   Vigdor, Neil. "Group opposes senator's bell-ringing for Salvation Army." *Connecticut Post* (Norwalk), December 8, 2017. https://www.ctpost.com/local/article/Group-opposes-senator-s-bell-ringing-for-12417364.php.

"We urge you to consider supporting only secular charities in the future," the group wrote. "This will ensure that representatives do not give the appearance of promoting an overtly Christian mission and will prevent citizens from feeling ostracized by their elected representatives because of their religious beliefs or sexual preference."

I just can't imagine people infected with such a deep-seated hatred of Christianity.

What kind of a vile human being would find pleasure in watching people go hungry for Christmas or watching a homeless child shiver outside in the cold?

"Their whole premise is I should not work with any organization that has any religious ties because it may offend someone in the community," Sen. Logan told the *Todd Starnes Radio Show.*

The money raised by the bell ringers funds a variety of Salvation Army ministries, from homeless shelters to addiction programs to providing warm coats for children.

Sen. Logan dismissed arguments from the Freedom From Religion Foundation that helping the Salvation Army was a separation of church and state issue.

"It doesn't mean lawmakers like myself are supposed to turn our back to our faith. That is not the intent," he told the *Todd Starnes Radio Show.* "It's utterly ridiculous. The purpose of ringing those bells is to raise money for the needy."

So Sen. Logan did what any red-blooded, freedom-loving American would do.

"I decided to ring even more bells for the Salvation Army," he defiantly declared. "We've raised more money than ever now—thanks to all the attention." (A development that is certain to curdle the atheists' eggnog.)

He has also received correspondence from the good, church-going people of Wisconsin, who are irate at the FFRF troublemakers.

"They want it to be known that not everyone in Wisconsin is against the Salvation Army," he said.

So here's to Sen. George Logan, an American patriot. He rang the Salvation Army's bells and he jingled the atheists' bells.

ATHEISTS COMPLAIN ABOUT MILITARY HANDING OUT CHRISTMAS BASKETS

The Military Religious Freedom Foundation has engaged in some pretty despicable behavior over the years, from demanding that the Baby Jesus be removed from military bases to complaining about Bibles on missing man tables.

But their attack on the airmen at Grand Forks Air Force Base (AFB) in North Dakota was so outrageous, even the Grinch was wondering, "Dude, what the hell?"

The MRFF was infuriated because airmen were encouraged to volunteer with the Salvation Army to hand out food baskets and gifts to families in need.

MRFF founder Mikey Weinstein said he was contacted by forty military personnel who felt humiliated and oppressed by the invitation to assist the Salvation Army.[172]

"We have no issue with the Salvation Army per se here as the total fault lies with the Air Force commanders who are effectively ordering their subordinates to assist the Salvation Army," Weinstein told me. "The Salvation Army is not at fault in this scenario."

He blamed U.S. Air Force commanders who sent the invitation to volunteer and told me they should be "court-martialed" for what he called an "unconstitutional outrage."

"They have completely ripped asunder good order, morale, discipline, and unit cohesion," Weinstein told news blog Crooks and Liars. "Our clients feel humiliated, confused and terrified."

---

172   Williams, Tess. "Air Force volunteer work with Salvation Army raises questions." *Military Religious Freedom Foundation*. December 14, 2018. http://militaryreligiousfreedom.org/press-releases/DutyHours_NotForReligiousVoluntelling.pdf.

Weinstein, in a letter to the Grand Forks AFB public affairs office, called the invitation a "disgraceful civil rights violation."

To their credit, it appears the Air Force Base has pretty much ignored Weinstein's Scrooge-like rantings. They did not respond to calls regarding the story.

First Liberty Institute jumped to defend not only the Air Force base but also the airmen who volunteered for the Salvation Army's Christmas event.

"Such participation is not only permissible but is consistent with the highest standards of the Air Force mission," First Liberty Institute attorney Michael Berry wrote in a letter to base officials and provided to *Starnes Country*.

First Liberty rightly noted that MRFF's complaint is unfounded and unsupported by the law, as well as military regulations.

"The Constitution does not prohibit active duty service members, reservists or Department of Defense employees from voluntarily participating in community service events with the Salvation Army," Berry wrote.

And military regulations clearly point out that volunteer service is permitted so long as there is no Department of Defense endorsement of any non-federal entity.

"Excluding the Salvation Army purely because of its religious identity and character sends the wrong message, and exhibits the kind of anti-religious hostility against which the Constitution guards," Berry noted.

The attorney pointed out that the Salvation Army is a well-known, faith-based, community service organization that is held in the utmost regard.

"Indeed, the Salvation Army, whose motto is 'Doing the Most Good,' meets the high standards required for inclusion in the Combined Federal Campaign," Berry said, referring to the official workplace giving program of the federal government.

"The MRFF's demands that you exclude such an organization from voluntary community service participation purely because of its religious identity not only defies logic, but is unsupported by law," Berry wrote.

How sad that the cold-hearted Grinches who lurk in the dark shadows of the Military Religious Freedom Foundation's headquarters got their tinsel in a twist because airmen wanted to make sure needy children would be able to celebrate Christmas.

MRS. CLAUS IS NOW A MISTER

Mrs. Claus is now a mister in a gay-themed Christmas storybook for children that had CNN and the rest of the mainstream media all aflutter.

Santa's Husband tells the story of a black Kris Kringle and his white husband living in holy matrimony at the North Pole.[173]

I don't mean to curdle your eggnog, but the storybook was written for children as young as four years old.

Yes, good readers. Now you can tuck in your preschoolers on Christmas Eve and regale them with tales of Frosty and the Sugar Plum Fairy and a jolly old gay elf who slides down chimneys and stuffs holiday stockings.

"As this charming book reminds us, Santa Claus can come in all shapes and colors and sizes—just like the children and families he visits all over the world each Christmas Eve," read a description of the book on Amazon.com.[174]

---

173   Starnes, Todd. "Ho! Ho! What?!? Children's Book Depicts Santa as Gay, Black Man." *Todd Starnes* (blog). December 20, 2017. https://www.toddstarnes.com/faith/ho-ho-childrens-book-depicts-santa-gay-black-man/.

174   Starnes, Todd. "Ho! Ho! What?!? Children's Book Depicts Santa as Gay, Black Man." *Todd Starnes* (blog). December 20, 2017. https://www.toddstarnes.com/faith/ho-ho-childrens-book-depicts-santa-gay-black-man/.

Author Daniel Kibblesmith, a writer for *The Late Show With Stephen Colbert*, told CNN he was inspired to write the book "by the annual tradition we have in this country of pretending that there's a giant war on Christmas, and that traditional Christmas is under attack."

Mr. Kibblesmith also took exception with the generally held belief that Santa Claus is a white guy.

"We were reading all of the news about Mall of America hiring a black Santa Claus last year and me and my now wife made a joke on Twitter that if we ever had a child they would only know about black Santa Claus and if they saw a white Santa Claus at the mall we would just explain 'Well, that's his husband,'" he told CNN.

Mr. Kibblesmith's politically correct version of Santa Claus is all the rage among mainstream media types—pretty much the same crowd that celebrates depictions of Jesus as a gay man.

The book is "as true and humble a Christmas tale as any Santa enthusiast could want," declared *Chicago Tribune* writer Rex Huppke.

"And that is the beauty of this holiday tale," he wrote. "The fact that Santa Claus is black and gay has little bearing on the story. What it's really about is accepting that every family sees Christmas in a different way."

Esquire heralded the book as "war on Christmas trolling at its finest."

"The all-ages book about a black, gay Santa takes on the Yuletide zealots with a warm smile," one headline screamed.

"In a lot of ways, it was just a reaction to people who wanted to police Christmas and keep it all to themselves, without acknowledging the reality of how diverse the country is, and how diverse our traditions have become—not just with people from different religions, but just with pop culture becoming one of the driving forces behind it," Mr. Kibblesmith told *Esquire*.

Mr. Kibblesmith does not offer any advice for parents on how to address questions that might arise from curious youngsters. Like, for example, why does Mrs. Claus have a beard?

Well, I suppose it could've been worse. Santa could've been married to a gender fluid, androgynous elf or a non-binary reindeer with a red nose.

CHAPTER 10

THE DAY A BUNCH OF MISSISSIPPI BOYS STOOD IN THE GAP

IN THE OPENING chapter of this book, I told you that I still have hope for America. In spite of the overwhelming onslaught against our faith and our freedom, I am hopeful.

There are still moms and dads who have committed to raising up a generation of young Americans who have pledged allegiance to our way of life. They are the freedom generation.

And I love telling their stories on my radio program and in my newspaper column. One of my favorite stories came by way of a reader from the Mississippi Gulf Coast. There are good people in that part of the country.

One of those stories involved Navy veteran Jerry Wayne Pino, who died on December 12, 2016 in Long Beach, Mississippi. He was seventy years old.

We don't know that much about Jerry. He was born in Baton Rouge and joined the Navy in New Orleans. He was a petty officer third class in Vietnam. That's the extent of his biography.

No family. No friends. He died alone.

Jerry's body lay unclaimed for several weeks at Riemann Family Funeral Homes.

"No one stepped forward," funeral home worker Cathy Warden told me. "He just didn't have any family."

Miss Cathy explained the situation to her colleague, Eva Boomer, and together they decided something must be done to give this veteran a proper send-off.

"Something had to be done with respect," Miss Cathy said. "We had to give him what he deserved. Nobody should go alone."

Miss Eva, who is also a veteran, wondered if some of the boys at Long Beach High School might be willing to serve as pallbearers. It was a longshot, though, seeing how most of the students were out on Christmas break.

But Miss Cathy called her teenage son, Bryce, who in turn texted some of his friends—and within a matter of minutes, six young men had volunteered to serve at a stranger's funeral.[175]

Nobody should go alone.

"It was the right thing to do," seventeen-year-old Bailey Griffin told me. "He served our country. He fought for our rights. For him to be buried with nobody there was just sad. I told myself I was going to do it and I did it."

They buried Petty Officer Third Class Jerry Pino on a Tuesday. The sun was shining and there was a cool gulf coast breeze meandering through the Biloxi National Cemetery. An honor guard stood at attention.

The boys were smartly dressed in khaki pants and buttoned-down shirts and neck ties. They solemnly took their places on either side of the flag-draped coffin and escorted a man they did not know to his final resting place.

"I went out there for the service and cried the whole way through," Miss Cathy said. "He had no one there. This veteran had nobody standing there but these boys."

But what happened at the end of the funeral was incredibly moving and poignant.

175　Magandy, Kate. "Pallbearer: 'No one should be buried without people who care present.'" *SunHerald* (Biloxi), Last modified December 30, 2016. https://www.sunherald.com/news/local/military/article123524654.html.

The flag that had draped Jerry's coffin was folded and presented to the six young men from Long Beach High School, home of the Bearcats.

"It touched my heart," Miss Cathy said.

The *Sun Herald* newspaper shared a message from the mother of one of the young pallbearers.

"Proud mom when he told me that no one should be buried without people who care present, especially a veteran," Stacie Tripp wrote on Facebook.

Evidence that moms and dads are doing something right in Long Beach, that's what Miss Cathy said.

"Our community is teaching these boys from the heart how it should be—how to care," she said.

They are still trying to figure out what to do with the flag that draped Jerry's coffin. It's being encased in glass, along with a plaque that bears his name.

There's talk about putting the flag on display at the high school or perhaps inside the locker room where four of the pallbearers play football.

It would be a fitting tribute to a man who died alone, but who was buried surrounded by his fellow countrymen.

And oh what a lesson for the rest of us, demonstrated by a group of young boys from Mississippi who committed in their hearts that nobody should go alone—especially a veteran.

CHAPTER 11

THEY TOLD ME I HAD TO TAKE JESUS OUT OF MY SPEECH

EVERY FALL, I host a weekend retreat at the Billy Graham Training Center at The Cove in Asheville, North Carolina. We call it church camp for grown-ups. And I would encourage you to join us!

It's a wonderful weekend to be inspired, encouraged by fellowship with Christians from around the nation, and surrounded by the beauty of the North Carolina mountains.

One of the highlights of our weekend is a religious liberty panel featuring some of the major players in stories that I have covered on Fox News.

One of our favorite guests was Sam Blackledge, an eighteen-year-old high school student who made national headlines after he was banned from delivering his graduation speech.[176]

Sam had worked hard on his valedictorian address. He had written a wonderful speech declaring to his teachers and classmates that he is a follower of Jesus Christ.

---

176 "High school valedictorian forced to remove all references to his faith from graduation remarks." *First Liberty*. Accessed May 29, 2019. https://firstliberty.org/cases/blackledge/#simple1.

But administrators at West Prairie High School in Illinois would not let him deliver that speech because the content was not appropriate for a high school graduation ceremony.

Just a few hours before the ceremony, he was summoned to the principal's office, where school and district administrators delivered their edict.

"They said they didn't want to make it a religious ceremony," Sam said. "They told me that if I took out Christ I could say everything else."

The young man with the 4.0 grade point average pleaded his case, explaining that he only wanted to convey to the audience about how his personal relationship with Christ had impacted his life.

"The principal told me it wasn't appropriate for the setting," he said.

School leaders then said they feared those in the audience might think Sam was speaking on behalf of the school district.

"I offered to begin my speech with a disclaimer but they turned that down too—twice," he said.

Sam told me he was devastated.

"I never felt that feeling before," he said. "It was terrible. I felt like I wanted to cry. I had basically—for months—I knew I wanted to talk about Christ in my graduation speech. For that to be taken away…"

School leaders gave Sam the opportunity to remove all the references to Christ, but he declined to do so.

"The most important thing in my life is Christ," he said. "Christ is the only reason I was a valedictorian. He's the reason I got that 4.0. If it wasn't for him I wouldn't be up there. I was giving Him the credit for that."

They offered to let Sam say a few brief remarks—provided he would not mention the name of Jesus. He agreed with their terms.

"I believe as a Christian we should respect the authority above us," Sam said. "I told them I would not disrespect them. I told them

I would respect their wishes. And I told them the reason why is because I'm a Christian."

The following day our friends at First Liberty Institute learned about Sam's plight and provided him with legal counsel pro bono.

"School officials should remember that students retain their constitutional rights to freedom of expression from the schoolhouse gates, all the way through the graduation ceremony," First Liberty Institute attorney Jeremy Dys told me. "These school officials ruined the only high school graduation Sam will ever know. How many more graduations have to be ruined before school officials will learn that the First Amendment protects student remarks at graduation?"

We now know the answer—none.

Not too long after Sam had graduated, the school district settled out of court with First Liberty and they have assured the attorneys that future valedictorians will not be censored.

But there was still the issue of Sam's terrific speech that no one had heard. So I decided to invite Sam to The Cove so he could deliver his graduation remarks before a crowd of several hundred Christians. I also invited Sam's parents to be our guests and they were more than happy to attend our gathering.

Here's the full text of Sam's address at The Cove:

Sherlock Holmes and his partner Watson were out camping and after a long night they quickly fell asleep. Awakening in the middle of the night, Holmes asked Watson what do you see? He responded by saying, "I see millions of stars." And Holmes proceeded, "Well what does that tell you?" Watson then pondered the question and said, "Astronomically speaking, it tells me there are millions of galaxies and potentially billions of planets. Astrologically it tells me that Saturn is in Leo. Timewise, it appears to be approximately a quarter past three. Meteorologically, it seems we'll have a beautiful day tomorrow, and theologically I see that this is a vast universe and we are just a minute part of the great whole. Why Holmes what do you see?" Holmes was silent for a moment and then speaks, "Watson you idiot, somebody has stolen our tent."

We as humans are really good at focusing on useless details all while missing the essentials. Class of 2018, we are all branching out into our own paths, each in different directions, yet todos estamos buscando para las mismas cuatro cosas. I am convinced that each of us are in pursuit of the same four things. A life devoid of evil, full of justice, full of love, and full of forgiveness. Evil, justice, love and forgiveness.

First, a life devoid of evil. Parents, I know that you greatly desire that your graduate's life would be devoid of evil and full of good. No one wants life to consist of unfair circumstances. What do we see in the news almost every day, we see mistreatment, murder, EVIL. And why do these things receive so much coverage, I believe that it is because people are obsessed with this longing for goodness.

Second, justice. If we stay on the topic of news for a second, we realize another reoccurring theme, and that is equality or justice. Race, gender, equal pay, sexual orientation, the list goes on and on. Every person wants to be treated fairly. And graduates, I know that when we leave from here we want a fair shot at life.

And thirdly, love. I imagine that the next time I see some of you, you will be married, and maybe even have kids. And I know that the driving force of that is love. We all look for love, from our parents, our friendships, and maybe in the future, our spouses.

Finally, I hope that you guys are successful in all that you do, but I'd be mistaken not to notice that we are bound to make mistakes. I find it significant that even the word "Human" has become the definition of messing up and being imperfect. With that in mind, we all need forgiveness.

So, we all want lives devoid of evil; we are looking for justice; we'll miss our families and make new ones because of love, and some of us are going to blow it big time and hope the rest of our peers are willing to forgive us. Evil, justice, love, and forgiveness.

I want you to think for a moment, is there any event in history where these four converged in one place? Where did Evil, Justice, Love and Forgiveness converge at a moment in history? Can I take you to a hill called Calvary and show you the person of Jesus Christ?

The Cross of Christ shows us our own evil hearts, that we would put an innocent man up to die. Christ came to show us God's justice in dealing with the unfairness of the world. The Cross demonstrates to us the very love of God who died in our place and how we find at the end of the day that without his forgiveness we would never make it.

Graduates, I hope your life is devoid of evil, full of justice, full of love, and full of forgiveness. I think our parents however, could attest that trying to manage this on our own is more than difficult. The most important thing in your life is to find that intimacy with God. He will guide you, he will hold you, and he will take you through safely in your journey. As you search for goodness, justice, love, and forgiveness, know that only God is big enough to provide that for you.

Thank you, Class of 2018, it's been real, it's been good, it's been real good·

Well, let me tell you there was not a dry eye in the room as several hundred people gave Sam a standing ovation. This brave young man remained faithful to God. He took a stand and his faithfulness was blessed many times over.

CHAPTER 12

READING, WRITING, AND RADICALS

By this point in the book, some of you have already evacuated to your apocalypse bunker. Some of you might be wondering, how did we get to the point where wanting to make America great again is the unpardonable sin? Who is responsible for brainwashing half the country into believing Trump supporters burn crosses in their backyards?

The answer to that question might very well trigger microaggressions among our conservative readers. In many communities across the fruited plain, your local schoolhouse has been turned into a far-left indoctrination center.

The culture jihadists laid siege to the nation's public education system many years ago and they won the war without having to fire a single shot. Many parents were simply disengaged and many taxpayers simply did not care how their hard-earned money was being used by local school districts.

There was a time when teachers ruled their classrooms with a yellow yard stick. The children would pledge allegiance to the flag and bow their heads for prayer. They would learn how to read and write and do long form division. They would play rough-and-tumble sports on the playground and eat pizza in the cafe-gym-natorium at lunch. Little did we realize that the 1970s were the good old days.

In the 21st century, teachers need government-issue Kevlar vests and a concealed carry permit. And even that's not enough to protect the teachers from a mob of unruly students. The kids can't read or write because they're too busy trying to determine where they are on the gender spectrum. Contact sports are banned because heaven forbid a child gets a boo-boo. And now everybody gets a trophy because heaven forbid a child's ego gets bruised.

They're serving meatless mystery meat and shots of wheatgrass in the cafe-gym-natorium, which could explain why the children are in a perpetually bad mood.

And don't even think about asking the kids to pledge allegiance. Nowadays the godless urchins take a knee to protest the flag and the only people praying are the teachers, asking the Good Lord to find them another job.

Radical progressives have assumed control of public education from preschool all the way through graduate school. That's how the Left has been able to facilitate massive cultural change in such a short amount of time.

Many public schools are teaching our children to hate America— to hate our way of life. That's why a shocking percentage of American young people believe there should be limits on free speech. That's why a disturbing number of millennials favor socialism over capitalism. That's why we have seen a massive surge in the number of people who cannot determine if they are male or female.

The crackdown on freedom of speech is frightening. A number of schools have even gotten into the business of banning books. Classics like *Huckleberry Finn*, *Little House on the Prairie*, and *To Kill A Mockingbird* have been banished from libraries over racial sensitivities.

New Jersey lawmakers introduced a resolution calling on school districts to specifically remove *Huckleberry Finn* from the school curriculum, citing its depiction of the antebellum South and the use of an offensive racial epithet. It did not seem to matter that the book included anti-racist and anti-slavery themes.

So, if the culture jihadists can ban *Little House on the Prairie*, is it really that much of a stretch to imagine a day in American life when the academics would banish the Holy Bible?

Beginning in 2020, many Advanced Placement students will be using an American History textbook that depicts President Trump as mentally ill and his supporters as racists.[177]

The textbook, published by Pearson Education, is titled, *By the People: A History of the United States.* The final section of the book, "The Angry Election of 2016," is especially critical of the president.[178]

"Most thought that Trump was too extreme a candidate to win the nomination, but his extremism, his anti-establishment rhetoric, and, some said, his not very hidden racism connected with a significant number of primary voters," the author wrote.

The author goes on to describe the president's supporters as "mostly older, often rural or suburban, and overwhelmingly white."

"Clinton's supporters feared that the election had been determined by people who were afraid of a rapidly developing ethnic diversity of the country, discomfort with their candidate's gender and nostalgia for an earlier time in the nation's history," the textbook reads. "They also worried about the mental stability of the president-elect and the anger that he and his supporters brought to the nation."

In other words, Advanced Placement students are going to be taught that President Trump is mentally insane and his supporters are a bunch of irredeemable deplorables. Such descriptions would be laughable, but this garbage is being shoved into the minds of impressionable American teenagers.

Ronald Reagan once said that "our most precious resources, our greatest hope for the future, are the minds and hearts of our people, especially our children."

---

177 Ellis, Christian. "Did High School Textbook Cross Line, Referring to Trump 'Mental Stability' and 'Not Very Hidden Racism'?" *CBN News.* April 24, 2019. https://www1.cbn.com/cbnnews/us/2019/april/high-school-history-textbook-labels-trump-as-insane-and-racist.

178 Starnes, Todd. "New High School Textbook Describes Trump as Mentally Ill, Supporters as Racist." *Todd Starnes* (blog). April 23, 2019. https://www.toddstarnes.com/campus/new-high-school-textbook-describes-trump-as-mentally-ill-supporters-as-racist/.

And yet we have entrusted our most precious resources to a bunch of degenerate propagandists who hate everything about the land of the free and the home of the brave. In his 1989 farewell address, Reagan warned the nation about what was to come.

"An informed patriotism is what we want," he said. "And are we doing a good enough job teaching our children what America is and what she represents in the long history of the world?"

Consider the answer to Reagan's question as you read these dispatches from America's classrooms.

KIDS GOT MORE STUPID UNDER OBAMA ADMINISTRATION

American school kids became more stupid under the Obama administration, according to rankings released by the Organization for Economic Cooperation and Development (OECD).[179]

In 2017, the OECD released the results of a worldwide exam administered every three years to fifteen-year-olds in seventy-two countries. The exam monitors reading, math, and science knowledge.

Based on their findings, the United States saw an eleven-point drop in math scores and nearly flat levels for reading and science.[180]

The Land of the Free, Home of the Brave, fell below the OECD average—and failed to crack the top ten in all three categories.

In other words, thanks to the Obama administration's education policies, kids in the Slovak Republic are more proficient in multiplication.

---

179   Starnes, Todd. "America's kids got more stupid in reading, math and science while Team Obama was in charge." Fox News. February 9, 2017. https://www.foxnews.com/opinion/americas-kids-got-more-stupid-in-reading-math-and-science-while-team-obama-was-in-charge.

180   Desilver, Drew. "U.S. students' academic achievement still lags that of their peers in many other countries." *Pew Research Center*. February 15, 2017. https://www.pewresearch.org/fact-tank/2017/02/15/u-s-students-internationally-math-science/.

In fairness, American teenagers may not know long form division, but by golly they know their non-binary gender pronouns. Yes sir, they do!

But you can't blame the kids for being dumb as rocks.

Instead of aspiring to greatness, public schools across the fruited plain are programming kids to be mediocre.

It doesn't matter if Little Johnny thinks five plus four is twelve.

Modern-day classrooms are safe spaces where everybody's a winner—everybody gets a gold star.

There's just one problem with that philosophy. When Little Johnny becomes Big Johnny, he's going to be living off the taxpayer dime. And good luck making change down at the Piggly Wiggly.

SCHOOL DISTRICT TALENT SHOW FEATURES EROTIC DRAG QUEEN SHOW

What in the name of RuPaul is wrong with the New York City Board of Education?

Parents are furious after children as young as five years old were exposed to an erotic drag show performance at what was supposed to be a school district talent show.

"My first reaction was what the hell is going on," parent Raquel Morales told me.[181]

The *New York Daily News* described the lewd performance as "complete with gyrations, tongue gymnastics and a flashed G-string."[182]

---

181   Starnes, Todd. "Gyrating drag queen's erotic performance shocks audience at grade school talent show." Fox News. June 2, 2017. https://www.foxnews.com/opinion/gyrating-drag-queens-erotic-performance-shocks-audience-at-grade-school-talent-show.

182   Chapman, Ben. "Parents 'horrified' after man performs surprise drag show at Manhattan school talent event." *Daily News* (New York), June 1, 2017. https://www.nydailynews.com/new-york/education/parents-horrified-man-performs-drag-show-nyc-school-article-1.3213718.

The performance shocked and enraged parents, who could not believe the school district would allow a grown man to spread his legs and display his crotch to wide-eyed children.

"I left the show the minute he started sticking his tongue out," one parent told the *Daily News*. "I had my children with me and I wasn't going to allow them to see that."

Ms. Morales filmed the seven-minute routine on her cell phone and provided me with a copy. It's jaw-dropping, folks. And when the drag queen dropped to the floor and began writhing in a sexually suggestive manner, the auditorium erupted.

"Once he got to that part it was chaos," Ms. Morales said. "People were yelling and leaving. A lot of parents were saying had they known this was going to happen they would have taken their kids out after they had performed."

The talent show was emceed by District 4 Superintendent Alexandra Estrella. And the individual who performed in drag was identified as the president of the Public School 96 Parent Association.

"The school district told me the performance was about LGBT awareness," she said.

I reached out to the district as well as the board of education, multiple times. So far, they have not returned my telephone calls.

There are several issues that need to be addressed. First, who signed off on a school program that featured a kindergarten choir and a gyrating, adult drag queen? Second, why is that person still employed by the school district? Third, why hasn't the school district publicly apologized to traumatized parents and their children?

Ms. Morales made it a point to explain that her objection had nothing to do with the LGBT movement.

"I'm 100 percent against discrimination," she said.

This is about age-appropriate behavior—and what happened in that auditorium was not age appropriate.

"The superintendent was the emcee—and she has a responsibility to protect all children," she said. "That wasn't a child performing. It was an adult."

Moving forward, I recommend the school district adopt a policy to govern future grade school talent shows:

If a drag queen wants to spread his legs and show off his G-string he should do that at a nightclub—not a public school talent show.

TEACHER ORDERED TO REMOVE BOOKS WRITTEN BY CONSERVATIVES FROM SUMMER READING LIST

The summer reading list for Gene Ponder's AP Government and Economics class at Spanish Fort High School in Alabama is causing some trouble.[183]

Mr. Ponder filled his list with books authored by conservatives—and libertarians. I know, right? Imagine that—a *conservative* public school teacher! Sweet mercy, America! Miracles do happen.

Mr. Ponder's summer reading list was a bonus assignment and included writers like Ann Coulter and Mark Levin and Ronald Reagan and Thomas Sowell.

They could choose from books like *God & Government, Black Rednecks and White Liberals, Liberty and Tyranny: A Conservative Manifesto, FairTax: The Truth*, and *48 Liberal Lies About American History (That You Probably Learned in School)*.

In other words, Mr. Ponder was providing the children with an alternative to the liberal propaganda that has saturated public school textbooks.

Well, you can probably guess what happened soon after the reading list was posted. The flat-tax hit the fan, as they say.

One local resident actually called the conservative authors "terrifying."

Gulf Coast News Today reported that critics complained about what they called the "perceived lack of diversity of ideas, as well

---

183   Starnes, Todd. "Alabama school bans Reagan, Coulter, Levin summer reading list." Fox News. June 23, 2017. https://www.foxnews.com/opinion/alabama-school-bans-reagan-coulter-levin-summer-reading-list.

as whether it met the reading levels required for a 12th grade AP class."

If those kids were reading Mark Levin books, they were more than likely reading well above the Advanced Placement requirements.

"The slant on this list is inappropriate and unbalanced," one person wrote on Facebook, demanding a "more rounded reading list for these developing minds."

The Baldwin County Board of Education got wind of the controversy and faster than you can say left-wing censorship, Mr. Ponder was ordered to pull his reading list and cancel the assignment.

"Mr. Ponder's reading list that is going around on social media has not been endorsed by the school system," Superintendent Eddie Tyler said in a statement. "The list has been removed by the teacher. Baldwin County Public Schools has a process to vet and approve reading lists so that a variety of sources are used. I expect all employees to follow our processes, procedures and policies."[184]

Yeah, right.

Why do I get the feeling the controversy surrounding Mr. Ponder's reading list was more about politics instead of procedures?

Mr. Ponder should have the kids read some of my politically incorrect books. That ought to give the youngsters a jaw-dropping dose of reality.

STUDENTS ORDERED TO STOP CHANTING "USA, USA"

There are a lot of patriotic students at Vista Del Lago High School in Folsom, California. So, you can imagine their shock when

---

184   Owens, Eric. "Check Out This High School Teacher's Hilariously One-Sided AP Government Summer Reading List." *The Daily Caller*. June 22, 2017. https://dailycaller.com/2017/06/22/check-out-this-high-school-teachers-hilariously-one-sided-ap-government-summer-reading-list/.

they were warned that chanting "U-S-A" at sporting events and pep rallies could appear to be inappropriate and intolerant.[185]

Television station CBS 13 in Sacramento reported that school leaders feared the chants could come across as intolerant and offensive to some. They wrote, "at some schools across the country, the chants appeared to be used in derogatory ways toward opponents of different ethnicities."[186]

"We can communicate an unintended message," the school's principal wrote in a letter to parents.

What would the unintended message be—that young people still love the red, white, and blue and that they want to make America great again?

Folsom Cordova Unified Communications Director Daniel Thigpen told the television station they have not banned the chant. They just want young people to be more considerate when they chant.

"To practice empathy, to practice kindness and to practice patriotism—you can do both," Thigpen said.

The school's principal suggested there are appropriate times to chant, like following the national anthem or the Pledge of Allegiance.

"I think it's really sad that chanting USA in our country has even become a negative thing," one parent told the television station.

The California Interscholastic Federation notified school districts across the state about concerns that the "USA" chant might be used in a derogatory manner.

But that does not appear to be the case at Vista Del Lago High School.

---

185   Starnes, Todd. "School Fears 'USA' Chant Could be Intolerant and Offensive." *Todd Starnes* (blog). September 14, 2017. https://www.toddstarnes.com/uncategorized/school-fears-usa-chant-could-be-intolerant-and-offensive/.

186   Greenwood, Angela. "Folsom School Warns 'USA' Chant Could Send 'Unintended Message.'" *CBS Sacramento*. September 14, 2017. https://sacramento.cbslocal.com/2017/09/14/high-school-usa-chant/.

"To say USA, you know, we're all the same," student Ryan Bernal told the television station. "We're all American. It doesn't matter what your skin tone is or where you're from."

That young man has more common sense that most of the grown-ups in charge of the school district.

"We're all one," Ryan said. "We all stand as one together."

It should be stressed that there's never been a complaint about the "USA" chants—not one.

The only people expressing angst about public demonstrations of American pride are school staffers.

Perhaps the school district should be more concerned about the unintended message that sends.

HEY KIDS, WHAT DO UNICORNS AND GOD HAVE IN COMMON?

A Georgia middle school is apologizing after middle school students were presented a poem that described God as a "mythical creature like a unicorn."

The 2017 lesson was part of a classroom discussion about Greek mythology at Cedartown Middle School.[187]

"God is like a mythical creature, a unicorn with silver blood," the controversial poem declared.

"The idea of god makes young children laugh and feel safe at night," the poet wrote. "But when you grow older and see the evil in the world and the face of death like a shadow behind the eyes of every living thing, then where is God?"

---

187   Starnes, Todd. "School Lesson Describes God as 'Mythical Creature—Like a Unicorn.'" *Todd Starnes* (blog). September 5, 2017. https://www.toddstarnes.com/uncategorized/school-lesson-describes-god-as-mythical-creature-like-a-unicorn/.

And if that wasn't enough to convince the youngsters to renounce their faith and become godless atheists, the poet concluded with a final splash of anti-deity flourish.

"Then God is revealed in all his foolishness, a naked lie, a childish dream, a mythical creature like the unicorn," the poet wrote.

Let's just say the poem went over like a unicorn blowing pixie dust out its backside.

Outraged parents contacted Fox 5 in Atlanta and faster than you could say "Puff the Magic Dragon," the school district apologized.[188]

"We recognize that it was an unfortunate mistake to have included the work as part of our classes here at our school," the Polk County, Georgia school district stated.

"We had meaningful conversations and believe that the inclusion of this article to have been made not by malicious intent nor the desire to denounce the faith or beliefs of any of our students, staff or community members," the district went on to state.

Principal Shannon Hulsey said she completely understands why parents were upset.

"They felt that it was very disrespectful to God and it (the poem) didn't really have anything to do with unicorns," she told Fox 5.

She said the teachers involved in the lesson pulled the poem out of a folder full of material on ancient mythology.

"This was a mistake. In no way whatsoever would we want to defame God or go anywhere in that direction at the school," she told the television station.

The lesson here is that parents saw something and said something. If we are truly going to restore American values, we must be willing to take a stand in our hometowns. Together, we can make a difference. Just ask the good people of Cedartown, Georgia.

---

188   "Parents upset after 'Unicorn' poem used in school." Fox 5. Last modified September 5, 2017. http://www.fox5atlanta.com/news/ parents-upset-after-unicorn-poem-questioning-god-used-in-school.

YOUNGSTERS TOLD TO STOP USING 5-LETTER WORDS— LIKE "JESUS"

It's not all that unusual for moms and dads to receive letters from their child's teacher, especially regarding inappropriate classroom behavior. But a letter written by a first-grade teacher and sent to parents in McCordsville, Indiana caused quite a stir.

The teacher urged parents to encourage their children to stop using religious words in the classroom.

"I have had a group of about five students using the words God, Jesus and Devil in conversation," the teacher wrote.[189]

Back when I was in grade school, my classmates would typically invoke the Good Lord's name—usually just before an exam.

She explained that she had "a talk" with the children regarding inappropriate classroom language, but the lesson did not seem to work.

"With McCordsville Elementary being a public school, we have many different religions and beliefs, and I do not want to upset a child/parent because of these words being used," she wrote to parents.

In other words, Jesus is not welcome in McCordsville Elementary School.

"If you go to church or discuss these things at home, please have a talk with your child about there being an appropriate time and place of talking about it," the teacher wrote.

In my last book, *The Deplorables' Guide to Making America Great Again*, I delivered a call to arms. I urged you to take a stand for your Constitutional rights; to take a stand in your neighborhoods.

And that's exactly what happened in McCordsville. One of the parents sent a copy of the teacher's Jesus-ban to a local Fox News

---

189   Starnes, Todd. "Teacher: Dear Parents, You're your Kids to Stop Talking About God." *Todd Starnes* (blog). August 30, 2017. https://www. toddstarnes.com/uncategorized/teacher-dear-parents-tell-your-kids-to-stop-taking-about-god/.

station—and faster than you could say, "God bless America," the school district backtracked.[190]

"Trying to limit a student's view on religion is a violation of a student's First Amendment rights," the district wrote in a statement.

Patriots took a stand and, as a result, a terrible wrong was made right.

Sadly, in many school districts, parents have capitulated and allowed their school districts to become public indoctrination centers for far-left activists; schools where words like "Jesus" are banned, but words like "gender fluid" are celebrated.

TEEN BOY TOLD TO TOLERATE GIRL UNDRESSING IN LOCKER ROOM

A teenage boy was told by school leaders that he had to "tolerate" undressing in front of a female student and to make it as "natural" as possible, according to a blockbuster lawsuit filed in a Pennsylvania federal district court.[191]

The lawsuit, filed by Alliance Defending Freedom and Independence Law Center (ILC), alleged that the Boyertown Area School District shamed the teenage boy and violated his personal privacy. They also alleged sexual harassment.

"No school should rob any student of this legally protected personal privacy," ILC attorney Randall Wenger said. "We trust that our children won't be forced into emotionally vulnerable situations

---

190 Wierks, Kylee. "McCordsville teacher asks first graders to stop talking about God at school." Last modified August 25, 2017. https://fox59. com/2017/08/25/mccordsville-teacher-asks-first-graders-to-stop-talking-about-god-at-school/.

191 Starnes, Todd. "School Orders Boy to 'Tolerate' Undressing with Girl and Make it 'Natural.'" *Todd Starnes* (blog). March 21, 2017. https://www.toddstarnes.com/uncategorized/school-orders-boy-to-tolerate-undressing-with-girl-and-make-it-natural/.

like this when they are in the care of our schools because it's a school's duty to protect and respect the bodily privacy and dignity of all students."[192]

In the case of "Joel Doe," they clearly ignored that duty.

In fall 2016, the teen boy was standing in his underwear inside a locker room at Boyertown Area High School preparing to change for a physical education class.

"He suddenly realized there was a member of the opposite sex changing with him in the locker room, who was at the time, wearing nothing but shorts and a bra," the lawsuit states.

The boy, along with several of his classmates, reported the incident to the assistant principal, named as a defendant.

"Dr. Foley indicated that the legality was up in the air but that students who mentally identify themselves with the opposite sex could choose the locker room and bathroom to use, and physical sex did not matter," the lawsuit states.

The teenage boy asked the assistant principal if there was anything that could be done to protect him from the situation.

"Dr. Foley told Joel Doe to 'tolerate' it and to make it as 'natural' as he possibly can," the lawsuit states.

As the boy got up to leave the office, the assistant principal allegedly told the youngster to again "be as natural as possible."

Even more disturbing, parents were not told of the school district's decision to let students of one sex use the locker rooms and bathrooms of students of the opposite sex.

"The District's directive to Joel Doe was that he must change with students of the opposite sex, and make it as natural as possible, and that anything less would be intolerant and bullying against students who profess a gender identity with the opposite sex," the lawsuit states.

---

192   "United States District Court. Joel Doe vs. Boyertown Area School District Complaint." 2017. http://www.adfmedia.org/files/DoeBoyertown Complaint.pdf.

The young man's parents made an appointment with school leaders and were told that the district is "all-inclusive."

The lawsuit alleges that Foley told the boy's parents their son could use the nurse's office to change, if he had a problem changing in front of girls.

Principal Brett Cooper, also a defendant, backed up the assistant principal's solution.

Supt. Richard Faidley suggested if "Joel Doe was uncomfortable changing with those of the opposite sex, or with using the nurse's office, then he could just withdraw from school and be home schooled."

The school district has yet to respond to the lawsuit.

Should the school district be found guilty, they should immediately fire Faidley, Cooper, and Foley. Their alleged behavior is beyond repulsive.

But the lawsuit clearly illustrates the radical sex and gender narrative being forced on every public school locker room in the nation.

And as evidenced by the school district's behavior, resistance to this perverse indoctrination seems to be futile.

UC BERKELEY SHUTS DOWN FREE SPEECH

The birthplace of the free speech movement has become its graveyard.[193]

Hundreds of liberals rioted at the University of California Berkeley, burning stores, throwing Molotov cocktails, and clashing with police.

The rampaging mob forced the university to shut down an event featuring gay conservative firebrand Milo Yiannopoulos.

---

193   Starnes, Todd. "Who knew there were so many
       homophobic, racist xenophobes at Berkeley." Fox News.
       February 2, 2017. https://www.foxnews.com/opinion/
       who-knew-there-were-so-many-homophobic-racist-xenophobes-at-berkeley.

"I'm outraged that Milo has been given a platform at UC Berkeley, and there should be no place for him here," visiting assistant art professor Samara Halperin told the *Daily Californian*. "He should be scared that people aren't going to stand for this."

Ironically, Milo had planned to deliver remarks defending free speech.

"One thing we do know for sure: the Left is absolutely terrified of free speech and will do literally anything to shut it down," he wrote on Facebook.

The British conservative journalist called the violence a "horrible spectacle and very humiliating for American higher education."

The crowd hurled fireworks at police officers and smashed windows at the Martin Luther King, Jr. Student Union. They also damaged buildings in downtown Berkeley, including a Starbucks and a number of banks.

The bloodthirsty mob targeted several supporters of President Trump. One young lady wearing a "Make America Great Again" hat was attacked during a television interview. An unknown man sprayed some sort of liquid in her face.

The *Daily Californian* reports another Trump supporter was grabbed by a crowd of agitators and thrown to the ground. He escaped, but they grabbed his red hat and set it on fire. And police had to rescue another man who was bloodied and beaten.

The university released a statement blaming the violence on outsiders who, they allege, came to the campus to cause mayhem.[194]

They also affirmed Milo's right to speak on the liberal campus.

"Chancellor Nicholas Dirks made it clear that while Yiannopoulos' views, tactics and rhetoric are profoundly contrary to

---

194   "Milo Yiannopoulos event canceled as violent protests
        erupt at UC Berkeley." *The Daily Californian*. Last modified
        February 2, 2017. http://www.dailycal.org/2017/02/01/
        milo-yiannopoulos-event-canceled-violent-protests-erupt-uc-berkeley/.

those of the campus, UC Berkeley is bound by the Constitution, the law and the university's values and Principles of Community, which include the enabling of free expression across the full spectrum of opinion and perspective."

Those are very nice words, but they are meaningless unless they are enforced. According to the university, not a single person was arrested. Not a single arrest, folks.

Did someone order the police officers to stand down? If so, who gave that order—and why?

Universities must guarantee free speech for all students, conservative and liberal. It's time for the federal government to eradicate this un-American infestation in higher education. No free speech, no federal dollars.

"No one's safety is at risk from different opinions," Milo told *Tucker Carlson Tonight*. "No one's physical safety is endangered by political ideas from a speaker on campus, but universities have sort of allowed this stuff to happen, and even in some cases encouraged it."

Ironically, it was a bunch of leftists who silenced a gay immigrant and vandalized a building named after a Civil Rights legend. Who knew there were so many homophobic, racist xenophobes at Berkeley?

LIBRARY EXPOSES KIDS TO SEX OFFENDER AT DRAG QUEEN STORYTIME

The Houston Public Library says they mistakenly allowed a convicted sex offender to read books to small children during a Drag Queen Storytime event and many parents are wondering what in the name of the Dewey Decimal System is wrong with the librarians.[195]

195　Talarico, Lauren. "Houston Public Library admits registered child sex offender read to kids in Drag Queen Storytime." *KHOU 11*. Last modified March 19, 2019. https://www.khou.com/article/news/local/houston-public-library-admits-registered-child-sex-offender-read-to-kids-in-drag-queen-storytime/285-becf3a0d-56c5-4f3c-96df-add07bbd002a.

Library officials confirm that Alberto Garza, a thirty-two-year-old drag queen who goes by the name Tatiana Mala Nina, was part of a recent children's program.

According to Department of Public Safety records, Garza was convicted of aggravated sexual assault of an eight-year-old child in 2009, the Houston Chronicle reported. He received five years of probation and community supervision.[196]

A registered child sex offender?

It turns out the public library failed to conduct a background check on Garza.

"In our review of our process and of this participant, we discovered that we failed to complete a background check as required by our own guidelines," the library said in a statement. "We deeply regret this oversight and the concern this may cause our customers. We realize this is a serious matter."

Parents may have never known their children were placed in danger had it not been for the work of Houston MassResistance, a pro-family activist group. They did what the library failed to do; they conducted a background check.

"If they had done their job and due diligence, if they had said wait…maybe it's not a good idea to have a sex offender who at 200 pounds and 5-foot-11 assaulted an 8-year-old boy," MassResistance spokesperson Tracy Shannon told reporters.

The library apologized to moms and dads and said the drag queen would no longer be involved in library activities.

"We may not all agree that having adult entertainers is the right way to entertain young children or promote literacy and adversity and acceptance and inclusion," Shannon told reporters. "But we can all agree that it's inappropriate to have a sex offender."

---

196   Scherer, Jasper. "Houston Library apologizes after registered sex offender participated in Drag Queen Storytime." *The Houston Chronicle* (Houston), Last modified March 17, 2019. https://www.chron.com/news/houston-texas/houston/article/Library-apologizes-for-letting-registered-sex-13693986.php.

Drag Queen Storytime is a national movement that has swept across libraries from coast to coast, introducing children as young as two years old to drag queens. Organizers say its mission is to promote love and acceptance. But critics say it has nothing to do with tolerance and everything to do with indoctrination.

In 2018, a drag queen in Lafayette, Louisiana all but admitted to city council members that storytime was about pushing an agenda.

"This is going to be the grooming of the next generation," Santana Pilar Andrews told council members. "We are trying to groom the next generation."[197]

Last year, Houston parents filed a lawsuit to stop Drag Queen Storytime, but a federal judge dismissed the case in January.

Clearly, there has been a breach of trust between the radical leftists who run the public library and the good church-going families of Houston.

The only way to repair the damage is for the city to fire the library's leadership, along with anyone else connected to this sordid affair. It is simply unacceptable to expose children to a convicted sex offender.

And in the future, librarians would be wise to do their homework before allowing anyone wearing a feather boa to regale children with recitations from "Rub-a-Dub-Dub Three Men in a Tub."[198]

---

197 Scherer, Jasper. "Houston Library apologizes after registered sex offender participated in Drag Queen Storytime." *The Houston Chronicle* (Houston), Last modified March 17, 2019. https://www.chron.com/news/houston-texas/houston/article/Library-apologizes-for-letting-registered-sex-13693986.php.

198 Starnes, Todd. "Todd Starnes: Sex offender reads to kids at library's drag queen story time—How the heck did that happen?" Fox News. March 18, 2019. https://www.foxnews.com/opinion/todd-starnes-sex-offender-reads-to-kids-at-librarys-drag-queen-story-time-how-the-heck-did-that-happen.

CHAPTER 13

THE FOOTBALL PLAYER WHO REFUSED TO TAKE A KNEE

CONNOR BREWER WAS fiercely loyal to his college football team. But he is also fiercely loyal to the United States of America.[199]

So when the Millikin University football team decided to protest the national anthem in 2016 by remaining inside the locker room—instead of on the sidelines—Connor was faced with a decision: would he join his teammates in their university-approved safe space or would he stand on the sidelines and honor America?

Connor chose to stand—alone.

A few weeks before, several Millikin football players took a page from disgraced NFL quarterback Colin Kaepernick by taking a knee during the national anthem.

The community outrage was apparently so severe the football team decided to "forge a new path."

"Rather than have our message be misunderstood or misconstrued, we are united in our decision to stay in the locker room until kickoff during which time we will engage in a moment of reflection to

---

199   Chasmar, Jessica. "Football player stands alone for anthem after teammates stay in locker room." *The Washington Times* (Washington, D.C.), October 18, 2016. https://www.washingtontimes.com/news/2016/oct/18/connor-brewer-millikin-u-football-player-stands-al/.

personally recognize the sacrifice of so many and renew our commitment to living up to those most important words: 'with liberty and justice for all,'" the team wrote in a statement that was published in the *Herald-Review*.

So instead of standing along the sidelines and showing a little respect for the United States, the football team chose to hunker down in their safe space for some "locker room" talk.

"Please let there be no doubt that we have the utmost respect for the sacrifice made by those who served or do serve in our armed forces, including many of our family and friends," the football team wrote. "Therefore, it is our desire to do nothing that could be viewed as disrespectful of their sacrifice."

University president Patrick White offered up a pile of academic gobbledygook in defense of the football squad.

"We all need to listen to voices and opinions different from our own and listen with our hearts and minds awake to difference," White wrote. "When the issues involve race and justice and differing contentions of what patriotism mean, all of us can stand more education."

Well, I'm fairly certain patriotism does not mean burning Old Glory or spitting on soldiers or cowering inside a locker room while "The Star-Spangled Banner" is being performed.

Historians may consider the events of October 16, 2016 as inconsequential, but that would be a shame.

Because it was the day an American citizen considered the cost and chose to defy the anti-American sentiment sweeping across the fruited plain. It was the day Connor Brewer, of Springfield, Illinois, stood resolute.

My column about Connor's act of patriotism struck a chord with my readers and radio show audience. I was inundated by hundreds of emails and messages all affirming their support for the brave football player.

I was especially touched by a poignant letter I received from a gold star mother, Debi Daniels.

"Reading your article about Connor broke my heart," she wrote. "It was the loneliness—that he had to be there by himself."

She asked me to reach out to Connor and I did.

"Please thank him for me," she said. "He has a lot of support."

And based on your well wishes and words of encouragement, it's clear to me that this young man who stood alone on the gridiron stands alone no more.

Mrs. Daniels said the recent controversy at Millikin University hit close to home for her family.

That's because her son Nickolas was a member of the varsity football program at Millikin back in 2004. He played offense and defense—he was one heck of an athlete.

In 2010, Nickolas enlisted in the Marines. The following year, he was killed in Afghanistan.

Lance Corporal Daniels was a decorated Marine, awarded the Purple Heart, Combat Action Ribbons, a National Defense Service Medal, a Global War on Terrorism Service Medal, and a Sea Service Deployment Ribbon.

So, you can understand why Mrs. Daniels has taken an interest in recent developments at the school.

"While I have stayed silent about this 'movement' this struck a tad close to home," she told me.

The Daniels family told me they understand the protests, but they "just think there is another way."

There's a reason we stand for the national anthem and we place our hand over our heart and pledge allegiance to the flag.

It's to honor men and women who shed blood so that we might be free. It's to remember that our freedom comes with a price.

So, when athletes take a knee, they don't just disrespect the American flag, they disrespect American heroes—like Lance Corporal Nickolas Daniels of Elmwood Park, Illinois.

CHAPTER 14

THE BIRDS AND BEES ARE DOING UNNATURAL THINGS

WHEN I ENROLLED in first grade at Hope P. Sullivan Elementary School in the 1970s, my classroom was populated with little girls and little boys. That's all God was creating back in those days. But according to the sex and gender revolutionaries, there are more genders than there are ice cream flavors at Baskin-Robbins. To help you understand, I've created a chart:

- o God
    - Male
    - Female
- o Facebook:
    - Agender
    - Androgyne
    - Androgynous
    - Bigender
    - Cis
    - Cisgender
    - Cis Female

- Cis Male
- Cis Man
- Cis Woman
- Cisgender Female
- Cisgender Male
- Cisgender Man
- Cisgender Woman
- Female to Male
- FTM
- Gender Fluid
- Gender Nonconforming
- Gender Questioning
- Gender Variant
- Genderqueer
- Intersex
- Male to Female
- MTF
- Neither
- Neutrois
- Non-binary
- Other
- Pangender
- Trans
- Trans*
- Trans Female
- Trans* Female

- Trans Male
- Trans* Male
- Trans Man
- Trans* Man
- Trans Person
- Trans* Person
- Trans Woman
- Trans* Woman
- Transfeminine
- Transgender
- Transgender Female
- Transgender Male
- Transgender Man
- Transgender Person
- Transgender Woman
- Transmasculine
- Transsexual
- Transsexual Female
- Transsexual Male
- Transsexual Man
- Transsexual Person
- Transsexual Woman
- Two-Spirit

Just in case you're wondering, Pangender has nothing to do with somebody doing something inappropriate with a cast iron skillet.

There is an effort afoot to completely redefine and deconstruct gender in America. Michigan State University actually told students to ignore the science and accept the identity people have chosen for themselves. They are literally teaching students to be anatomy deniers.

This is nothing more than an attack on Christianity and the Holy Bible. The leftists want to destroy God. The academic world has all but canonized the idea that, in the beginning, God did not create the world. This sacrilegious notion has been accepted as the gospel truth in not just government-run schools, but also in many churches.

There's just one problem with their theology—once you cast doubt on the first verse of the Bible, you cast doubt on all the verses that follow. If you can convince people that God did not create the sea creatures and the beasts of the field, you can pretty much throw everything else out the window, too.

You see, the leftists don't believe that man was made in God's image. They believe man made man in man's image. Cue the thunder and lightning.

And as you are about to discover, there is a terrible price to pay when academics and progressive theologians question the legitimacy and the inerrancy of Scripture—and basic human anatomy.

CHILD REBUKED FOR MISGENDERING CLASSMATE

In 2017, a first grader at a California charter school was sent to the principal's office after she accidentally "misgendered" a classmate in what's being called a "pronoun mishap."[200]

---

200 "Transgender reveal in kindergarten class leaves parents feeling 'betrayed.'" *CBS News*. August 22, 2017. https://www.cbsnews.com/news/ transgender-reveal-kindergarten-class-rocklin-academy-parents-upset/.

The incident occurred at Rocklin Academy, a school roiled by controversy after a kindergarten teacher led an in-class discussion on transgenderism that included a "gender reveal" for a little boy who was transitioning to a little girl. *For kindergartners.*[201]

Parents were furious because they were not informed in advance and were not given the chance to opt their five-year-olds out of the classroom transgender activity. However, school leaders informed moms and dads that they were not allowed to opt out, and the state did not require them to notify parents.

The "pronoun mishap" occurred during the first week of school, when a first-grader came across a classmate on the playground. She called the student by his given name—apparently unaware that the boy now identified as a girl.

"This innocent little first grader sees a classmate, calls him by the name she knew him last year and the boy reports it to a teacher," Capitol Resource Institute's Karen England told me. "The little girl gets in trouble on the playground and then gets called out of class to the principal's office."

Capitol Resource Institute is a California-based public policy group that specializes in strengthening families. And they are working with a number of parents at Rocklin Academy upset about the LGBT agenda being forced on their children.

England said the first grader was investigated by the principal to determine whether or not she had bullied the transgender child by calling him by his original name. After about an hour it was determined the little girl made an honest mistake and she was not punished or reprimanded.

"The daughter came home from school upset and crying, saying, 'Mommy, I got in trouble at school today,'" England told me.

---

201   Starnes, Todd. "First Grader Sent to Office, Investigated, for 'Pronoun Mishap.'" *Todd Starnes* (blog). August 25, 2017. https://www.toddstarnes. com/uncategorized/first-grader-sent-to-office-investigated- for-pronoun-mishap/.

The little girl's mother, who asked not to be identified, immediately contacted the school to find out what had happened.

"She was told that whenever there is a pronoun mishap with this biological boy who now claims to be a girl—the school must investigate," England said.

Capitol Resource Institute provided me with a letter the mother wrote—expressing her extreme concern over how the situation was handled.

"I stressed over and over with the principal that I am all for protecting the rights of [the transgender child], but my children have rights as well," the parent wrote. "It makes me sad that my daughter felt like she was punished for trying to be kind to the kid."

England said Alliance Defending Freedom (ADF), a nationally known religious liberty law firm, is currently investigating the playground incident as well as the classroom lesson on gender identity.

"Our focus is on ensuring that every student's privacy is protected and that parental rights, including the right to be notified that before children are exposed to gender identity teaching, are respected by the school officials," an ADF spokesman told me.

What's happening at Rocklin Academy is an example of how schools have become indoctrination grounds for the LGBT agenda. And the only way to stop the indoctrination is for moms and dads to take a stand. It may be unpleasant and it may be uncomfortable, but we've got to stand up to these activist bullies.

CHRISTIAN TEACHER FIRED FOR USING WRONG PRONOUN

A devout Christian teacher was fired from a government-run school in West Point, Virginia after he refused to call a girl who identifies as a boy by her preferred pronoun.[202]

The school district voted unanimously to fire Peter Vlaming, a veteran French teacher who was beloved by students. They accused him of "misgendering" a student.

"That discrimination then leads to creating a hostile learning environment. And the student had expressed that. The parent had expressed that," said West Point Superintendent Laura Abel told NBC News. "They felt disrespected."

Vlaming explained to school officials that his religious beliefs prevented him from using male pronouns when addressing a biological female. He had agreed to call the child by her new "masculine" name, but the school district rejected that compromise.

"I can't think of a worse way to treat a child than what was happening," said West Point High Principal Jonathan Hochman, "It was very threatening."

He was basically given a choice—either reject the teachings of the Bible and basic human biology or find another job.

"Tolerance is a two-way street," said Shawn Voyles, Vlaming's attorney. "My client respects this student's rights; he is simply asking that his rights be respected as well… The student is absolutely free to identify as the student pleases. The school board adopted one viewpoint and required Mr. Vlaming, at the cost of his job, to repeat that ideology, repeat that viewpoint. That's where it's compelled speech.

---

202   Starnes, Todd. "Teacher Fired For Refusing to Call a Transgender
       Student By Preferred Pronoun." *Todd Starnes* (blog). December 14, 2018.
       https://www.toddstarnes.com/show/teacher-fired-for-refusing-to-call-a-
       transgender-student-by-preferred-pronoun/.

That's where it violates his First Amendment right he still retains as a public employee."[203]

More than a hundred students walked out of class to show their support to Vlaming. Eighth grader Cassidy Heidelberg helped organize the middle school students' participation in the walkout. She agreed with other students that both sides should have their rights respected and valued.

"I don't think they should shut Mr. Vlaming and his rights out like that," Heidelberg told the *Virginia Gazette*. "He has four children, a wife and it's hard enough earning enough as a teacher."

High school junior Forrest Rohde told the newspaper he is outraged by the school board's decision.

"Everyone has rights, the student has rights, but so does Mr. Vlaming," Rohde said. "This is violating Mr. Vlaming's First Amendment rights of freedom of speech and religion. He cares about his students and we care about him."

So now a good and decent teacher, a father of four children, is unemployed—simply for following the tenets of his faith and refusing to comply with the sex and gender revolutionaries who run West Point High School.

SCHOOL: LITTLE BOYS CAN HAVE PERIODS

Boys and girls in the United Kingdom are being instructed by their teachers that little boys can have periods, the *Daily Mail* reported.[204]

203   Bolster, Karina. "West Point High teacher fired following transgender controversy." *NBC 12*. Last modified December 8, 2018. https://www.nbc12.com/2018/12/06/west-point-high-teacher-fights-dismissal-following-transgender-controversy/.

204   "Eight-year-old pupils to be told 'boys can have periods too' under new sex education lessons guidelines." *Daily Mail*. Last modified December 16, 2018. https://www.dailymail.co.uk/news/article-6500231/Eight-year-old-pupils-told-boys-periods-new-sex-education-guidelines.html.

Brighton and Hove City Council stated: "Trans boys and men and non-binary people may have periods."

The British school district went on to direct that language about menstruation must be inclusive of "all genders" and ordered that "bins for used period products are provided in all toilets" for children.

Tory MP David Davies called the school lessons absolutely insane.

"Learning about periods is already a difficult subject for children that age, so to throw in the idea girls who believe they are boys also have periods will leave them completely confused," he told the *Daily Mail.*

Even leading feminists are outraged by the reports that little boys can menstruate.

"To tell impressionable children that boys can also menstruate sidelines girls who should be getting support when they start their periods," Julie Bindel told the newspaper.

DADDY-DAUGHTER DANCES ARE NOW A NO-NO

A grade school in Staten Island, New York was forced to cancel its annual father-daughter dance because it violated a new school district policy regarding transgender and gender nonconforming students.[205]

The New York Department of Education directed schools to eliminate any gender-based practices like the daddy-daughter dance unless the activities served a clear education purpose, the *New York Post* first reported.[206]

---

205   Starnes, Todd. "School Cancels Father-Daughter Dance Over Gender Issues." *Todd Starnes* (blog). February 5, 2018. https://www.toddstarnes.com/values/school-cancels-father-daughter-dance-gender-issues/.

206   Sanders, Anna. "These parents defied NYC's no daddy-daughter dance rule." *New York Post* (New York), February 10, 2018. https://nypost.com/2018/02/10/nyc-schools-are-allowed-to-have-father-daughter-dances-after-all/.

"If this doesn't convince you that the PC/SJW [social justice warrior] movement has lost their minds I don't know what will," Donald Trump, Jr. tweeted. "This nonsense really needs to stop."

The PTA president at PS 65 blamed the cancellation on the district's new "Transgender and Gender Nonconforming Student Guidelines," the *Post* reported.

"Father-daughter dances inherently leave people out. Not just because of transgender status, just life in general," Jared Fox, the district's LGBT community liaison, told the newspaper. "These can be really uncomfortable and triggering events."

Yes, good readers, there are actually people in America who live in fear of being triggered by a grade school's daddy-daughter dance.

However, the LGBT liaison said there is no outright ban on father-daughter dances, provided they are inclusive.

"For a young trans girl, to be able to go to a father-daughter dance can feel very affirming because in this instance she's recognized as a daughter," Fox told the newspaper.

Parents are furious over what they see as a capitulation to political correctness and militant sex and gender revolutionaries.

"All this gender crap needs to just stop," mom Akaia Cameron told the *Post*.

"They're trying to take away everything that everybody grew up on and has come to know and I don't think it's fair or right," Matthew West, a thirty-two-year-old father of two daughters told the newspaper. "They should leave it the way it was—father-daughter, mother-son."

A district spokesperson told the *Post* that the school was ordered to make changes to ensure that all students and families were welcome to attend.

"The DOE . . . has strict guidelines about how we present information," the principal wrote in a note to parents. "They have a 'gender neutral' policy that must be adhered to at all times."

Penny Nance, the president of Concerned Women for America, said on the *Todd Starnes Radio Show* that she was heartbroken and deeply concerned by the cancellation.

"It's not in anyone's best interest to throw a wet blanket on any kind of a program in which schools are trying to strengthen the father-daughter relationship," Nance told me. "The people that are hurt by this are young women."

Nance said she fondly remembered her daughter getting dressed up and attending her first father-daughter dance.

"The whole point of that was to teach her how she was supposed to be treated—what it feels like to have a man honor you and give you respect and open a door for you and show you love and kindness. I am so grateful for those times between my daughter and my husband," Nance said.

"I want that for every single young woman in this country," she said.

Sadly, the young girls at PS 65 will no longer experience that precious dance with their fathers because the school district is afraid of stepping on the LGBT community's toes.

CANADIANS ORDERED TO SAY "PEOPLEKIND"

What in the name of Rocky and Bullwinkle is going on in Canada?

Last year, Canadian Prime Minister Justin Trudeau flipped out after a woman representing a religious charity used the word "mankind" during a town hall gathering.[207]

"We have received many awards throughout the whole world. However, unfortunately in Canada, our volunteering as a charitable religious organization is extremely difficult. Extremely," the woman told the gathering.

---

207   Starnes, Todd. "Canada's Prime Minister Corrects Woman: 'Peoplekind,' Not 'Mankind.'" *Todd Starnes* (blog). February 6, 2018. https://www.toddstarnes.com/show/canadas-prime-minister-corrects-woman-peoplekind-not-mankind/.

Now, that's true. Much like their brethren to the south, Canadian liberals loathe people of faith.

"That's why in actuality, we cannot do free volunteering to help our neighbors in need as we truly desire. So that's why we came here today, to ask you to also look into the policies that religious charitable organizations have in our legislation so that it can also be changed because maternal love is the love that is going to change the future of mankind," she said. "So we'd like you to—"

Trudeau interrupted and got a bit snippy with the poor lady.

"We like to say peoplekind, not necessarily mankind, more inclusive," he declared.[208]

Trudeau was in truth being dead serious, folks. Since he took office, the prime minister has been pushing a radical gender neutrality agenda.

Last year, lawmakers approved a law making it illegal to use the wrong gender pronouns. Critics fear those who do not subscribe to progressive gender theory could be accused of hate crimes, the *Daily Signal* reported.

Trudeau heralded the legislation, tweeting, "Great news. Bill C-16 has passed the Senate—making it illegal to discriminate based on gender identity or expression. #LoveisLove."

You might recall that our gender-neutral friends north of the border recently passed a bill to make the national anthem more gender inclusive.

The Canadians took out the phrase "in all thy sons command" and replaced it with "in all of us command."

The prime minister called it "another positive step towards gender equality."

---

208 Livsey, Anna. "Justin Trudeau tells woman to say 'peoplekind' not 'mankind.'" *The Guardian* (London), February 6, 2018. https://www.theguardian.com/world/2018/feb/07/justin-trudeau-tells-woman-to-say-peoplekind-not-mankind.

And you thought the sex and gender revolutionaries were radical on this side of the border, with their bans on daddy-daughter dances and Facebook's ever-growing list of brand-spanking new genders.

Jeezaloo, America.

I wonder if it's too late to amend President Trump's border security plans? Maybe we ought to consider building a wall on the northern border too. Eh?

NEW YORK CITY CRACKS DOWN ON POLITE CONVERSATION

Well, it turns out that man-spreading is not the most pressing threat facing the New York City subway system after all.[209]

And neither are the trains that break down in the underbelly of the city, leaving passengers stranded for hours with a continuously playing pan flute ensemble.

Nor is the most pressing issue the muggers or perverts manhandling women, or homeless people urinating on seats, or giant rats prowling subway stations.

No, ladies and gentlemen, the greatest threat facing the Big Apple's subway system is train conductors using the words "ladies and gentlemen."

The *New York Post* reports the Metropolitan Transit Authority (MTA) has ordered all subway personnel to refrain from addressing riders as "ladies and gentlemen."[210]

---

209   Starnes, Todd. "Ladies and Gentlemen No Longer Welcome on NYC Subways." *Townhall.* November 11, 2017. https://townhall.com/columnists/toddstarnes/2017/11/11/ladies-and-gentlemen-no-longer-welcome-on-nyc-subways-n2407854.

210   "MTA takes political correctness to ridiculous heights." *New York Post* (New York), November 9, 2017. https://nypost.com/2017/11/09/mta-takes-political-correctness-to-ridiculous-heights/.

Instead, staffers have been told they must use gender neutral words like "riders," "passengers," and "everyone," according to a memorandum obtained exclusively by the *Post*.

"Please don't use any greeting other than these," the memo reads.

Subway workers say political correctness has derailed the nation's largest subway system.

"They are trying to be politically correct," one worker told the *Post*. "They are acknowledging that they have some transgender riders. They don't want to offend anyone."

An MTA spokesperson told the *Post* that gender issues were a consideration for the move.

I suspect it was a preemptive strike by the MTA to avoid some sort of legal action taken by the LGBTQI and the letter A community.

Heaven help the poor cis-gender train conductor who inadvertently mis-genders a gender-fluid passenger.

Gender fluidity, by the way, is the latest fad in the sex and gender revolution. Followers ascribe to a belief that there's really no such thing as male or female.

For example, you could be a male passenger on the B Train at 34th Street-Herald Square, but you could identify as a female passenger by the time you reach Rockefeller Center.

I know, it's all very confusing, ladies and gentlemen (my apologies).

Lord only knows what the next stop is going to be on this gender-bender train ride into gender inclusivity. I wonder if they'd be okay if the conductors just hollered out, "You people"?

SCHOOL CHOOSES SEX COLUMNIST AS ROLE MODEL

Parents were furious after a California elementary school posted a bulletin board that addressed issues like sexual identity and encouraged children as young as four years old to break out of gender stereotypes.[211]

The bulletin board at Rancho Romero Elementary School also featured nationally syndicated sex columnist Dan Savage as a role model for children. Mr. Savage also hosts an annual porn festival.

"For him to be a role model for four-year-olds to eleven-year-olds is utterly disgusting," one anonymous parent said on the *Todd Starnes Radio Show*. "He's not someone you want to put up at an elementary school."

The bulletin board included Mr. Savage's photo (fully clothed), along with the following quote:

"A lot of kids are bullied because of their sexual identity or expression. It's often the effeminate boys and the masculine girls, the ones who violate gender norms and expectations who get bullied."

In 2012, Mr. Savage bullied a group of Christian teenagers who walked out of a journalism conference after he launched a profane attack on the Bible. He called them "pansy-a**ed."[212]

And there was that time he tried to infect a Republican candidate with a flu virus. And how can we forget about the time he wished congressional Republicans would "f***ing die?"

"The man does nothing but spew vitriol at people he does not like—like religious groups and conservatives," the anonymous parent said.

The parent, who has a first-grader and a fourth-grader at the public elementary school, said the gender bulletin board has created a firestorm. Of particular concern: the school used a unicorn as a propaganda tool.

211   Starnes, Todd. "Grade School Uses Sex Columnist, Unicorn to Promote Gender Identity." *Todd Starnes* (blog). January 24, 2018. https://www.toddstarnes.com/show/grade-school-uses-unicorn-sex-columnist-encourage-kids-question-gender/.

212   Shapiro, Ben. "Flashback: Obama Teams with Anti-Christian Bully Savage." *Breitbart*. April 30, 2012. https://www.breitbart.com/politics/2012/04/30/obama-white-house-disassociate-savage/.

The so-called "Gender Unicorn" introduced children to concepts like gender identity, gender expression, and gender presentation. It also included words like "sexually attracted to" and "romantically/ emotionally attracted to."

"A unicorn—an object loved by little children—was used to lure them to the bulletin board," the parent said on the *Todd Starnes Radio Show.* "It felt like it was a creepy way to lure a child over to the board and confuse them about gender."

The San Ramon Valley Unified School District said the bulletin board is meant to highlight a monthly theme.

"For January the theme for the month is 'breaking out of gender stereotypes,'" a district spokesperson said.

"The school has a parent-led Inclusion and Diversity Committee that maintains a bulletin board to highlight a different theme each month within the rubric that all students, staff and parents are safe and welcomed on campus," the spokesperson added.

The school did modify parts of the display after parents raised concerns about age-appropriate content. They said the initial content was only up for about four hours.

The school also acknowledged there was a quote and a photograph of Mr. Savage, the porn peddler.

"The quote and photo were removed as part of the revision," the spokesperson said.

There are still two questions that have yet to be resolved.

First, why is the school district using a unicorn to confuse children about things they ought not to be confused about?

And secondly, what was school leadership smoking when they decided that a person like Dan Savage would be a good role model for four-year-old children?

PLANNED PARENTHOOD WANTS
TRANSGENDER DISNEY PRINCESS

A Planned Parenthood chapter in Pennsylvania wants the next Disney princess to be a transgender union worker who illegally crossed the border to have an abortion.

"We need a disney [*sic*] princess who's had an abortion," read a tweet from Planned Parenthood Keystone's Twitter account. The tweet was later deleted.

LifeNews first reported the disturbing item and snagged a screenshot. Also on Planned Parenthood Keystone's Twitter wish list:[213]

o   A Disney princess who's had an abortion.

o   A Disney princess who's pro-choice.

o   A Disney princess who's an undocumented immigrant.

o   A Disney princess who's a union worker.

o   A Disney princess who's trans.

What in the name of Jiminy Cricket is wrong with those people?

"Today, we joined an ongoing Twitter conversation about the kinds of princesses people want to see in an attempt to make a point about the importance of telling stories that challenge stigma and championing stories that too often don't get told," Planned Parenthood president Melissa Reed told *USA Today* in a statement. "Upon reflection, we decided that the seriousness of the point we were trying

---

213   Bilger, Micaiah. "Planned Parenthood: 'We Need a Disney Princess Who's Had an Abortion.'" LifeNews. March 27, 2018.
https://www.lifenews.com/2018/03/27/planned-parenthood-we-need-a-disney-princess-whos-had-an-abortion/.

to make was not appropriate for the subject matter or context, and we removed the tweet."[214]

Conservatives and pro-lifers were outraged.

"Promoting abortion-positive messages to toddlers and school children (and their parents, family and friends)? Seriously?" wrote Michele Blood on Lifezette. "Let's face it, folks: Planned Parenthood is essentially an arm of the Democratic National Committee at this point. It operates as a spokesagency for liberals who are OK with taking the life of the unborn merely because a woman may choose to do so or feel like it."

Lila Rose, of Live Action, said Planned Parenthood Keystone's call to "promote abortions to impressionable little girls who admire Disney princesses is despicable."

"Planned Parenthood is pushing abortion on kids as young as possible, selling lies that abortion is something 'good,' empowering, and even noble,' she wrote on Twitter.

How about a Disney princess who doesn't try to cram pro-abortion propaganda down the throats of American children?

Imagine the plot of Disney's next Broadway blockbuster if Planned Parenthood had its way:

Cinderella catches Prince Charming cheating on her, so she gets knocked up by a Newsie and they travel South of the Border to get an abortion.

Wicked.

---

214   Hafner, Josh. "Planned Parenthood called for Disney princess 'who's had an abortion' in now-deleted tweet." *USA Today* (McLean), Last modified March 28, 2018. https://www.usatoday.com/story/news/nation-now/2018/03/27/planned-parenthood-called-disney-princess-whos-had-abortion-now-deleted-tweet/464016002/.

TEEN VOGUE TEACHES KIDS ABOUT ANAL SEX

Teen Vogue is defending its decision to publish a graphic tutorial to anal sex for children and teenagers—calling critics homophobic.[215]

"This is anal 101, for teens, beginners and all inquisitive folk," author Gigi Engle wrote in "A Guide to Anal Sex."

"Anal sex and anal stimulation can be awesome, and if you want to give it a go, you do that," wrote Engle, a self-described sex educator. "More power to you."

The original article did not include any references to practicing safe sex, but was later amended to include a line about condoms being "non-negotiable."[216]

"Here is the lowdown on everything you need to know about butt stuff," the writer declared.

Parents across the nation became enraged upon learning that *Teen Vogue* wanted to turn their children in sexual deviants.

"I was truly flabbergasted," Elizabeth Johnston told me on my radio program. "They should not be teaching sodomy to our children."

Johnston, known as The Activist Mommy, launched a national campaign to urge local stores and public libraries to pull *Teen Vogue* from bookshelves: #PULLTEENVOGUE.

"This is not a Republican issue or a Democrat issue. This is not a conservative issue or liberal issue. This is a parent issue," she told me.

More than ten million people have viewed a video of Johnston burning a copy of *Teen Vogue* in her backyard.

Phillip Picardi, the magazine's digital editorial director, fired back in a flurry of tweets, culminating with a photo of him embracing another man while holding up his middle finger.

---

215   Starnes, Todd. "Teen Vogue Defends Teaching Kids
       How to Engage in Sodomy." *Todd Starnes* (blog). July
       18, 2017. https://www.toddstarnes.com/uncategorized/
       teen-vogue-defends-teaching-kids-how-to-engage-in-sodomy/.
216   Engle, Gigi. "Anal Sex: What You Need to Know." *Teen Vogue*, May 16,
       2018. https://www.teenvogue.com/story/anal-sex-what-you-need-to-know.

He said they had been "inundated with hate mail saying we promote sodomy and want teens to get AIDS."

"How can you expect young women to not get pregnant without access to reproductive health care," he tweeted.

Picardi then accused his Catholic school of being "guilty of endangering all of us by sheer omission of FACTS. EDUCATION doesn't equal ENCOURAGEMENT."

Well, I think we can all agree that Hell would freeze over before a Catholic school would teach children about anal sex.

Picardi then played the phobic-card—a favorite among liberals.

"The backlash to this article is rooted in homophobia," he wrote. "It's also laced in arcane delusion about what it means to be a young person today."

"This has nothing to do with homophobia," Ms. Johnston told me. "This is about parents protecting their children from perversion."

Teen Vogue would have you believe it's offensive for parents to be offended by the smut they are peddling.

And in their perverse world, the magazine's editors would have you believe that a bunch of teens and tweens are frolicking across the fruited plain, having anal sex with Lord-knows-what. Remember the good old days when kids just used to play spin the bottle?

AIR FORCE: WORDS LIKE BOY, GIRL COULD OFFEND

The Air Force fears that words like boy, girl, colonial, and black-list might offend people, according to an email sent to Airmen at Joint Base San Antonio. An outraged Airman sent me a copy of the email as evidence that the military is still infected with Obama-era political correctness.[217]

---

217   Starnes, Todd. "Exclusive: Air Force Says Words Like 'Boy'
and 'Girl' Could be Offensive." *Todd Starnes* (blog). March
9, 2017. https://www.toddstarnes.com/uncategorized/
exclusive-air-force-says-words-like-boy-girl-could-be-offensive/.

The email included an attachment that listed a number of words and phrases that might be construed as offensive. Now, to be fair, there were some legitimately offensive and racially charged words and phrases on the list. But also included on the list were the words boy and girl.

The email was written by a senior Air Force leader and was sent to an untold number of personnel at Lackland Air Force Base. Airmen were advised to study a list of words and phrases that "may be construed as offensive." Here's a partial list of some of the dubious words and phrases deemed troublesome by the Air Force:

1. Boy

2. Girl

3. You People

4. Colonial

5. Blacklist

6. Blackmail

7. Blackball

8. Sounds Greek to me

9. Blondes have more fun

10. Too many chiefs, not enough Indians

"Please be cognizant that such conduct is 100 percent zero tolerance in or outside of the work climate," the email read. "Let's capitalize on our richly diverse climate, and help others seek assistance if they are struggling with compliance."

Based on my interpretation of the email, it's pretty clear that Airmen have been advised not to use those words in any sort of context, on or off base.

So, I reached out to the public affairs office at Lackland to find out why they had a problem with the words "boy" and "girl." Was it true that the Air Force had banned those words?

"The Air Force has no list of prohibited terms," a public affairs spokesperson told me. "It was sent out by an individual simply reminding Airmen to be respectful to others."

Apparently, the words "100 percent zero tolerance" don't have the same meaning in Air Force vernacular.

This is a case of the Air Force getting caught red-handed trying to advance a politically correct agenda. And now that I've got a copy of the evidence, they are attempting to whitewash the situation.

It's time for the Pentagon to root out Obama-era political correctness in the Armed Forces. We must never again allow the greatest fighting force on the planet to be used as a social engineering petri dish.

The Airmen I know are brave men and women who are devoted to their calling to protect our great nation. I sincerely doubt they give two hoots about political correctness.

That being said, there could be one or two folks in the military who contracted microaggressions that were triggered by someone uttering the words "boy" or "girl."

Perhaps those individuals might consider seeking treatment for their affliction inside a designated safe space at a nearby public university, instead of Joint Base San Antonio.

CHAPTER 15

IT'S NOT A SIN TO WEAR A MAGA HAT

THE YOUNG MEN of Covington Catholic High School have been subjected to nothing short of a political inquisition because of their faith, the color of their skin, and their devotion to making America great again. And they are owed an apology.[218]

The boys had been in Washington, D.C. to participate in the annual March For Life. Later in the day, they assembled outside the Lincoln Memorial to wait for school buses. And that's where the trouble started.

According to the mainstream media, the boys surrounded and terrorized Native American activist Nathan Phillips. A video clip showed what the media described as a teenage boy wearing a MAGA hat blocking Phillips and staring him down.

"It was getting ugly, and I was thinking, 'I've got to find myself an exit out of this situation and finish my song at the Lincoln Memorial,'" Phillips told the *Washington Post*. "I started going that way, and that guy in the hat stood in my way and we were at an impasse. He just blocked my way and wouldn't allow me to retreat."

---

218   Chamberlain, Samuel. "Kentucky student seen in viral confrontation with Native American speaks out." Fox News. Accessed May 29, 2019. https://www.foxnews.com/us/kentucky-student-seen-in-viral-confrontation-with-native-american-speaks-out.

Phillips told the *Detroit Free Press* that he had seen the white Catholic students "attacking these four black individuals."

"There was that moment when I realized I've put myself between beast and prey," he told the newspaper. "These young men were beastly and these old black individuals was their prey, and I stood in between them and so they needed their pounds of flesh and they were looking at me for that."

It was all untrue, of course, but that did not stop the mainstream media from going nuclear.

"Boys in 'Make America Great Again' Hats Mob Native Elder at Indigenous Peoples March," read *The New York Times* story.

"The Catholic Church's Shameful History of Native American Abuses," the *Washington Post* declared.

Even conservative outlets like the *National Review* turned on the Catholic boys—without bothering to check their facts.

"The Covington Students Might as Well Have Just Spit on the Cross," read a screed written by *National Review* Deputy Editor Nicholas Frankovich.

"They mock a serious, frail-looking older man and gloat in their momentary role as Roman soldiers to his Christ," he wrote.

Seriously? The *National Review* compared this activist to Jesus Christ? Sweet mercy.

As a result of the media coverage, the students and their families have been terrorized and publicly shamed. Some students were identified and targeted by leftist activists.

And now, thanks to irrefutable video evidence, we know that the entire story was a hoax—a flat-out lie.

The videos, which I have personally viewed, show that Phillips and some of his associates were the ones who instigated the confrontation. It was Phillips who thrust his drum in the face of the teenage boy wearing the MAGA hat.

"White people go back to Europe where you came from," one of the activists shouted at the Catholic students. "This is not your land."

And the young man in the so-called "stare down" can be seen trying to calm down a classmate while one of the adult activists cursed the child.

The boys were also accused of chanting, "Build that wall." However, based on the videos I've seen, there is no evidence to back up those accusations.

Oh, and those black protesters turned out to be members of the Black Hebrew Israelites, a radical group known for being anti-gay. The video clearly shows the black protesters berating the teenage boys with all sorts of racial and homophobic slurs.

"Your president is a homosexual," one of the grown men told the boys. "Your president is a homosexual. Greek was a bunch of homosexuals, just like the Romans. You proud of sodomy?"

"You give fa***ts rights," the man shouted.

At that point, the Catholic school boys jeered in protest and disgust. One of the boys could be heard rebuking the Black Hebrew Israelites for using anti-gay language.

And yet, that information was completely left out of the mainstream media news coverage.

"Covington Catholic High School students surrounded, intimidated and chanted over Native Americans singing about indigenous people's strength and spirit," read the lead paragraph on Cincinnati.com.

In context, it appears that what really happened on the steps of the Lincoln Memorial is that a group of Catholic school boys was targeted and harassed by grown adults just because they were white, Catholic Trump supporters.

But the mainstream media doesn't care about the truth because they believe people who support President Trump and believe in God are irredeemable deplorables.

"Don't let your Catholic school's students wear MAGA hats on a field trip for the March for Life," *The New York Times* columnist Ross Douthat wrote on Twitter.

As I have thoroughly documented in this book, it's not the first time that people have been attacked for wearing those ball caps. And I doubt it will be the last. The good news is that Nick Sandmann is fighting back—filing lawsuits against many of the mainstream media outlets that smeared his name.

There are a whole lot of grown-ups who owe those good and decent teenage boys an apology, starting with the liars in the mainstream media. But it's next to impossible for American newsrooms to do any soul searching, seeing how one must have a soul to search. But they should pay heed to what I'm about to tell you. It is not a sin to wear a Make America Great Again ball cap. But it is a sin to bear false witness.

In the meantime, maybe it's time for parents to sit down with their sons and have long talks about the dangers of being a pro-life, pro-Trump Christian in America. Young men need to know they might be targeted and profiled for wearing a MAGA hat. Society will judge them by the color of their skin instead of the content of their character.

Just before this book was published, attorneys representing the Sandmann family began filing multi-million-dollar lawsuits against a number of mainstream media companies and individual reporters. They must be held accountable for their actions.

To truly understand how heinous the news coverage was, you need to understand what really happened that day on the Washington Mall. Nicholas and his family gave me permission to share with you his recollections of that fateful moment.

STATEMENT OF NICK SANDMANN, COVINGTON CATHOLIC HIGH SCHOOL JUNIOR, REGARDING INCIDENT AT THE LINCOLN MEMORIAL:[219]

I am providing this factual account of what happened on Friday afternoon at the Lincoln Memorial to correct misinformation and outright lies being spread about my family and me.

I am the student in the video who was confronted by the Native American protestor. I arrived at the Lincoln Memorial at 4:30 p.m. I was told to be there by 5:30 p.m., when our busses were due to leave Washington for the trip back to Kentucky. We had been attending the March for Life rally and then had split up into small groups to do sightseeing.

When we arrived, we noticed four African American protestors who were also on the steps of the Lincoln Memorial. I am not sure what they were protesting, and I did not interact with them. I did hear them direct derogatory insults at our school group.

The protestors said hateful things. They called us "racists," "bigots," "white crackers," "faggots," and "incest kids." They also taunted an African American student from my school by telling him that we would "harvest his organs." I have no idea what that insult means, but it was startling to hear.

Because we were being loudly attacked and taunted in public, a student in our group asked one of our teacher chaperones for permission to begin our school spirit chants to counter the hateful things that were being shouted at our group. The chants are commonly used at sporting events. They are all positive in nature and sound like what you would hear at any high school. Our chaperone gave us permission to use our school chants. We would not have done that without obtaining permission from the adults in charge of our group.

---

219 "Statement of nick Sandmann, Covington Catholic High School junior, regarding incident at Lincoln Memorial." CNN. Last modified January 23, 2019. https://www.cnn.com/2019/01/20/us/covington-kentucky-student-statement/index.html.

At no time did I hear any student chant anything other than the school spirit chants. I did not witness or hear any students chant "build that wall" or anything hateful or racist at any time. Assertions to the contrary are simply false. Our chants were loud because we wanted to drown out the hateful comments that were being shouted at us by the protestors.

After a few minutes of chanting, the Native American protestors, who I hadn't previously noticed, approached our group. The Native American protestors had drums and were accompanied by at least one person with a camera.

The protestor everyone has seen in the video began playing his drum as he waded into the crowd, which parted for him. I did not see anyone try to block his path. He locked eyes with me and approached me, coming within inches of my face. He played his drum the entire time he was in my face.

I never interacted with this protestor. I did not speak to him. I did not make any hand gestures or other aggressive moves. To be honest, I was startled and confused as to why he had approached me. We had already been yelled at by another group of protestors, and when the second group approached I was worried that a situation was getting out of control where adults were attempting to provoke teenagers.

I believed that by remaining motionless and calm, I was helping to diffuse the situation. I realized everyone had cameras and that perhaps a group of adults was trying to provoke a group of teenagers into a larger conflict. I said a silent prayer that the situation would not get out of hand.

During the period of the drumming, a member of the protestor's entourage began yelling at a fellow student that we "stole our land" and that we should "go back to Europe." I heard one of my fellow students begin to respond. I motioned to my classmate and tried to get him to stop engaging with the protestor, as I was still in the mindset that we needed to calm down tensions.

I never felt like I was blocking the Native American protestor. He did not make any attempt to go around me. It was clear to me that he had singled me out for a confrontation, although I am not sure why.

The engagement ended when one of our teachers told me the busses had arrived and it was time to go. I obeyed my teacher and simply walked to the busses. At that moment, I thought I had diffused the situation by remaining calm, and I was thankful nothing physical had occurred.

I never understood why either of the two groups of protestors were engaging with us, or exactly what they were protesting at the Lincoln Memorial. We were simply there to meet a bus, not become central players in a media spectacle. This is the first time in my life I've ever encountered any sort of public protest, let alone this kind of confrontation or demonstration.

I was not intentionally making faces at the protestor. I did smile at one point because I wanted him to know that I was not going to become angry, intimidated or be provoked into a larger confrontation. I am a faithful Christian and practicing Catholic, and I always try to live up to the ideals my faith teaches me—to remain respectful of others, and to take no action that would lead to conflict or violence.

I harbor no ill will for this person. I respect this person's right to protest and engage in free speech activities, and I support his chanting on the steps of the Lincoln Memorial any day of the week. I believe he should re-think his tactics of invading the personal space of others, but that is his choice to make.

I am being called every name in the book, including a racist, and I will not stand for this mob-like character assassination of my family's name. My parents were not on the trip, and I strive to represent my family in a respectful way in all public settings.

I have received physical and death threats via social media, as well as hateful insults. One person threatened to harm me at school, and one person claims to live in my neighborhood. My parents are receiving death and professional threats because of the social media mob that has formed over this issue.

I love my school, my teachers and my classmates. I work hard to achieve good grades and to participate in several extracurricular activities. I am mortified that so many people have come to believe something that did not happen—that students from my school were chanting or acting in a racist fashion toward African Americans or Native Americans. I did not do that, do not have hateful feelings in my heart, and did not witness any of my classmates doing that.

I cannot speak for everyone, only for myself. But I can tell you my experience with Covington Catholic is that students are respectful of all races and cultures. We also support everyone's right to free speech.

I am not going to comment on the words or account of Mr. Phillips, as I don't know him and would not presume to know what is in his heart or mind. Nor am I going to comment further on the other protestors, as I don't know their hearts or minds, either.

I have read that Mr. Phillips is a veteran of the United States Marines. I thank him for his service and am grateful to anyone who puts on the uniform to defend our nation. If anyone has earned the right to speak freely, it is a U.S. Marine veteran.

I can only speak for myself and what I observed and felt at the time. But I would caution everyone passing judgment based on a few seconds of video to watch the longer video clips that are on the internet, as they show a much different story than is being portrayed by people with agendas.

I provided this account of events to the Diocese of Covington so they may know exactly what happened, and I stand ready and willing to cooperate with any investigation they are conducting.

CHAPTER 16

THE CULTURAL CLEANSING OF THE SOUTH

DURING MY EARLY years at Fox News, I had the chance to interview one half of a popular country music duo. I made an off-handed comment about why people love country music—specifically because unlike soy latte sipping pop stars, country music stars drive pickup trucks, drink sweet tea, own guns, and love America.

While I meant for the comment to be a joke, it really is the gospel truth. For most of its existence, the country music industry has been a standard-bearer of American values, except for a few songs about bar fights and conduct unbecoming a Baptist in a trailer park.

A few minutes after the interview, my producer came back to my desk with a concerned look on her face. After the interview had concluded, the country music star called back and was not too happy. He told my producer he was angry and he took great offense at my comments. He accused me of stereotyping country music singers and fans. It turns out this particular country music singer enjoyed sipping soy milk lattes while flitting about Nashville in one of those battery-powered metrosexual foreign-made cars.

Little did I know at the time that country music had become infected with a malaise known as culture creep. It's sort of like kudzu. Once it starts growing on something, you can't get rid of it.

And sure enough, ten years after my interview with that leftist crooner, the industry that gave us Hank and Johnny and George had been taken over by fellows squeezed into skinny jeans, reeking of essential oils, and dishing about their bromances onstage at the Grand Ole Opry.

Let me put it this way—if Minnie Pearl were in a bar fight with a bunch of those Bromance Boys at a honkey-tonk on Lower Broadway, she'd smack the spray-on tan right off their moisturized faces.

Billboard Magazine blew the lid off the butter beans in 2018 by reporting that the Country Music industry was more liberal than it let on. Not long after the Dixie Chicks were excommunicated in 2003 for their on-stage attacks against President Bush, a group of liberal music executives formed a coalition.[220]

"Fifteen years later, this contrast has never been more apparent," *Billboard* reported. "The past year in Nashville - a city that consistently votes blue - has transformed the town from comfortably silent to one vociferously at odds with the conservative political agenda."[221]

"Liberal used to be a dirty word in country music," the *Tampa Bay Times* declared. "But today, more artists are speaking out on gun control, LGBTQ rights and immigration. And some are stumping for a Democratic wave on Election Day."[222]

In other words, the denim and diamond crowd on Lower Broadway just got woke. The *Times* went so far as to say a blue hue

---

220 "Dixie Chicks pulled from air after bashing Bush." CNN. March 14, 2003. http://www.cnn.com/2003/SHOWBIZ/Music/03/14/dixie.chicks.reut/.

221 Moss, Marissa R. "The Country Music Industry Is More Liberal Than It Lets On: Will More Start To Speak Up?" *Billboard*. June 5, 2018. https://www.billboard.com/articles/columns/country/8458774/why-liberal-country-music-artists-executives-dont-speak-up.

222 Cridlin, Jay. "Nashville's blue wave: 15 years after the Dixie Chicks, country artists make a liberal political shift." *Tampa Bay Times* (Tampa), November 1, 2018. https://www.tampabay.com/things-to-do/music/nashvilles-blue-wave-15-years-after-the-dixie-chicks-country-artists-make-a-liberal-political-shift-20181101/.

had settled over Music Row. The question is whether country music fans will follow their favorite musicians to the left side of the stage.

And that brings me to an incident that occurred in 2018, when one of country music's most powerful executives said gun-toting, Bible-clinging fans like former Arkansas Gov. Mike Huckabee are no longer welcome.[223]

The controversy started when the Country Music Association triggered a massive outbreak of microaggressions after they appointed Huckabee to the board of its charitable foundation. Huckabee has been a longtime supporter of music education, so his appointment to a charitable board that supports music programs for young people was a perfect fit.

However, a mob of social justice warriors, led by openly gay country music executive Jason Owen, protested, calling Huckabee's appointment "grossly offensive" and "heartbreaking."

"This man has made it clear that my family is not welcome in his America," the owner of Sandbox Entertainment wrote in a letter to the CMA. "And the CMA has opened their arms to him, making him feel welcome and relevant."

Owen, whose roster includes Faith Hill, Little Big Town, Kacey Musgraves, and Midland, threatened to pull out of the CMA Foundation over Huckabee's appointment.

"Huckabee speaks of the sort of things that would suggest my family is morally beneath his and uses language that has a profoundly negative impact upon young people all across this country," he wrote.

For the record, Huckabee is a born-again, Southern Baptist preacher who follows the teachings of the Holy Bible. And that

223 Watts, Cindy and Dave Paulson. "Mike Huckabee resigns from CMA foundation board amid controversy." *Tennessean*. Last modified March 2, 2018. https://www.tennessean.com/story/entertainment/music/2018/03/01/mike-huckabee-resigns-cma-foundation-board-following-controversy/385920002/.

includes the Bible's directives on marriage. And I'd also be willing to bet a gallon of sweet tea and a bucket of chicken that a good many country music fans go to church, own a gun, and share the same beliefs as Gov. Huckabee. That's why there are more country music songs about God and pickup trucks and honky-tonks instead of Chevy Volts and juice bars.

Owen also objected to the former governor's involvement with the National Rifle Association, calling it "harmful and damaging."

"What a shameful choice," he wrote. "I will not participate in any organization that elevates people like this to positions that amplify their sick voices."

Has it really come to this, America? Must we renounce our religious beliefs and bow down to those who will not tolerate tolerance? Does the Country Music industry really consider their base to be people with "sick voices"?

Less than twenty-four hours later, Huckabee resigned from the CMA Foundation Board and wrote an open letter to the industry titled "Hate Wins." The governor permitted me to share his letter in this book and it's worth reading:

Dear Board Members:

It appears that I will make history as having the shortest tenure in the history of the CMA Foundation Board. I genuinely regret that some in the industry were so outraged by my appointment that they bullied the CMA and the Foundation with economic threats and vowed to withhold support for the programs for students if I remained. I had NO idea I was that influential! I'm somewhat flattered to be of such consequence when all I thought I was doing was voluntarily serving on a non-profit board without pay in order to continue my decades of advocacy for the arts and especially music.

The message here is "Hate Wins." Bullies succeeded in making it untenable to have "someone like me" involved. I would imagine however that many of the people who buy tickets and music are not that "unlike me."

I hereby tender my resignation effective immediately. I hope this will end the unnecessary distraction and deterrent to the core mission of the Foundation which is to help kids acquire musical instruments and have an opportunity to participate in music programs as students.

Since I will not be able to continue in what I had hoped to be useful service in this endeavor, I wanted to at least put some things on the record. I have no expectation that it will change the irrational vitriol directed toward you or me for my religious or political views that necessitated my abrupt departure, but I want you to know what you would never know by reading intolerant and vicious statements on the internet about who I am or what led me to want to be a part of your efforts to empower kids with the gift of music. So please bear with me.

Music changed my life. I grew up dirt poor in south Arkansas. No male upstream from me in my entire family ever even graduated from high school. I had no reason to believe that my life would consist of anything but scratching out a meager living and hoping to pay rent in a house I would never own just as generations before me had done.

Music changed that. The gift of an electric guitar by my parents when I was 11 put in my hands a future. It took them a year to pay for the $99 guitar they bought from the J. C. Penney catalog. Granted, I was never good enough to make a full-time living at music, but the confidence I gained by playing, being in front of people, and competing against myself and the low expectations I grew up with was transformative.

No need to recite my entire history, but I was especially baffled that I was accused of not being supportive of public education. I am the PRODUCT of public education. As Governor my own children were the first children of a Governor in 50 years to have their entire education grades 1-12 in the PUBLIC schools of Arkansas. I fought to give teachers the largest pay raise in state history. I successfully led the effort to allow teachers to retire with full benefits after 28 years of service after my two Democrat predecessors vetoed the same bill. I personally shepherded through legislation that mandated both music AND arts programs for EVERY student in grades 1-12 and taught by fully certified teachers. We were one of the only states to have ever done that.

I was Chairman for 2 years of the Education Commission of the States, comprised of all 50 Governors, education leaders in the Senate and House from all 50 state legislatures, and the state education chief for each of the 50 states. My chosen theme and agenda for those two years was music education for every child. I launched an initiative "Play it Again, Arkansas" that promoted donation of musical instruments that would be professionally refurbished and provided to students whose parents couldn't afford the rent or purchase of an instrument allowing them to be in the school band. I traveled repeatedly to DC with the NAMM Foundation to advocate for music education and have worked with them for several years to urge states to mandate music and arts education. Now someone who has never met me threatens to wreck valuable programs of the CMA Foundation because of a personal contempt for my faith and politics. I am willing to get out of the way for the sake of the students the Foundation will hopefully help.

If the industry doesn't want people of faith or who hold conservative and traditional political views to buy tickets and music, they should be forthcoming and say it. Surely neither the artists or the business people of the industry want that.

Until recently, the arts was the one place America could set aside political, geographical, racial, religious, and economic barriers and come together. If the arts community becomes part of the polarization instead of bridging communities and people over the power of civil norms as reflected in the arts, then we as a civilization may not be long for this earth.

All of us have deep passions about our beliefs. I do about mine. But I hate no one. I wish upon NO ONE the loss of life or livelihood because that person sees things differently than me.

I hope that the music and entertainment industry will become more tolerant and inclusive and recognize that a true love for kids having access to the arts is more important than a dislike for someone or a group of people because of who they are or what they believe.

My sincere thanks to the CMA Foundation for believing I had something to contribute. I regret that my presence caused controversy and threats to vital support for deserving kids. Kids wanting to learn music shouldn't be the victims of adults who demand that only certain people can be in the room or be heard.

I wish you nothing but good will and success at reaching students across America who need music as much as I did. At the end of the day, I'm not worth the fight, but the kids are. Never stop fighting for THEM![224]

Sincerely,

Mike Huckabee

Governor Huckabee was a guest on my radio program the day after he mailed the letter. He was quick to point out that he harbored no ill will toward the Country Music Association Foundation.

"I'm not mad at them. I feel sad that we are in a place in our country—the last place where people could get together and find common ground for civilized behavior—which was the arts—is now becoming itself a polarized place in society and that's just tragic," the governor said.

---

224 Huckabee, Mike. "Hate wins." *Mike Huckabee* (blog). March 2, 2018. https://www.mikehuckabee.com/ news?id=eba2a1da-4aaa-4ced-8435-1ef4d2b9b3a9&CommentPage=6.

And the culprits are people like Jason Owen who scream about tolerance while privately trying to destroy anyone who does not conform to his personal moral code. Again, Governor Huckabee was deemed unfit because of his Christian convictions regarding marriage and because of his membership in the National Rifle Association.

"What is inclusion if inclusion only means people who have a very strong, and very far left-of-center point of view? That's not inclusion," the governor told me. "When people on the left say love, they mean hate. When they say tolerant, they mean intolerant. When they say diversity, what they really mean is conformity."

In reality, an overwhelming number of Americans and Country Music fans share the governor's moral code, not Jason Owen's. So why didn't Governor Huckabee demand that Owen be removed from his position on the CMA Foundation? It's because the governor is a tolerant man and he understood that the foundation is not about gay marriage or gun control. The foundation is about music education.

Folks, I'd be lying if I said I was not concerned about Governor Huckabee's public flogging. As difficult as it may be, we have to ask whether the country music industry has been overrun by a bunch of anti-Christian, gun-hating bullies.

I certainly hope that is not the case, but one thing is mighty clear—we're not in Cornfield County anymore, Hee Haw fans. And as the following dispatches from the front lines of the culture war will demonstrate, there is a full-scale cultural cleansing underway in the Southern states.

OLE MISS BANS THE DIXIE FIGHT SONG

The University of Mississippi has officially dumped "Dixie" so they can be more inclusive. I fear old times there will soon be forgotten, folks.

"The newly expanded and renovated Vaught-Hemingway Stadium will further highlight our best traditions and create new ones that give the Ole Miss Rebels the best home field advantage in college football," the university announced.[225]

"Dixie" was first played by the Ole Miss band around 1948, *Mississippi Today* reports.

"Because the Pride of the South is such a large part of our overall experience and tradition, the Athletics Department asked them to create a new and modern pregame show that does not include Dixie and is more inclusive for all fans," the university declared.

More inclusive, eh?

Perhaps they could consult with Beyonce or Jay-Z. I'm certain the university will find some inspiration from her 2016 Super Bowl Halftime performance.

It's only a matter of time before Ole Miss replaces fried catfish and sweet tea with fermented soy sandwiches and beverages made from lawn clippings—all for the sake of inclusivity.

Allen Coon, a student government leader, was thrilled with the university's decision.

"It's an important step forward for our university as we attempt to reconcile and understand our relationship with our Old South past," Coon told the *Commercial Appeal*. "Ending the use of 'Dixie' promotes inclusivity and makes room for traditions that all UM students can connect with."[226]

In its quest to be politically correct, I wonder if Ole Miss will also ban various genres of music that include offensive lyrics about women? And what about modern-day music that employs the use of a certain racial epithet? Would Ole Miss consider rap and hip-hop taboo, too? It's doubtful.

---

225   Wierman, McKenna. "Vaught-Hemingway Stadium: The heart of Ole Miss." *The Daily Mississippian* (Oxford), August 22, 2016. https://thedmonline.com/vaught-hemingway-heart-ole-miss/.

226   Maxey, Ron. "Ole Miss to stop playing Dixie at football games this fall." *The Commercial Appeal*. August 19, 2016. http://archive.commercialappeal.com/mobile-topstories/ole-miss-to-stop-playing-dixie-at-football-games-this-fall-3a722e9d-dbe3-5ccc-e053-0100007fc761-390725801.html.

Ole Miss has been shedding its Southern heritage for quite some time now. Confederate flags have been effectively banned since 1997, reports *Mississippi Today*. Last year, they banned the Mississippi State flag.[227]

Colonel Rebel, the school's mascot, was sidelined from games in 2003 because critics said he looked too much like a white plantation owner. He was replaced by a black bear. And in 2009, they told the band to stop playing "From Dixie With Love," in part because fans were yelling "The South will rise again" during the song.[228]

A reader of the *Oxford Eagle*, the official newspaper of record, summed up the sentiment of many Mississippians.

"Ole Miss is despicable for doing this," the gentleman wrote. "The university keeps bowing before the boot of political correctness."

And it ain't over, folks. It would be foolish to think the progressive academic elites have concluded their quest to eradicate Southern culture and traditions. It won't be long before someone mounts a campaign to remove the word "Rebel" from the school's athletic teams.

The only question is whether that happens before or after one of those perpetually offended, liberal snowflakes files a federal lawsuit demanding the university change its name.

I can already imagine the headlines:

- "Students Say 'Ole Miss' Causes Microaggressions"

- "Safe Spaces Overrun by Victims of 'Ole Miss' White Privilege"

- "President Ocasio-Cortez Signs Executive Order Renaming 'Ole Miss' the University of Obama"

---

227 Svrluga, Susan. "Old Miss takes down its state flag with Confederate emblem." *The Washington Post* (Washington, D.C.), October 26, 2015. https://www.washingtonpost.com/news/grade-point/wp/2015/10/26/ole-miss-takes-down-its-state-flag-with-confederate-emblem/?noredirect=on&utm_term=.c28919cc9da1.

228 Maxey, Ron. "From Colonel Reb to Rebel Black Bear to — a Landshark? Ole Miss considering mascot change." *Commercial Appeal*. Last modified September 18, 2017. https://www.commercialappeal.com/story/news/2017/09/18/ole-miss-football-mascot-sec-colonel-reb-rebel-black-bear-landshark-students/678339001/.

Come to think of it, that last headline may not be all that far-fetched.

Meanwhile, progressive liberals continue to bulldoze across the Southern states burning, torching, and tearing down every vestige and cultural tradition of the Deep South, much like General Sherman did during the Civil War. Look away Dixieland—just look away.

NORTH CAROLINA TOWN DETERMINES "DIXIE" IS OFFENSIVE

Cultural progressives in Winston-Salem, North Carolina want to change the name of the Dixie Classic Fair.

They say the word "Dixie" is offensive.

Councilman James Taylor told FOX8 that some folks find the word "offensive" and some folks are "angry" with the name. He said that as a progressive city, they need a name that "everyone can appreciate."[229]

They're trying to dig up a dead Confederate general in Memphis. They want to sand blast Robert E. Lee's face off the side of Stone Mountain, Georgia. And Lord only knows what they want to do with Aunt Jemima and Uncle Ben.[230]

The Dixie Classic Fair has been around since the 1950s, and nobody around town seems to be all that irate, according to FOX8. They said their reporters could not find a single person who took offense at the name.

---

229 Hennessey, Michael. "'Dixie Classic Fair' name in question, council member says some find it 'offensive.'" Fox 8. August 11, 2015. https://myfox8.com/2015/08/11/dixie-classic-fair-name-in-question-council-member-says-some-find-it-offensive/.

230 Shah, Khushbu. "The KKK's Mount Rushmore: the problem with Stone Mountain." *The Guardian* (London). https://www.theguardian.com/cities/ng-interactive/2018/oct/24/stone-mountain-is-it-time-to-remove-americas-biggest-confederate-memorial.

"I thought it was ridiculous," resident Dina Nelson told the television station. "I mean, there's no reason to change the name of the Dixie Classic Fair. I mean, it's a Southern name—but there's nothing racist about it."

If the cultural cleansers succeed in their quest to ban the word Dixie, don't be surprised if they start banning Dixie Cups and Winn Dixie and the Dixie Chicks.

I really hope they don't try to ban Dixie Cups, folks. How else would you be able to drink Dixie Beer with Hollywood star Dixie Carter?

GONE WITH THE WIND IS GONE WITH THE WIND

Common sense has even gone with the wind in my hometown of Memphis, Tennessee.

The famed Orpheum Theatre announced it will no longer show summertime screenings of *Gone with the Wind*, ending a thirty-four-year Mid-South tradition. The Orpheum Theatre Group told me they made the decision to exclude the classic film from its 2018 summer movie series over "specific inquiries from patrons."[231]

"As an organization whose stated mission is to 'entertain, educate and enlighten the communities it serves,' the Orpheum cannot show a film that is insensitive to a large segment of its local population," the theatre company said in a statement to the *Todd Starnes Show*.

Television station WREG noted in its coverage that the African American population of Memphis is about 64 percent.

---

231 Beifuss, John. "'Gone with the Wind' is gone - from Memphis theatre after 34 years." *USA Today*. Last modified August 28, 2017. https://www.commercialappeal.com/story/news/2017/08/25/gone-wind-gone-orpheum/601949001/.

"While title selections for the series are typically made in the spring of each year, the Orpheum has made this determination early in response to specific inquiries from patrons," the statement read.

It's bad enough that Memphis leaders wanted to dig up the dead body of Confederate General Nathan Bedford Forrest from a local park, but now they want to ban Prissy and Scarlett and Rhett and Aunt Pittypat. This cultural cleansing of my hometown has gone too far.[232]

Brett Batterson, the president of the Orpheum Theatre Group, told the *Commercial Appeal* the decision was made before the violence in Charlottesville, Virginia.

"This is about the Orpheum wanting to be inclusive and welcoming to all of Memphis," he told the newspaper.

Frankly, Mr. Batterson, I don't give a damn.

But since the Orpheum is all about inclusiveness, perhaps Mr. Batterson could explain why the theatre company is run by a white man? And why is it that an overwhelming number of board members are white? Why, the whole business smacks of white privilege, if you ask me.

Sadly, I predicted that it would be only a matter of time before the culture jihadists targeted Tara.

And now our beloved film is gone with the wind, done in by a bunch of meddling, no-account thespian carpetbaggers (to be fair, I am not sure where Mr. Batterson's people are from, but I don't think they're from around the Mid-South).

Many Memphians must be wondering what has come over this here town. To borrow a phrase from *Gone with the Wind*, Liberals have come over it. Same as they've come over all of us.

But there's no use crying in our sweet tea, Southerners. We must stand up to the scourge of the intolerant liberals. We must stand up

---

232   Watts, Micaela. "Nathan Bedford Forrest descendants sue Memphis, demand return of equestrian statue." *Commercial Appeal.* Last modified December 18, 2018. https://www.commercialappeal.com/story/news/2018/12/18/memphis-sued-over-confederate-statue-nathan-bedford-forrest-descendants/2346955002/.

and fight. In the words of Scarlett O'Hara, as God is my witness, we're not gonna let them lick us.

DIGGING UP DEAD CONFEDERATE WAR HEROES

For the past several years, progressives have been waging a culture jihad across the nation, turning our nation's heritage into a pile of rubble. They've been bulldozing our history much like the Islamic Radicals have been doing in Iraq. Sadly, my hometown of Memphis, Tennessee, has suffered a similar fate.

While most of the good citizens of Memphis were attending Wednesday night church services, the mayor and city council were busy finalizing a despicable plot to bypass the law and desecrate a Civil War gravesite.

In October 2017, the Tennessee Historical Commission refused to allow city leaders to remove statues of Nathan Bedford Forrest and Jefferson Davis from two city parks. The city initiated mediation with the state, but that, too, was unsuccessful.[233]

Instead of following the ruling, the mayor and the city council concocted a nefarious plan to disobey the law and take down the statues in the dark of night.

The city council voted in the early afternoon to sell two public parks to a newly formed nonprofit group chaired by a county commissioner. (Anybody smell a rat?)[234]

---

233 Horton, Alex. "Tennessee lawmakers punish Memphis for removing statue of Confederate and KKK leader." *The Washington Post* (Washington, D.C.), April 18, 2018. https://www.washingtonpost.com/news/post-nation/wp/2018/04/18/tennessee-lawmakers-punish-memphis-for-removing-statue-of-confederate-and-kkk-leader/?utm_term=.d265aacc140a.

234 Wamsley, Laurel. "Finding a Legal Loophole, Memphis Takes Down Its Confederate Statues." *NPR*. December 21, 2017. https://www.npr.org/sections/thetwo-way/2017/12/21/572654031/finding-a-legal-loophole-memphis-takes-down-its-confederate-statues.

The two parks, both prized pieces of real estate, were sold for $1,000 each. What kind of a shady real estate deal is that?

While the city council was voting, heavy machinery and an army of police officers were being dispatched to both parks. Did the nonprofit pick up the tab for the police officers and the heavy machinery? Or were taxpayers forced to foot the bill?

"The law allows a private entity to remove items such as statues from its own land," Mayor Jim Strickland told bewildered citizens.

After the city council passed the sham real estate deal, the cowardly mayor issued a notice on social media.

"Health Science Park and Memphis Park have been sold," the mayor declared. "Operations on those sites tonight are being conducted by a private entity and are compliant with state law."

Within a matter of hours both statues were removed in the darkness of night.

"The City made a decision to willfully violate state law and remove the statues of Forrest and Davis," said Thomas Strain of the Sons of Confederate Veterans. "This is a direct violation of state law and we must allow the state to pursue this case in a lawful manner."

James Patterson, the commander of the Tennessee division of the Sons of Confederate Veterans, called it a "well-organized, behind the scenes plan by the city."

"They are willfully violating the Heritage Preservation Act. The City has broken state law," Patterson said.

Beyond that, the bodies of Nathan Bedford Forrest and his wife are buried in one of the parks. Therefore, it was my contention that the mayor and city council are also guilty of desecration.

My fury had nothing to do with the monuments or the memorials. It had nothing to do with selling off prime real estate at a bargain-basement price. My fury had to do with the flagrant disregard of the law.

Mayor Jim Strickland and the Memphis City Council flouted that law. They violated their oath of office and they desecrated a gravesite.

At the time, I urged the governor and the state legislature to launch an immediate investigation of the corruption that has infested Memphis City Hall. The law demanded it. And I said on my radio program that I looked forward to the day when Mayor Jim Strickland and members of the city council were removed from office and hauled out of City Hall in handcuffs.

The mayor did not take kindly to my remarks—and he took me to task in the local media. He called me a liar. I reckon the mayor must have his own version of the truth, like Oprah.

THE DAY DOLLY PARTON GOT STAMPEDED

Dolly Parton's famous "Dixie Stampede" just got trampled by a politically correct mob. The popular dinner show with locations in Pigeon Forge, Tennessee and Branson, Missouri, will now be called "Dolly Parton's Stampede."[235]

For nearly thirty years, the Dixie Stampede has been a family-friendly dinner show attraction—featuring great food and expert horsemanship, and steeped in Civil War history. The Starnes family has attended on numerous occasions (we sat on the Southern side).

It's unclear what, specifically, Miss Dolly will be stampeding in the culturally-cleansed revision. And it's also not clear why the sudden name change (but I have a suspicion).

"Our shows currently are identified by where they are located," Miss Dolly said in a press statement. "Some examples are Smoky Mountain Adventures or Dixie Stampede. We also recognize that attitudes change and feel that by streamlining the names of our shows, it will remove any confusion or concerns about our shows and will help our efforts to expand into new cities."

---

235   Jones, Maggie. "Dolly Parton's Dixie Stampede gets name change, now called Stampede." *Knox News*. Last modified January 9, 2018. https://www.knoxnews.com/story/entertainment/2018/01/09/dolly-partons-dixie-stampede-gets-name-change-now-called-stampede/1017388001/.

A few years back, Slate sent a Yankee reporter to Pigeon Force to write a scathing review of the Dixie Stampede, described as the "Lost Cause of the Confederacy meets Cirque du Soleil."

The writer went on to call the show a "lily-white extravaganza" that celebrates the "Old South." Again, Miss Dolly did not say what influenced the decision to culturally cleanse the Dixie Stampede—but others share my thoughts.

"Well, like everybody else, I love Dolly, and I love all that she's done for our community, which is her community, and I'm disappointed that they're yielding to political correctness," Knox County Mayor Tim Burchett told the *Knoxville News Sentinel.* "What's next? Are we going to change the name of Dixie cups and the Dixie sugar company?"

THE WAR ON THE SOUTHERN DRAWL

As you know, I'm a Son of the South. And even though I've lived in New York City for the past decade, I still take my tea sweet, my chicken fried, and my biscuits buttered. I'm proud to call myself a gun-toting, Bible-clinging Tennessee Volunteer.

So you can imagine my befuddlement when I learned the Oak Ridge National Laboratory wanted to crack down on workers who have Southern accents by holding a "Southern Accent Reduction" course.[236]

In other words, them government folks want to learn us rednecks how to talk right. Bless their hearts.

The *Knoxville News Sentinel* reported that the government-managed facility wanted to bring in a "nationally certified speech pathologist and accent reduction trainer."

---

236   Greenblatt, Alan. "Y'all Keep Talking: Lab Scratches 'Southern Accent Reduction' Course." *NPR.* July 29, 2014. https://www.npr.org/sections/thetwo-way/2014/07/29/336364371/yall-keep-talking-lab-scratches-southern-accent-reduction-course.

"Feel confident in a meeting when you need to speak with a more neutral American accent, and be remembered for what you say and not how you say it," read a notice that was sent to workers.

A neutral American accent? That sounds about as appealing as a fermented soy sandwich with a side of bean curd.

Needless to say, Oak Ridge's edict stirred up a mess of trouble and they eventually called off the class.

"Given the way that it came across, they decided to cancel it," lab spokesman David Keim told the newspaper.

So what's wrong with a Southern drawl?

Scientific American reported in 2012 that some Americans say a Southern accent sounds "ignorant."[237]

"Studies have shown that whether you are from the North or South, a Southern twang pegs the speaker as comparatively dimwitted, but also likely to be a nicer person than folks who speak like a Yankee," the publication reported in 2012.

Folks, if Southern-fried stereotypes like that don't grip your grits, I don't know what will. For the record, Southerners do not talk funny. We just like to savor our vowels; let them linger for a bit.

I'm beginning to wonder if this attack on Southern diction is part of a much larger crusade to eradicate our way of life and our traditions. A few weeks ago, a liberal reader took me to task for mentioning that Tennesseans enjoy eating catfish and hush puppies. The reader accused me of stereotyping. I tried to explain to the guy that I happened to be from Tennessee and I enjoy eating both fried catfish and hush puppies. It's not stereotyping. It's just good eatin'.

I mentioned that encounter on my Facebook page and soon my newsfeed lit up with irate readers. A fan from southern New York

---

237   Fields, R. Douglas. "Why Does a Southern Drawl Sound Uneducated to Some?" *Scientific American*. December 7, 2012. http://blogs.scientificamerican.com/guest-blog/2012/12/07/why-does-a-southern-drawl-sound-uneducated-to-some/.

mentioned that he loved catfish. Some church ladies from Alabama said they eat their fish with a side of white beans. And a guy from Dallas reminded me that the catfish are actually bigger in Texas.

Why, I even received correspondence from someone living among the liberals of the Pacific Northwest. He said they've been known to throw down with some deep-fried halibut and cornbread.

The general consensus among my readers and radio listeners is that folks who don't like the Southern way of life should just mind their own business. That being said, it's probably a good thing I didn't mention that I enjoy hoe cakes, too.

I have noticed, though, that Southern traditions are under assault. They're serving barbecue tofu in Asheville and tuna tartar at the Opryland Hotel. Just the other day, I was in Texas and ordered a glass of sweet tea and a buttermilk biscuit. The waitress told me they had stopped serving sweet tea and that the only bread product they had was something called a bran muffin with flax seed. I'm sure it's quite tasty, if you happen to be a constipated bird.

Friends, the South is suffering from something called culture creep and it's spreading across Dixie like kudzu. One day your neighborhood diner is serving unsweetened tea, and the next day, your neighborhood is home to a yoga shop, a Prius dealership, and a farm-to-table restaurant serving eggs delivered by an Amish midwife.

I'm a bit disappointed Oak Ridge decided to cancel the class, though. I was looking forward to watching the feds teach a bunch of good ole boys how to converse like federal government bureaucrats.

It's not every day you get to see somebody talk out their wazoo.

TWO-SLICE HILLY

There is a bipartisan rule in the Deep South: You never question the authenticity of a Southern woman's homemade pecan pie. Ever.

You can debate the merits of cornbread dressing versus chestnut stuffing. You can argue over roasting the turkey instead of deep-frying the turkey. You can even thumb your nose at Aunt Maylene's prized ambrosia.

But it is considered ill-mannered and uncouth to suggest a Southern woman would sully the sanctity of the Thanksgiving Day table with a store-bought pecan pie. And that brings me to one of the most absurd conspiracy theories to hit the Trump Administration.

White House Press Secretary Sarah Sanders, a daughter of the great state of Arkansas, had been doing some baking, and she posted a picture of her culinary masterpiece on Twitter.

"I don't cook much these days, but managed this Chocolate Pecan Pie for Thanksgiving at the family farm," she wrote.

The delicious pie stirred the suspicions of CNN political analyst April Ryan, who all but accused the White House press secretary of faking the pie.[238]

"Show it to us on a table," Ms. Ryan tweeted.

For the sake of full disclosure, Ms. Ryan blocked me on Twitter, so I'm relying on images of her tweets from my Fox News colleagues.

"I am not trying to be funny but folks are already saying #piegate and #fakepie. Show it to us on the table with folks eating it and a pic of you cooking it. I am getting the biggest laugh out of this. I am thankful for this laugh on Black Friday," Ryan tweeted.

Ms. Ryan has some nerve, questioning the authenticity of a Southern woman's homemade pecan pie. She may as well have accused Ms. Sanders of bringing a bucket of store-bought chicken to the Wednesday Night Church Fellowship Supper. So, I reached out to Ms. Sanders to get to the bottom of the pie dish.

"Of course I made the pie," Sanders told me. "I make it for every holiday family gathering and have for years."

---

238   Roberts, Molly. "Sarah Huckabee Sanders, 'fake news' and real pics." *The Washington Post* (Washington, D.C.), December 14, 2017. https://www.washingtonpost.com/blogs/post-partisan/wp/2017/12/14/sarah-huckabee-sanders-fake-news-and-real-pies/?utm_term=.97506afe9dc3.

A source close to the Sanders and Huckabee families confirmed to me the authenticity and the tastiness of the pecan pies.

Ms. Sanders was using a recipe handed down to her by her mother and her grandmother.

"I also used to make them for my neighbors on my street at Christmas every year," Sanders said.

In spite of Ms. Ryan's injurious and slanderous accusations, Ms. Sanders offered to bake her a pie, accompanied by a #fakenews hashtag. Ms. Ryan added insult to injury by telling Ms. Sanders she would decline a slice of the chocolate pecan pie.

"Okay I want to watch you bake it and put it on the table," she tweeted. "But forgive I won't eat it. Remember you guys don't like the press."

Perhaps Ms. Ryan was familiar with that infamous pie scene from *The Help* and feared it might spark another viral hashtag: "Two-Slice Hilly."

JESUS, CHEERLEADERS, AND DODGE COUNTY, GEORGIA

You would be hard-pressed to find anybody in Dodge County, Georgia who does not stand for the national anthem or take a knee to pray. That's just how it is.

So when the Dodge County High School cheerleaders started selling T-shirts that read, "In Dodge County, we stand for the flag, kneel for the cross," nobody thought it would cause a controversy. But, sweet mercy, did it cause a stink.[239]

Dodge County School Board member Shirley Ikedionwu posted a scathing message on Facebook calling the shirts "politically divisive."

---

239   Baker, Pepper. "T-shirts cause controversy in dodge County." *WMAZ-TV*. Last modified August 15, 2018. https://www.13wmaz.com/article/news/local/t-shirts-cause-controversy-in-dodge-county/93-584487596.

"This shirt is not only one-sided but offensive," she wrote. "I can't imagine how our children would feel entering a place that is supposed to be welcoming and accepting of students from all walks of life, beliefs, and perspectives—but instead, they are faced with this type of exclusionary message."

Proceeds from the patriotic shirts were going to help fund cheerleading competitions. But that did not seem to satisfy the school board member's anger. Ikedionwu wrote that she personally contacted school system administrators to voice her concerns.

"At this point, the shirt will no longer be sold," she declared.

But that's when local residents and businesses got involved and decided to sell the T-shirts off campus.

"I'm standing because it has the United States flag on it and the cross. Those are two things I will back any day of the week," said Nikki Mullis, the manager of White Hat Auto in Eastland.

Mullis, who was a guest on my radio show, said that people are calling to purchase shirts from across the world. They even shipped three shirts to Afghanistan.

"This ain't just Georgia anymore," she said. "We are a community that when something happens we are all together."

Credit manager Amanda Parker tells me never in a million years would she have thought there would be a controversy over Old Glory and the Lord.

"We are just a small town in Eastman, Georgia and we're standing up for our Christian faith and what we believe in," she said.

But there were some folks around town who were triggered by the patriotic message.

"It stands for the hurt of black people getting killed, beat by police officers and getting off with it," one resident told television station WMAZ. "So therefore, we as black people, some of us have taken that, to us, that's what it looks like."

To be clear, there is nothing on the shirt that comes even close to promoting police brutality.

"I don't see anything wrong with that shirt," resident Bill Tripp told me. "The South is known for being the Bible Belt. If you can't stand for the flag and you can't stand for the cross—I don't know what you can stand for."

I reckon there are more than a few folks around Dodge County who would offer an "amen" to that sentiment.

HEY OBAMA, KISS MY GRITS

When President Obama promised to fundamentally transform America, we had no idea he was secretly plotting to ban biscuits and grits.

The 2010 Healthy Hunger Free Kids Act strictly limited calories, fat, salt, sugar, and just about everything else that makes food edible—including grits. It was the War of Culinary Aggression.[240]

"We could originally serve half whole grains but that changed in 2012 when we had to start serving 100 percent whole grains," said Stephanie Dillard, the child nutrition director for Geneva County Schools in Alabama. That meant no more grits.

"And grits are a staple in the South," Ms. Dillard told me. "Students really want to eat their grits."

I'm fairly certain that, had Southerners known President Obama had taken away their biscuits and grits, Mitt Romney would've won the South in a landslide.

My New York editor sent me an email reminding me that I have a diverse readership and I should probably include a working definition of the word "grits." The word "diverse" is a polite way of saying I have a number of Yankee readers.

---

240   U.S. Department of Agriculture. *Healthy Hunger-Free Kids Act.* Washington, D.C.: USDA Food and Nutrition Service, 2013. https://www.fns.usda.gov/school-meals/healthy-hunger-free-kids-act.

So for all y'all up in the Bronx, grits are made from stone-ground corn and prepared with lots of butter. Grits are also versatile, meaning you can eat them for breakfast or supper (which is the meal called "dinner" north of the Mason-Dixon Line).

"Grits and fish go well together," Ms. Dillard said. "Students love that."

Of course, the folks from South Carolina are renowned for shrimp and grits, and I know a few folks in Mississippi who toss a few eggs in theirs. I'm from Tennessee and we prefer a little cheese in our grits, but I digress.

The Obama administration also had a problem with traditional Southern buttermilk biscuits made from Martha White Flour.[241]

"Biscuits have to be 100 percent whole grain," Ms. Dillard said. "It's not the kind of biscuit you would see at a restaurant."

Nor is it the kind of biscuit you would see on your grandmother's dining room table or a Wednesday night church supper. Why, no self-respecting Southerner would ever serve such an atrocity.

I had the unfortunate experience of eating one of those government-approved biscuits. I wouldn't wish that culinary apostasy on Bernie Sanders.

"It's hard to find good, fluffy, 100 percent whole grain biscuits," Ms. Dillard told me.

I'm not terribly surprised. The South has a better chance of rising than a 100-percent whole grain, government-approved biscuit.

"The students have gotten used to them," she said. "They really aren't that bad."

---

241   Hamburger, Tom. "Michelle Obama's school lunch agenda faces backlash from some school nutrition officials." *The Washington Post* (Washington, D.C.), May 30, 2014. https://www.washingtonpost.com/politics/michelle-obamas-school-lunch-agenda-faces-backlash-from-some-school-nutrition-officials/2014/05/29/6a8e4af6-e744-11e3-afc6-a1dd9407abcf_story.html?noredirect=on&utm_term=.2144b10af5de.

My friend, the Southern humorist Shellie Rushing Tomlinson, seems to think whole grain biscuits are a Communist plot.[242]

"No freedom honoring nation should force whole grain cathead biscuits on their young," she told me.

Like Grandmother Starnes used to say, biscuits should only be made from buttermilk and Martha White Flour, the way the Good Lord intended.

All that to say, a delegation of school nutritionists recently paid a visit to Congress to politely inform lawmakers that the Obama-era food rules were overcooking their grits.

"We're asking for some flexibility so we can serve 50 percent whole grains," Ms. Dillard said. "If we can have that, we would be allowed to serve our grits."

The School Nutrition Association is lobbying for a relaxation of the rules too. But they took me to task for saying President Obama had banned grits.

"There's no ban on one kind of food—it just has to fit within the criteria," their spokesperson told me.

Grits don't fit into their criteria, so in my estimation that means they're banned.

For what it's worth, Miss Shellie stands with the good people of Alabama as they try to bring back grits.

"May God have favor on their efforts," she said. "Grits can heal America."

We now ask Democrats and Republicans in Congress to do the right thing and restore biscuits and grits to their rightful place. And the next time the federal government decides to outlaw basic Southern provisions, We the People should rise up and tell Uncle Sam to kiss our grits.[243]

---

242 Tomlinson, Shellie Rushing. *Shellie Rushing Tomlinson* (blog). Accessed May 29, 2019. http://www.belleofallthingssouthern.com.

243 Starnes, Todd. "Southern Schools: Let Us Eat Grits!" *Todd Starnes* (blog). April 21, 2017. https://www.toddstarnes.com/uncategorized/southern-schools-let-us-eat-grits/.

FIRST THEY CAME FOR DAISY DUKE, THEN THEY CAME FOR THE GENERAL LEE

If you still doubt there is a full-fledged cultural cleansing of the Southern States, consider the plight of the beloved General Lee (from the Dukes of Hazzard, not the Civil War.)

Warner Brothers announced they will remove the Confederate Flag from atop one of the most famous cars in television history. They will also ban any Dukes of Hazzard merchandise that once sported the Confederate flag.[244]

Maybe they could just paint a rainbow flag on top and rename it the General Sherman. He culturally cleansed the South, too. Just ask the good people of Atlanta.

Sears, Walmart, and eBay have also announced they will no longer sell Confederate merchandise. And that could explain why Sears is on life support.

Meanwhile, lawmakers are debating whether to remove state flags and rename schools and parks and streets named after Confederate war heroes. In Washington, they're talking about removing Confederate statues from the U.S. Capitol. Senator Mitch McConnell wants a statue of Jefferson Davis evicted from the Kentucky statehouse.[245] And retired Senator Harry Reid wants UNLV to rename its Runnin' Rebels mascot.[246]

---

244   Kreps, Daniel. "Warner Bros. Bans 'Dukes of Hazzard' Car with Confederate Flag." *Rolling Stone*. June 24, 2015. https://www.rollingstone.com/tv/tv-news/ warner-bros-bans-dukes-of-hazzard-car-with-confederate-flag-58510/.

245   Kelly, Nora. "Mitch McConnell to Kentucky Capitol: Lose the Jefferson Davis Statue." *The Atlantic*. June 23, 2015. https://www.theatlantic.com/ politics/archive/2015/06/mitch-mcconnell-to-kentucky-capitol-lose-the-jefferson-davis-statue/448515/.

246   "Senator Harry Reid urges UNLV to reconsider 'Runnin' Rebels nickname." *Sports Illustrated*. June 23, 2015. https://www.si.com/college-basketball/2015/06/23/ senator-harry-reid-unlv-runnin-rebels-confederate-flag-mascot.

It's only a matter of time before the cultural revolutionaries literally destroy films like *Gone with the Wind* and *Forrest Gump* and burn copies of *Tom Sawyer* and *Huckleberry Finn*. Stalin and Lenin would be bursting with pride.

And mark my words: the Left's cultural crusade will not stop with the Confederate Flag. They will use the perception of racism and hatred to whitewash history and silence dissent.

And one day, very soon, I predict they will come after another flag—the one with broad stripes and bright stars. So, don't be terribly surprised when even Republicans stand idly by as they burn the Star-Spangled Banner.

Run Forrest, Run.

CHAPTER 17

A FOOTBALL COACH WITH A HIGHER CALLING

As I MENTIONED earlier in the book, I host a gathering in North Carolina at the Billy Graham Training Center. We jokingly refer to our weekend of fellowship as "church camp for grown-ups" without extreme sports.

It's an intimate gathering of about several hundred of my readers and viewers and listeners from all over the country. And I'm honored to say that we've made many long-lasting friendships out of our time at The Cove. On a side note, you can find more information on my website, toddstarnes.com.

One of my favorite moments is our Saturday afternoon panel discussion where I get to introduce and interview some of the folks who have been the subjects of my columns on religious liberty. In 2018, Joe Kennedy, the former assistant football coach at Bremerton High School in Washington State, was my special guest.

Coach Joe, a former Marine Corps gunnery sergeant, was fired after he refused to stop taking a knee to pray after football games. His story has resonated with people of faith across the nation and his testimony has inspired millions.[247]

---

247   "School district fires football coach Joe Kennedy over prayer." *First Liberty*. Accessed May 29, 2019. https://firstliberty.org/cases/coachkennedy/.

I consider Coach Joe to be one of my modern-day heroes of the faith. He faced a Shadrach, Meschah, and Abednego moment. Do you obey God or do you obey the government? He faced down a mob of culture jihadists and he discovered that God was still by his side—even when he was thrown into a fiery political furnace. And now he's fighting in the courts to get back his job.

Here's the back story:

Since 2008, Coach Kennedy has taken a knee at the fifty-yard line at the conclusion of every football game to offer a brief, quiet prayer of thanksgiving, for player safety, sportsmanship, and spirited competition.

The coach's petition to the Almighty usually lasted about thirty seconds. He did not proselytize nor did he compel players or anyone else to participate. In other words, it was just a private prayer, not a Billy Graham Crusade.

He was inspired to pray after watching *Facing the Giants*, a faith-based film about a high school football team.

"Coach Kennedy made a covenant with God that he would give thanks through prayer, at the end of each game, for what the players had accomplished and for the opportunity to be part of their lives through the game of football," the lawsuit states.[248]

Over time, some of the teenage players asked if they could join him in prayer and the coach replied, "This is a free country. You can do what you want."

The lawsuit also points out that other coaches engaged in religious expression at the beginning and the end of football games. The lawsuit specifically mentioned David Boynton, an assistant coach who delivered a Buddhist chant near the fifty-yard line.

---

248   Starnes, Todd. "A faithful coach wants his job back." Fox News. Last modified August 10, 2016. https://www.foxnews.com/opinion/a-faithful-coach-wants-his-job-back.

"Coach Boynton has never been suspended, let alone dismissed, on the basis of his religious expression," the lawsuit states.

It's not quite clear what led to the school district's investigation, but on September 17, 2015, Coach Kennedy received a letter informing him that the district was conducting an inquiry into a policy regarding "religious-related activities and practices."

The district directed the coach to refrain from praying around students or doing anything that might cause people to think he was praying. He was forbidden from bowing his head or kneeling, too.

However, Coach Kennedy chose to defy the district's demands, and on October 23, 2015, he walked out to the fifty-yard line after the football game and prayed. On October 28, 2015, the coach was placed on paid administrative leave and banned from participating in the football program.

"The District stated it had placed Coach Kennedy on administrative leave because he 'engaged in overt, public religious displays on the football field while on duty as a coach,'" the lawsuit states.

In November 2015, Coach Kennedy received a poor performance evaluation, after years of receiving stellar performance reviews.

The evaluation recommended that the coach not be rehired "based on his alleged failure to follow District policy regarding religious expression, and his alleged failure to supervise students after games."

In January 2016, Coach Kennedy's contract was not renewed.

"They fired him for praying," said Michael Berry, the coach's attorney. Berry is with First Liberty Institute, one of the nation's largest law firms handling religious liberty cases.

The coach is not asking for a single penny in his lawsuit; he just wants his job back.

"All we really want for him—is to be back on the sideline coaching those kids—and nothing more," Berry said.

Attorney Berry said they tried to reach out to the school district on a number of occasions, but the district's attorney declined to meet.

So, on January 30, 2016, the coach filed a discrimination charge with the Equal Employment Opportunity Commission. In June of that year, the Department of Justice issued a right-to-sue letter. But the legal road has been rocky for the coach and his attorneys.

A three-judge panel of the U.S. Ninth Circuit Court of Appeals ruled the Bremerton School District was justified in suspending Coach Joe Kennedy after he took a knee and prayed silently at midfield after football games.

"When Kennedy kneeled and prayed on the fifty-yard line immediately after games while in view of students and parents, he spoke as a public employee, not as a private citizen, and his speech therefore was constitutionally unprotected," the 9th Circuit wrote. "An objective student observer would see an influential supervisor do something no ordinary citizen could do—perform a Christian religious act on secured school property while surrounded by players—simply because he is a coach."

Franklin Graham, the president of Samaritan's Purse and the Billy Graham Evangelistic Association, spoke out against the ruling on my radio program.

"It's sad this has happened but it really doesn't surprise me," Graham said. "We find these courts and these judges are making these decisions against the will of the people. We have judges out there who hate God and hate His standards and disrespect the people who follow God."

The case is still making its way through the courts, but as it now stands, the 9th Circuit believes they can ban all coaches from praying individually in public just because they can be seen. Is this really the kind of America contemplated by our Constitution?

"Now all coaches across the country stand under the prospect of being prevented from engaging in any outward displays of religion," First Liberty Institute attorney Jeremy Dys told me. "That includes crossing yourself or even taking a knee to pray."

That's right, folks—not even Catholic coaches will be allowed to cross themselves in public, the attorney said.

Coach Kennedy told me during our 2018 interview at the Billy Graham Training Center that he has no regrets.

"I wouldn't do anything differently," he said. "I've always taught my guys to stand up for what they believe in—even if it's not popular."

Coach Kennedy is also leading by example, demonstrating that sometimes there is a price to pay for doing the right thing. But as we learned in Sunday school, good will eventually triumph over evil.

And I suspect there are lots of folks in Bremerton who would rather stand alongside a Christian Marine Corps veteran than a bunch of godless school district bureaucrats.

But thanks to activist judges, we live in a nation that has been fundamentally transformed. It's a nation where football players can take a knee to disrespect the flag, but a coach can't take a knee to pray to the Almighty.

CHAPTER 18

WATCHMEN ON THE WALL

THIS IS A very serious moment in our history.

On Election Day in 2020, Americans will stand at a crossroad. Do we cling to freedom and liberty, or do we surrender the Republic to the socialists and secularists? Do we stand up for the First Amendment or do we allow ourselves to be silenced? Do we defend the right to bear arms or will we stand down and allow ourselves to be disarmed? Do we stand up for the unborn or do we turn a blind eye to a modern-day Holocaust?

Dr. Dobson was right when he told us the issues facing our nation are not just political, they are also spiritual. The culture jihadists want to destroy the American family. The sex and gender revolutionaries want to redefine what God defined. The secularists want to evict Christians from the public marketplace.

These are very real struggles that require a spiritual solution. You see, the first step to taking back the state house is to get back to the church house.

A recent Gallup study revealed that church attendance in America is on the decline. Even more troubling is that the number of non-religious people has more than doubled to 19 percent.[249] Consider Gallup's findings:

---

249   Lardieri, Alexi. "A Poll Finds U.S. Membership in Religious Institutions Hits an All-Time Low." *U.S. News and World Report.* April 18, 2019. https://www.usnews.com/news/national-news/articles/2019-04-18/gallup-poll-finds-us-membership-in-religious-institutions-is-at-an-all-time-low.

- o 77 percent of Americans identify with some organized religion, down from 90 percent in 1998–2000

- o 52 percent of American adults are members of a church, compared with 69 percent a decade ago

- o 39 percent of Catholics attend church weekly; 45 percent of Protestants

The 2017 Pew Survey on Faith documented similar findings. They discovered that the share of Americans who believe in God with absolute certainty has declined. One-third of Americans say they do not believe in the God of the Bible.[250]

Yet in spite of the findings, I still have hope for America. It bears repeating, my hope is built on the blood and the righteousness of Jesus Christ. Our current national maladies can be cured by something as simple as an old-fashioned, Holy Ghost revival meeting! If you really want to make America great again, we have to start at the foot of the cross.

There's no doubt, billowing storms of political change are gathering, but there are still rays of sunlight piercing through the clouds.

One day I received a letter from Deb Zippel, one of my faithful readers in Minnesota. Her daughter is studying to be an agricultural education teacher and she happened to be attending the annual gathering of the Future Farmers of America (FFA) Organization meeting in Indianapolis.

Jaci Deitrick, an FFA member from Newcastle, Oklahoma, walked onto the stage and delivered a stirring rendition of "God Bless the USA."[251]

---

250 "Religious Landscape Study." *Pew Research Center.* Accessed May 29, 2019. https://www.pewforum.org/religious-landscape-study/.
251 Jaci Deitrick sings God Bless the USA, 90th National FFA Convention." https://vimeo.com/241061630

"Ladies and gentlemen, we live in the greatest country in the world and that's only because we have men and women fighting daily for that freedom," she told the massive crowd. "Thank you for standing."

And that's exactly what they did. Tens of thousands of young people rose to their feet and began singing along with the vocalist.

And when she started crooning about those lakes in Minnesota and the hills in Tennessee—well, the young patriots dutifully let out hoots and hollers.

When the singer concluded the song, the entire audience erupted with boisterous chants of "USA USA."

You would be hard pressed to find any snowflakes laden with microaggressions in the FFA.

"These kids are the ones that get it," Deb told me. "They are hard working. They don't expect it to be handed to them."

Deb said her daughter worked two jobs to pay her way through college, "including getting up at 4 a.m. to milk cows and working at an organic farm and squishing potato bugs by hand."

It's that kind of hard work and determination that makes America the most exceptional nation on the planet.

I wrote this book for the good people of Akin, Illinois, a small town in the heartland. It's a place where the crops are bountiful and so are the patriots.

They don't even have a post office in Akin, but they do have a church. And around this part of the country, church is what folks do.

So you can understand the concern among townsfolk when the salutatorian at Akin Grade School was told he could not deliver his graduation speech because it was too religious.[252]

252 "Student Banned from Giving Faith-Filled Graduation Speech Still Found a Way." *CBN News*. May 28, 2017. https://www1.cbn.com/cbnnews/us/2017/may/how-student-banned-from-giving-graduation-speech-centered-on-his-faith-still-did-it.

Seth Clark, thirteen, was mighty proud of that speech. He referenced God and quoted from the Bible and even mentioned his Christian faith.

But just hours before graduation, Seth was told that he would not be permitted to deliver his remarks.

"As a public school, it is our duty to educate students, regardless of how different they or their beliefs may be," Superintendent Kelly Clark wrote in a prepared statement to the Benton Evening News.

"While students are welcome to pray or pursue their faith without disrupting school or infringing upon the rights of others, the United States Constitution prohibits the school district from incorporating such activities as part of school-sponsored events, and when the context causes a captive audience to listen or compels other students to participate," her statement read.

But that's not where our story ends.

Word began to spread around Akin that Seth's faith-based speech was not permitted on school property. And folks decided something needed to be done to right this wrong. Seth needed to be able to deliver the speech that God had placed on his heart to deliver.

It just so happened that a neighbor of the Clarks owned a house across from the school and he invited Seth to deliver the speech on his property.

"When it came time for the valedictorian and the salutatorian to deliver their speeches, they invited the audience to join them across the street at the house," Becky Clark said.

And sure enough, that's exactly what happened. Dozens of folks piled onto the front yard of the home and listened intently as young Seth delivered his address. It was a scene right out of a Currier and Ives lithograph.

"It was the proudest moment of my life," Mrs. Clark said. "He is more courageous at the age of thirteen than I am at the age of forty-three."

She said her son is a tender-hearted person who just wants to be a man of God.

"This is not an attention thing for him," she said. "He wanted to share what was on his heart about God."

And I must tell you about the football team at Burroughs High School in Southern California. The young men wanted to honor our military and send a message to the National Football League.

On game night, the team ran onto the field waving large American flags as Lee Greenwood's beloved, "God Bless the USA" played on the public address system.

"The kids have been frustrated with what's going on across the country with players taking a knee," head coach Todd Mather me. "I told the kids that politics don't have a place in high school sports. I told them we stand for the national anthem. That's what you do as an American in this country."

And that's exactly what they did during the homecoming game, bringing the audience to tears.

"There wasn't a dry eye in the stands—including myself," the coach said.

At the conclusion of the song, the game announcer told the crowd they were living in the "best country on the face of this Earth."

"At Burroughs football game—we are standing," he declared. "We are standing for the national anthem."

"It was absolutely amazing," parent Tina Haugen said. "Our community is unbelievably patriotic. Everybody was clapping and cheering."

The young men on the football team and the good citizens of Ridgecrest should be commended for their public display of patriotism. They reminded the nation that there are plenty of folks across the fruited plain who are proud to be Americans.

This book is written for next-generation patriots like Seth Clark and the Future Farmers of America and the Burroughs High School football team. They resolved to stand up to the culture jihadists, not with brute force, but with old-fashioned resolve. Happy warriors, all.

Earlier, I detailed how leftists had been infected with Trump Derangement Syndrome. And I'm sure we all shared a chuckle at some of the outlandish bouts of TDS. But in reality, it's no laughing matter. Conservatives have been targeted in the streets and on social media. Elected leaders have openly called for violence against Trump supporters.[253] And many of our fellow patriots have been beaten, physically accosted. Others have been bullied into silence.

But we cannot be silent. We must speak out. Our voices must be heard. But we cannot co-opt the tactics of the culture jihadists. So, what, exactly, are we supposed to do?

Well, I believe Press Secretary Sarah Sanders, former Florida Attorney General Pam Bondi, and Transportation Secretary Elaine Chao provide us with the answer to that question. We must raise our voices without raising our fists.

To recap, Ms. Bondi and her date were accosted outside a movie theater, which, ironically, was showing a documentary about Mr. Rogers. Her security team urged her to go out the back door to escape the mob. But she refused to duck and run.[254]

"No way. I will not be intimidated," she told me on my syndicated radio program. "We are walking out the door we came in."

She refused to be bullied.

Ms. Sanders was enjoying a night out on the town with her family when the owner of the Red Hen ordered her to leave the restaurant.

253   Ehrlich, Jamie. "Maxine Waters encourages supporters to harass Trump administration officials." CNN Politics. Last modified June 25, 2018. https://www.cnn.com/2018/06/25/politics/maxine-waters-trump-officials/index.html.

254   Wilson, Kate and Steve Contorno. "Pam Bondi confronted by protesters outside Mister Rogers movie." *The Buzz.* June 23, 2018. https://www.tampabay.com/florida-politics/buzz/2018/06/23/pam-bondi-confronted-by-protesters-outside-screening-of-mr-rogers-movie/.

Ms. Sanders could've caused a scene, but instead she displayed civility and grace in the face of humiliating bigotry.[255]

And then there's Ms. Chao, the wife of Senate Majority Leader Mitch McConnell. They were accosted by students at Georgetown University, but instead of ducking into the car, Secretary Chao went toe-to-toe with the mob. She did not back down.[256]

Those three conservative ladies set a bold example for all of us to follow. We must stand up to the far left. We must do so with grace and civility, but sometimes, as one of my callers from Gadsden, Alabama once said, "Sometimes the hoops come off, the hair goes up—and it's time for an old fashioned come-to-Jesus meeting."

So consider this your call to arms, happy warriors. We are tasked with defending a noble cause and a noble faith. Sure, we've taken more than a few sucker punches and the enemies of freedom have us surrounded. No doubt that our numbers are dwindling, but we are still in the fight. Because we are Americans.

Lieutenant General Lewis Burwell "Chesty" Puller was the most decorated Marine in the history of the nation. To say that this leatherneck was a badass would be a great understatement.

His bravery and valor are legendary and still today Marines invoke his name.

Puller was also known for his quips and one in particular is appropriate for our political fight with the culture jihadists.

---

255 Vespa, Matt. "Red Hen Nightmare: Restaurant That Refused To Serve Sarah Sanders Is Torpedoing The Town's Tourism Business." *Townhall.* September 3, 2018. https://townhall.com/tipsheet/mattvespa/2018/09/03/red-hen-nightmare-restaurant-that-refused-to-serve-sarah-sanders-is-torpedoing-t-n2515501.

256 Viebeck, Elise. "'You leave my husband alone!': Elaine Chao, Mitch McConnell confronted over family separations." *The Washington Post* (Washington, D.C.), June 26, 2018. https://www.washingtonpost.com/news/powerpost/wp/2018/06/26/you-leave-my-husband-alone-elaine-chao-mitch-mcconnell-confronted-over-family-separations/?utm_term=.60df1788ef38.

Puller and his troops were surrounded by enemy fighters in Korea. He told his men, "All right, they're on our left, they're on our right, they're in front of us, they're behind us … they can't get away this time."

In other words, be men and women of courage. It is imperative that gun-toting, Bible-clinging patriots rise up with a mighty voice and declare that this Great American Experiment is worth saving.

And remember, our battle is not against flesh and blood. Our battle is against the rulers of darkness of this world, against spiritual wickedness in high places.

In closing, I leave you with these words, written by George Washington on July 2, 1776: "The fate of the unborn millions will now depend, under God, on the courage and conduct of this army. Let us, therefore, rely upon the goodness of the cause and the aid of the Supreme Being, in whose hands victory, is, to animate and encourage us to great and noble actions."[257]

Onward to great and noble actions, my fellow countrymen. God speed, America!

---

257   Washington Library. "Address to the Continental Army Before the
       Battle of Long Island | Tuesday, August 27, 1776." Washington,
       D.C.: Center for Digital History. Accessed May 23, 2019. https://
       www.mountvernon.org/library/digitalhistory/quotes/article/
       the-time-is-now-near-at-hand-which-must-probably-determine-whether-
       americans-are-to-be-freemen-or-slaves-whether-they-are-to-have-any-
       property-they-can-call-their-own-whether-their-houses-and-farms-are-to-
       be-pillaged-and-destroyed-and-themselves-consigned/.